THE ELECTION A-Z

urbanepublications.com

THE ELECTION
A-Z

Insights, Intrigue and Spin from
50 Years of Political Reporting

NICHOLAS JONES

First published in Great Britain in 2015
by Urbane Publications Ltd
Suite 3, Brown Europe House,
33/34 Gleamingwood Drive,
Chatham, Kent ME5 8RZ

A CIP catalogue record for this book is available
from the British Library.

Paperback ISBN 978-1-9106922-7-1
mobi ISBN 978-1-9106922-9-5
epub ISBN 978-1-9106922-8-8

Cover design and typeset by Chandler Book Design
Cover image: © David Carillet | Dreamstime.com

Printed and bound by
CPI Group (UK) Ltd,
Croydon, CR0 4YY

urbanepublications.com

CONTENTS

Introduction   1

A.   election advertising   11

B.   battle buses   23

C.   constituents   33

D.   deposits   39

E.   election timing   47

F.   fragmentation   59

G.   political gaffes   69

H.   heckling   81

I.   interviews   91

J.   journalists   99

K.   kitchens   109

L.   Liberal Democrats   119

M.   the monstering of Miliband   129

N.   nationalists   141

O.   opinion polls   153

P.   photo-opportunities   165

Q.   Queen   175

R.   results evening   183

S.   Scotland   193

T.   trade unions   201

U.   UKIP   209

V.   votes   217

W.   political wives   223

X.   Xavier (Michael Portillo)   237

Y.   youth vote   249

Z.   Zelig   257

index   267

about the author   275

Introduction

When discussing with my publisher Matthew Smith our ideas for *The Election A-Z* we thought the outcome of the 2015 general election would be so close there was every likelihood that another coalition government would be inevitable. Little did we know an electorate that was being described as the most unpredictable since the Second World War was about to deliver a result that would be far more decisive than the pollsters and pundits had forecast – a verdict by the voters that would have devastating consequences few had anticipated.

Matthew's aim in commissioning this book was to use the experiences and conclusion of the 2015 campaign as an opportunity to reflect on the highlights and lessons of past general elections. This was my 14th in the five decades I have spent reporting political and industrial affairs. Matthew's invitation to write a fifth election book was an offer I could not resist, a chance to share my thoughts and observations on the highs and lows of electioneering, the strange encounters and off-beat events that have made the campaigns that I have reported so memorable.

We could hardly have chosen a more momentous starting point: against all the odds polling day in May 2015 delivered a Conservative government with an outright majority; shattered the Labour party; decimated the Liberal Democrats; produced an historic landslide for the Scottish National party that redrew the political map of Scotland; and saw the United Kingdom Independence party gain the third largest share of the popular vote yet return only a single MP to the House of Commons.

Journalists share the same doubts as politicians the closer we get to polling day. Like them we sense those times when the mood of the country seems definitely on the turn, but when we also have to acknowledge that the direction of that shift in opinion is too difficult to identify with any accuracy, and when we all have to accept that until the votes are counted no-one can be sure which way the electorate has gone. Two closely-fought general elections in 1974, following on from two elections in rapid succession in the mid-1960s, determined the shape of my career. I was hooked on politics after seeing Harold Wilson lead Labour to victory in 1964 against a Conservative government that had been in power for so long.

Wilson held on to office so tenaciously, fighting four further elections. Labour's two defeats, by Edward Heath and then by Margaret Thatcher in 1979, were defining moments in my career. In the late 1970s I had been assigned by the BBC to report the industrial disputes that dogged James Callaghan's Premiership, only to find that Mrs Thatcher's victory was about to keep reporters on the labour beat fully occupied. The Conservatives' assault on trade union power, plus the break-up of the nationalised industries, dominated the headlines for much of her decade in power.

When I returned to Westminster in the late 1980s the Thatcher years were drawing to a close. Her successor

John Major led the Conservatives to victory against the odds in 1992, and then began the rise of New Labour and the long haul to Tony Blair's historic landslide in 1997. Labour's 13 years in power ended with an indecisive result in 2010, and the formation of a Conservative-Liberal Democrat government, the first coalition of the post-war years. For months the country was led to believe by opinion poll surveys that another hung parliament would again be the outcome in 2015. The pollsters were unanimous in their prediction that the two largest parties were neck-and-neck, and that both the Conservative Prime Minister David Cameron and the Labour leader Ed Miliband might have a chance of gaining power, either through another coalition or perhaps by leading a minority government.

The near certainty of these repeated forecasts that the country was heading for a second indecisive result generated endless speculation about the likely line-up of a future coalition. All manner of scenarios and questions came into play: What chance did Miliband have of convincing the electorate he was a prime minister in waiting, when set against Cameron's five years in office? Would the SNP deliver the wipe-out of Labour in Scotland that had been so widely predicted? Were Liberal Democrat MPs right in believing that the loyalty of their supporters would be enough to see them through on polling day? After topping the poll in the 2014 elections to the European Parliament, were UKIP about to make further inroads into the Conservative and Labour vote?

So many scenarios were being floated that election reporting became something of a turn-off for the public at large, but from the moment the polling stations closed the edifice of conjecture that had prepared the country for another hung parliament started to collapse. An exit poll commissioned by broadcasters for the results night television programmes was released at 10 p.m. and unexpectedly it put the Conservatives well ahead. Cameron and his election strategists had always been convinced they were doing better than the polls suggested. At last they had the confirmation they had been waiting desperately to hear. Miliband and his campaign team were mortified, scarcely believing the exit poll prediction of 316 seats for the Conservatives with Labour trailing on 238. Miliband had to abandon any thought of a speech claiming he had the right to lead the next government, and instead he had to ready himself for resignation. Early declarations were confirming Labour's worst fears: hard-fought target seats were being retained by the Conservatives who were soon well on their way to an eventual outright majority of 331 seats, an outcome that Cameron declared was 'the sweetest victory of all' when he arrived at party headquarters from the count in his Witney constituency.

Labour finished with 232 MPs on 30.4 per cent of the vote, their lowest share since Michael Foot's defeat in 1983. In his resignation speech Miliband stood by the thrust of his campaign, the advancement of policies that would have reduced inequality, the case 'for a country that works for working people once again'. Almost immediately a battered and bruised parliamentary party, bereft of leading figures such as the shadow chancellor Ed Balls, set in motion an election to choose Miliband's successor. Labour's virtual wipe-out in Scotland, where the party held only one out of 41 seats, was a catastrophic set back. The inexorable advance of the SNP had not only destroyed a previously impregnable Labour's power base, but had also done incalculable electoral damage south of the border, having strengthened support for Cameron.

Miliband never succeeded in countering the Conservatives' claim that the nationalists would have become the dominant force if he had needed the support of the SNP leader Nicola Sturgeon when attempting to lead a coalition or minority government. Under her leadership, she had turned defeat in the 2014 referendum on Scottish independence into a launch pad for a bid to become Scotland's voice at Westminster, a campaign that generated unprecedented swings in the SNP's favour and a virtual clean sweep of Scotland's 59 constituencies leaving the Conservatives, Labour and Liberal Democrats each with a single seat.

Fear of an SNP-dominated coalition was exploited ruthlessly by the Conservatives as Ms Sturgeon piled on the pressure for Miliband to co-operate with her so that together Labour and the SNP could 'lock David Cameron out of Downing Street'. Backed to the hilt by Conservative-supporting newspapers, Cameron's Australian election strategist Lynton Crosby pursued tactics that succeeded in driving a wedge that peeled off wavering supporters from both Labour and the Liberal Democrats. The prospect that Ms Sturgeon would be able to dictate policy on both spending cuts and the future of the Trident nuclear deterrent, fuelled a succession of scare stories that warned of what would happen if a Miliband-led government came under the influence of the 'most dangerous woman in Britain'.

From the outset Miliband had stood out against media proprietors, repeatedly mentioning Rupert Murdoch by name. Labour's manifesto called for the introduction of a system of press self-regulation endorsed by Royal Charter, and proposed a review of the concentration of media holdings. In return Miliband was constantly denigrated by newspapers such as the *Sun*, *Daily Mail* and *Daily Telegraph* to a degree that shocked Labour's American election strategist David Axelrod, a former adviser to President Barack Obama. Axelrod considered the

British press was more partisan and aggressive in its reporting than even the biased pro-Republican coverage of Murdoch's American television channel Fox News.

Labour's post-election analysis, like that of the Liberal Democrats, acknowledged that their basic strategic error was to have been misled by opinion polls that were still predicting a dead heat right up until polling day. If Miliband's team had known the pollsters' forecasts were so inaccurate, they say he would have concentrated their attack on the dangers of a second Conservative government rather than getting side tracked into a debate about for conditions for another coalition. The Liberal Democrats' campaign team argued that they too had been blindsided by the inaccuracy of the polls. If their leader Nick Clegg had realised the Conservatives had a clear lead, he would have strengthened the Liberal Democrats' argument that only they could moderate a lurch to the right by a future Tory government.

Clegg, for five years the Deputy Prime Minister, paid a devastating price for having led his 57 MPs into coalition with the Conservatives. He and his colleagues accepted Cameron's invitation to put party politics aside in the national interest so that together they could tackle the financial crisis left by the crash of 2008, a brave but risky decision that became increasingly toxic after a string of tactical errors. Until seeing with utter disbelief the exit poll forecast of 10 seats they had remained confident of retaining at least 30, but when abandoned by so many previously loyal supporters disaffected by the Liberal Democrats' role in coalition, they could not withstand the Conservatives' advance. Brutal eviction from all the constituencies the Liberal Democrats held in south-west England, as well as from other strongholds that had been theirs for decades, reduced their number to eight MPs, the lowest since the 1970s. The near annihilation of a party that had seemed assured in its role as the third force in British politics was such a calamitous outcome Clegg had no option but join Miliband in standing down, their two resignations taking place within an hour of each other.

Barely a month had passed, and the eight surviving MPs had just set about deciding who should replace Clegg, when their woeful plight was made even worse by the sudden death of their former leader Charles Kennedy, one of ten Liberal Democrats in Scotland who lost their seats in the tidal wave of support for the SNP. Kennedy led his party's opposition in 2003 to Tony Blair's backing for the US invasion of Iraq. His reward in 2005 was securing almost six million votes, and the election of 62 Liberal Democrat MPs, the best result since 1923 and the days of the leadership of Lloyd George. Kennedy was said by colleagues to be the only Liberal Democrat MP who declined to vote in favour of entering a coalition with Cameron. He feared being re-branded Liberal Conservatives would drive 'a strategic coach and horses' through the realignment of the centre left, and damage if not destroy what he believed was a great Liberal tradition. In his concession speech at the count after losing Ross, Skye and Lochaber by 5,000 votes, a seat he had held for 32 years, he told his supporters they would be able to tell their grandchildren they were there the night of the long skean dhus (knives).

Opinion pollsters who had called the shots throughout the pre-election period, commanding widespread attention in the news media, ran for cover when faced by a barrage of complaints for having misled the country and encouraged Labour and Liberal Democrats to pursue election strategies that assumed another coalition was imminent. Hundreds of polls were published during an extended campaign and

11 released on the eve of the election were unanimous in predicting a dead heat, a lamentable record that prompted the British Polling Council to launch an inquiry to discover why all the polling companies had so under-estimated the scale of the Conservatives' lead over Labour.

A promise by the pollsters to follow any recommendations to re-adjust the systems they used did little to lessen the demands for a ban on the publication of polls for up to seven days before an election. The clamour to change the voting system also gathered pace after a study by the Electoral Reform Society showed that the 2015 result was the most disproportionate in the history of UK elections. The lottery of first-past-the-post had piled up 7.4 million votes for UKIP, the Liberal Democrats and the Greens yet the three parties finished up with only 10 MPs between them. Their combined share of the vote was 24.3 per cent, but a winner-takes-all voting system meant the Conservatives, who gained 11.3 million votes, a 36.9 per cent share, returned with a grand total of 331 MPs. An alliance formed by leaders of the smaller parties gave their support to a petition calling for the introduction of proportional representation. If a single transferable vote system had been in place the ERS calculated that UKIP would have gained 54 seats, Liberal Democrats 26 and Greens 3. Conservatives would have remained the largest party, but their tally would have fallen to 276, forcing them to find coalition partners. Cameron's outright majority of 12, well under John Major's 1992 margin of 21, was a far shakier mandate than he would have preferred as he prepared for the referendum on the UK's membership on European Union that his government had promised to hold before the end of 2017. One legacy of the 2010 coalition was a change in the law to fixed five-year parliaments, an arrangement that Labour hoped would give the party time to rebuild support after its catastrophic losses in Scotland and its continued failure to win seats in southern England. The Liberal Democrats too faced an uphill task to restore their credibility with the electorate.

UK 2015 general election result					
	Seats	gains	losses	votes	share
Conservative	331	35	11	11,334,576	36.9
Labour	232	22	48	9,347,304	30.4
Scottish National party	56	50	0	1,454,436	4.7
Liberal Democrat	8	0	49	2,415,862	7.9
Sinn Fein	4	0	1	176,232	0.6
Plaid Cymru	3	0	0	181,704	0.6
SDLP	3	0	0	99,809	0.3
Ulster Unionist	2	2	0	114,935	0.4
UKIP	1	1	0	3,881,099	12.6
Green	1	0	0	1,157,613	3.8

election advertising

Political advertising is always a contentious issue in general election campaigns thanks to the ingenuity of Britain's advertising and public relations industries. Donations from big business have invariably given the Conservatives far greater fire power than Labour. As well as their financial superiority, there is the added flair and creativity that derives from a strong association with the world of commercial promotion. Advertising agencies and public relations consultants tend to have a far closer affinity with management rather than workers, with employers rather than trade unions, and by the very nature of their business they have to maintain an effective working relationship with media proprietors, who themselves have a heavy bias towards the Conservatives.

Posters and newspaper advertisements, which for so long were the two most widely used forms of paid-for election advertising, have found their previous dominance has been increasingly challenged by far more sophisticated and targeted forms of communication such as direct mail, telephone canvassing and most recently by advertising and marketing via the internet. A significant shift was seen in the 2010 general election, when much of the expenditure started to move from billboards and press advertising towards spending on social media and direct marketing, a trend that accelerated still further during the 2015 campaign.

Online political promotion has the advantage for party activists of being outside the scope of regulatory frameworks. Unlike radio and television, political content on the internet is not monitored or assessed by the broadcasting regulator Ofcom. Equally the remit of the Advertising Standards Authority does not extend to political advertising. Nonetheless there are self-imposed tests of taste and decency that newspapers apply to all advertisements; billboard contractors have similar voluntary restraints. But unencumbered by any such inhibitions, the internet offers a virtual free for all, a platform for abuse and often inaccuracy that is not permitted in traditional media outlets. An image that might once have been destined to appear in a newspaper advertisement or poster can be far more daring in an online format, and more importantly can transmitted digitally within an instant. Twitter, Facebook, YouTube and a limitless range of other sites all provide opportunities for political promotion, and a constant dialogue with a much more targeted audience.

Since the 2005 election the parties have had to contend with an ever growing army of internet insurgents only too keen to parody political campaigns. Online mischief reached new heights in the lead-up to polling day in 2010, and again in 2015. As in-house designers and copywriters stepped up the intensity of their lines of attack, becoming ever more aggressive and hurtful, so they became the targets for retaliation from activists supporting their opponents. An ability to photo shop and spoof any and every political message did tend to have a levelling effect on the internet, but in terms of originality and overall impact the Conservatives' had the edge over their opponents, benefiting once again from their traditional links with advertising and the wider communications industry.

Election strategists are eager for more research into the extent to which online campaigning helps deliver electors to polling stations, especially as many older voters do not spend so much of their time on the internet, but the 2015 election did mark another milestone in extending still further the vast reach of social media. There was a rapid increase in paid-for messaging by the Conservatives, and a great deal of effort went into preparing online advertisements and commentaries for posting on Facebook and YouTube.

Instead of using advertising to establish a national presence, the party stepped up its direct marketing in marginal constituencies. Liberal Democrat constituencies in the south-west of England were among those targeted, and a clean sweep of seats previously held by their former coalition partners was a vindication of the tactics adopted by the Conservatives' Australian election strategist Lynton Crosby and his colleague Jim Messina, who masterminded Barack Obama's re-election in 2012. Their strategy was to identify potential Tory voters and then target them via direct mail and social media. On the basis of his data and research, Messina was said to have predicted a week before polling day that support for the Conservatives was continuing to build and that David Cameron would win at least 306 seats, far higher than the polls were predicting at the time.

Having switched resources to expensive but targeted promotion and marketing, the Conservatives concluded there was little to be gained from repeating the national advertising of previous elections. Posters on hoardings across the country and full-page newspaper advertisements were used in the past to create momentum. Wherever voters went, and whatever their popular paper, there was often a paid-for reminder of the party's key themes. Blanket coverage of that nature has become far too costly, given the need to concentrate advertising in the areas around the seats that are being targeted and to pay for extra promotional activity online. The lack of posters except in marginal constituencies was a notable feature of the 2015 campaign. More than half the seats in the country rarely if ever change hands, and the absence of the usual billboard reminders was a source of disappointment to many party workers. Except in hotly contested seats there were also far fewer posters being displayed by householders in their front windows and gardens, another pointer to the shift that has taken place.

Although online messaging has hastened the demise of traditional forms of election advertising many of the challenges remain the same. Compressing a political message into a few words, and then creating a relevant illustration, are tasks that require a highly disciplined approach, whether from a left or right wing perspective. Whatever the political direction, election slogans do matter, and the choice is limited: should it be positive, perhaps a much-heralded pledge alongside an image of the party leader, or a negative approach, attacking rival policies and personalities? Either way political parties have to be bold and assertive if they are to make an impact. They hope their claims and counter-claims might be newsworthy, perhaps attract the attention of political journalists, and gain extra publicity. Their efforts are not always risk free: catchy phrases that appeared both relevant and correct at the start of a campaign can get overtaken by events, backfire or get mocked by their opponents.

Party election broadcasts are another much valued platform, but their content and timing is strictly regulated. Political advertising is banned on television and radio, unlike the USA where vast fortunes are spent on the attack advertisements that dominate American television and have done so much to debase the discourse between Democrats and Republicans during presidential and congressional elections. In many ways Britain's tabloid newspapers perform a similar role as attack dogs, abusing politicians and trivialising their work. Their editorial freedom to de-stabilise governments or opposition, and to pump out propaganda on behalf of the party of their choice, is seen as one of the conditions of a free press.

While in no way seeking to minimise the disparity resulting from the might of Conservative funding and the pro-Tory weighting of the national press, there are at least some limits on party spending once an election is underway. Another balancing factor is a regulated system of broadcasting that cannot take sides politically and is required to a give a platform to minority parties. Inevitably, blatant bias and character assassination in the pages of the national press can have a lasting effect, but research has shown that what perhaps has the greatest influence before electors decide how to vote is the opportunity to see and hear what a party leader says, to listen how they respond to difficult questions, a chance for voters to form a judgment on the capability and trustworthiness of a future prime minister. A peak audience of 9.9 million for the UK's first televised leaders' debate in 2010 was an indication of the demand for direct access and the vast appetite for a chance to see a considered discussions between the leading contenders.

While politicians on the left insist they are at a perpetual disadvantage because of an in-built press bias in favour of the Conservatives, which they claim feeds across to broadcast and online coverage, Tony Blair's historic landslide in the 1997 general election demonstrated that the Labour party was capable of harnessing the support of hitherto hostile newspapers. Like Margaret Thatcher before him, Blair succeeded in winning over and then retaining the support of the media proprietors. British prime ministers do tend to be pretty invincible during that perhaps brief period when they have an impregnable parliamentary majority and the overwhelming support of the national press. Mrs Thatcher was backed to the hilt by most newspapers during her assault on trade union power in the bitter industrial disputes of the 1980s, just as Blair had widespread support from the popular press was when he joined forces with George Bush and took Britain into the Iraq War in 2003.

For good or for ill, the national press continues to retain considerable influence over the course of day to day politics. Circulations might have fallen sharply but the content, tone and editorial direction of the daily newspapers often dominates the wider news agenda; their story lines get picked up online and then initiate and sustain much of the commentary on social media. Political advertising in the press and on posters, by magnifying the positive or negative messages of the opposing sides, feeds into that broader conversation. The more provocative the advertisements, the greater the chance they will grab the attention of newspapers, radio and television and bolster the narrative that each party is attempting to promote.

Every election tends to generate heated arguments over the legitimacy, and sometimes the truthfulness, of the claims that are being made. However manufactured or synthetic the row that might develop, journalists seize on such stories as they are a welcome diversion from the tedium of complicated arguments over policy issues. Politicians scrapping with each other can liven up radio and television coverage, and provide good copy for the newspapers.

Some advertisements are so imaginative in capturing a political mood or moment that their impact endures long after the election in which they first appeared. To the dismay of their opponents an image or statement devised by advertising agency can earn a place in political folklore. When reprinted in newspapers or featured in television programmes they provide an instant visual reminder of past failings or abuses.

The Saatchis' infamous 'Labour isn't working' poster, with a dole queue snaking off into the distance, developed a life of its own during the 1979 general election campaign, and perhaps not surprisingly given the number of times the image has since been reproduced, was voted best poster of the century by the advertising magazine Campaign in 1999. Its longevity results from an association with one of the defining chapters of Britain's post-war political history, the so-called 'Winter of Discontent' that culminated in the defeat of the then Labour government and Mrs Thatcher's election as Prime Minister.

When it first appeared in August 1978, the Conservative party was on the offensive, fearing that Labour might go to the country that autumn. In the event, despite the build-up being generated by his supporters and in the press, Prime Minister James Callaghan opted against a snap general election, deciding instead to soldier on for another year. Callaghan failed to take seriously warnings from the trade union movement that there was every likelihood of industrial action if his government tried to impose another round of wage restraint. Strikes that winter disrupted services across the public sector. The Saatchi poster, together with photographs of piles of uncollected rubbish, has become part of a tapestry of images used by the media to illustrate the decline and eventual defeat of the Callaghan government.

Maurice and Charles Saatchi, who had been working on the Conservatives' advertising account for just six months, could hardly believe their good fortune when the Chancellor of the Exchequer Denis Healey criticised the poster in the House of Commons. He accused the Conservatives of 'selling politics like soap-powder', claiming that the people in the photograph were not genuinely unemployed but actually a line of Saatchi employees. Healey had made the fatal mistake of helping to promote a Conservative poster that was immensely damaging to Labour's prospects, and in the process he generated the kind of publicity that the Saatchis craved. His failure to have taken the precaution of thinking through a counter-attack that he could have used to damage the Tories was a miscalculation that Labour avoided 18 years later when another Saatchi advertisement created headline news.

In the summer of 1996 John Major's government was hanging on, counting down to a general election the following spring, but his party was determined to mount the strongest possible campaign against the rise of New Labour and perhaps avert of what seemed the near certainty of a landslide victory for Blair. As part of their pre-election fight back, the Conservatives launched an advertising campaign that proclaimed 'New Labour, New Danger'. A pair of vivid red curtains, with a pair of red, bloodshot eyes staring out, were intended to represent the front behind which New Labour was hiding.

Within a few weeks of flaming red posters appearing all over the country, the shadow transport minister, Clare Short, inadvertently gave substance to the lurid imagery created by M&C Saatchi. In an interview for the New Statesman she justified her criticism of Blair's two leading spin doctors, Peter Mandelson and Alastair Campbell, by accusing them of having briefed journalists against her: 'Everything they do is in hiding…Everything we do is in the light…I sometimes call them the people who live in the dark.'

Maurice Saatchi was given two days by the Conservative Party chairman Dr Brian Mawhinney to update the 'New Labour, New Danger' campaign in time for the weekend press. The advertisement he presented for approval showed a photograph of Blair with a big grin on his face and red, demon-like eyes. It appeared in only three newspapers that August Sunday, one of which the *Mail on Sunday* used the claim that Blair was manipulating policy in 'a sinister way' as the basis for a front-page splash.

Summer parliamentary recesses often find political journalists at a loose end, idle hands looking for mischief, only too willing perhaps to be exploited by a spin doctor conversant in the black arts of media manipulation. I heard subsequently from the Conservatives' director of communications Charles Lewington, who was with Mawhinney when they approved the advertisement that Saatchi had been far more nervous about putting demon eyes on Blair than either of them, because he feared it would provoke a storm of protest.

Mandelson had sensed the Conservatives' vulnerability. In contrast to Healey's full-frontal attack, he launched a far more deadly assault by engineering what turned into a mini media frenzy. There appeared no limits, he said, to the depths to which the Tories would sink in personalising their negative attacks on New Labour. 'Tony Blair is a practising Christian…to portray him as the devil is a crass, clumsy move.' Mandelson' masterstroke was that he had gained the support of the Bishop of Oxford, the Right Reverend Richard Harries. He denounced the vilification of politicians. His contention was that 'when that vilifying draws on satanic imagery it is not only silly but potentially dangerous'.

Labour considered their protests had been more than justified when the Advertising Standards Authority decided that the advertisement breached the industry's code of conduct because it had depicted Blair as 'sinister and dishonest'. The ruling was one of the last of its kind. In 1999 the ASA excluded political advertising from its remit because of concerns about the legality of restraining freedom of speech around democratic elections.

There can be as many potential pitfalls with a positive rather than negative campaign. Billboard advertising promoting the Conservatives' pledge to protect spending on the NHS was constantly vandalised and spoofed online in the run-up to the 2010 election. The first poster featured an obviously air-brushed photograph of David Cameron wearing an open-necked shirt, alongside the slogan, 'We can't go on like this. I'll cut the deficit, not the NHS.'

Graffiti artists with paintbrushes began defacing hoardings up and down the country, eagerly taking advantage of the copywriter's failure to realise that the slogan was open to endless variations. Cameron's favourite was said to be the poster in Hereford which was altered to give him an Elvis Presley-style haircut and the slogan was tweaked to reference a line from one of Presley's hits: 'We can't go on like this. With Suspicious Minds.' Even more imaginative versions appeared online and Cameron's smooth, blemish-free face became the most mocked image of the campaign. For once tabloid attack dogs had to take a back seat as viral graffiti artists and vandals turned the Conservatives' billboards into a laughing stock.

The first poster to cut through the extended election of 2015 was launched two months from polling day, and went on to become the most parodied image of the campaign. M&C Saatchi's aim was to build on fears that a Labour-led minority government would end up under the control of the Scottish National party, a line of attack that would be exploited relentlessly by the Conservatives. A miniature Ed Miliband was seen peeping out of the top jacket pocket of the former First Minister of Scotland Alex Salmond, who led the SNP's campaign in the 2014 referendum on Scottish independence. By lunchtime on the day the poster was launched a rival version appeared online. David Cameron was depicted peering out of the jacket pocket of Nigel Farrage, leader of the United Kingdom Independence party.

Portraying Miliband and Cameron as mere playthings was a reminder of the lampooning of the 'two Davids' by Spitting Image during conflict in the 1980s over the leadership of the SDP-Liberal Alliance when David Owen's adoring sidekick David Steel was often shown tucked into his jacket pocket. In a review of the 2015 campaign for the *Guardian*, Margaret Thatcher's former media adviser Lord Tim Bell praised the Salmond-Miliband poster for being so single-minded and visually rewarding. 'It's also very funny. People are more likely to receive a message if you deliver it with humour than if you shout of them.'

An earlier much-criticised attempt to make capital out of the SNP's potential hold over Labour had pictured Miliband on the doorstep of 10 Downing Street standing beside Salmond and the Sinn Fein President Gerry Adams with the caption, 'Your worst nightmare ... just got even worse'. A YouTube version featured a soundtrack that included the noise of breaking glass. The launch a month later of the image of Miliband in Salmond's pocket immediately caught the attention of the media, and it was widely reproduced in press coverage. M&C Saatchi re-worked the poster when Salmond's successor Nicola Sturgeon was hailed the shock winner of the first televised leaders' debate. Shortly after the programme, finished the Conservatives rushed out an online version showing a hapless-looking Miliband peering out of the jacket pocket of a smiling and contented Ms Sturgeon. The same theme was adopted in a later poster that depicted the SNP leader as a puppet-master holding up a wriggling Miliband.

Posters may longer dominate hoardings across the country during elections, but they do often appear, if only briefly, on the side of advertising campaign vans or as a backdrop for news conferences. Their great value is online where images created by advertising agencies can be constantly refashioned to suit a changing news agenda. The durability of the 1978 'Labour isn't working' poster is a testament to the potency of the Saatchis' original concept and slogan. A Labour parody in the 2015 campaign replaced the line-up of jobless workers with a long queue of patients, some in wheelchairs, outside a waiting room, with the headline, 'The doctor can't see you now'. Cameron's outright majority, and Miliband's swift resignation from the leadership, appeared to have eliminated the possibility that he might once again be portrayed as a plaything of Ms Sturgeon, but there is every likelihood that many others will end up being depicted in the top pocket of a powerful politician.

B

battle buses

Political parties face a constant challenge trying to find new ways to grab voters' attention. Each election presents a fresh challenge as the parties struggle to exploit the very latest techniques in presentation and communication. Three televised leaders' debates transformed the 2010 general election, a reminder to the strategists if one were needed that yet another political game changer might be in the offing. In the seemingly interminable build-up to polling day in May 2015, party managers agonised over how best to come to terms with the explosion in online messaging and the whole of phenomenon of social media. Having seen the impact of Twitter, Facebook, YouTube, emails, text messages and the like during hectic campaigning ahead of the 2014 referendum on Scottish independence, they were desperate to take advantage of every electronic advance, hoping to steal a march on their rivals.

Election campaigns were far easier to plan and manage before the days of 24-hours news coverage, mobile phones and especially the immediacy of the internet. By the late 1970s the pace was quickening: BBC and ITV were expanding their regional news and current affairs output, and although breakfast television and rolling news were still some years away, local programmes provided an increasingly important platform for politicians. David Steel, who in 1979 was facing his first general election as leader of the Liberal party, was about to break new ground by introducing the election **battle bus**, a converted coach that became a mobile office and headquarters. Travelling by road from one campaign stop to the next was a long-established feature of American elections; party activists and journalists bonded well together, and became known as the Boys on the Bus.

Steel thought his US import might help satisfy the insatiable demand of television crews and photographers. What better way to provide action and lots of moving pictures as he criss-crossed the country to far flung constituencies than to arrive and depart in his own bus, complete with party logo and slogan. Steel looks back with fondness on what he claims was a first for British politics, as I do too, because I drove countless miles chasing after him.

My assignment for BBC Radio 4 was to stick as closely as possible to Steel for the duration of the campaign. Rather than join other journalists on board, I had to follow the battle bus in my BBC-issue Morris Marina because I needed to peel off when required in order to file reports from the nearest BBC local radio station, and then re-join the pack at his next engagement.

Steel's decision to take to the road was news in itself because leading politicians were having to be provided with an unprecedented level of police security following the death in March 1979 of the Conservative MP Airey Neave, who was killed when a magnetic car bomb exploded under his Vauxhall Cavalier as he drove out of the underground car park at the House of Commons.

His assassination, claimed by the Irish National Liberation Army, had shocked and alarmed MPs and peers, and only added to the turmoil created by the defeat two days earlier of the Prime Minister James Callaghan. The Labour government had lost a House of Commons motion of no confidence by one vote 311-310, and the day before Neave was killed, MPs had been coming to terms with the finality of events the night before. Parliament would have to be dissolved and Callaghan forced to hold a general election in early May.

Neave had been a staunch supporter of Margaret Thatcher, who had called for the vote of no confidence. His assassination was thought to have been timed to exploit the political uncertainty at Westminster. After her election as Conservative Party leader in 1975 she had appointed Neave head of her private office and later he was promoted to shadow Secretary of State for Northern Ireland. He had backed the Army's hard line against both Loyalist and Republican paramilitaries, and the targeting of one of Mrs Thatcher's closest confidants so soon after Callaghan's defeat had put the entire political establishment on edge.

Journalists shared that sense of vulnerability as we were all having to come to terms with the implications of a fatal terrorist attack inside the precincts of the Palace of Westminster. Neave, MP for Abingdon, had been on good terms with political correspondents. I first made contact with him in the late 1960s, during my years as local government reporter for the *Oxford Mail*, and then subsequently in the mid to late 1970s when reporting for the BBC from Belfast. Having filed reports from the scene of some of the many explosions and shootings during the Troubles, I realised after Neave's death that security for the general election would be like no other. When journalists had our first sight of the battle bus we were told Steel would be accompanied throughout the campaign by a team of three plain clothes police officers; I assumed they would be armed but I did not inquire too closely.

I recall Steel and his campaign team being rather taken aback by the level of protection, but he told me he had been given a pretty chilling explanation as to why he was considered especially vulnerable. 'I had heard in a roundabout way from Ted Heath's personal assistant why the threat to the leader of the Liberal Party was being taken so seriously. Apparently an attempt on my life would have the greatest potential for publicity because I was sees as a soft target, likely to have the most minimal level of protection.' Notwithstanding the potential gravity of the circumstances, he seemed undaunted by prospect of having police officers in constant attendance, although as we toured the country the reaction to their presence ranged from disbelief and bewilderment to a touch of anxiety at local party headquarters that previously had rarely if ever commanded the attention of the Police.

Steel was one of only 13 Liberal MPs and the constituencies they represented were hundreds of miles apart, so resources were stretched as the party made preparations to contest not far short of 600 seats. Hiring a battle bus to inject excitement into the campaign built on the success of Steel's predecessor Jeremy Thorpe whose astute political showmanship had helped generate a revival in Liberal fortunes in the mid-1970s. In the general election of February 1974 the Liberals polled more than 6 million votes, their highest share since the 1920s, securing 14 seats, but in the October election six months later, despite once again being whisked around the country in helicopters and hovercraft, Thorpe failed to achieve the same turnout and the Liberals lost one of their MPs.

Steel's belief that his battle bus might prove just as eye catching in the 1979 election was fulfilled. National and regional television news programmes were able to draw on a great variety of footage as we sped along main roads or pulled into town centres. He had a ready-made, distinctive backdrop for interviews and to their great satisfaction, camera crews were able to provide arrival and departure shots that were a step up from the predictable image of a party leader arriving at a railway station or climbing out of a car. Television correspondents need a constant supply of tracking shots to illustrate their commentaries and images of Steel on the move were in demand in order to provide balanced coverage.

Each weekend we returned to the Scottish Borders so that Steel could spend time campaigning in his constituency of Roxburgh, Selkirk and Peebles. His home was in the village of Ettrickbridge where I had use of a radio line and microphone tucked into the corner of a former schoolroom that doubled up as the village playgroup. Once Steel had finished attending meetings, or perhaps giving evening speeches in the constituency, the role of the duty police officer was to accompany him home. Having safely 'delivered' the leader, the officer could re-join his colleagues back at their hotel at Selkirk. They were soon very familiar with the ten minute drive along empty roads and apparently enjoyed seeing who could clock up the shortest time for the journey, a dash of excitement in what otherwise had become a rather uneventful tour of duty.

Margaret Thatcher's clear victory over Callaghan put paid to Steel's hopes of a recovery in Liberal fortunes. The party lost just over a million votes and another two MPs, but the battle bus had made its mark, and from its humble beginnings as a rather modest charabanc would morph in subsequent elections into a high-tech mobile communications centre.

When Steel's successor Paddy Ashdown toured the country in a canary yellow campaign coach in the 1992 general election, the battle bus rosette went to the Conservatives. In the second week of the campaign we all assembled in Smith Square for the delivery outside Conservative Central Office of John Major's pride and joy. His enthusiasm was infectious as he showed off what he said was his 'fabulous' travelling campaign headquarters; it came complete with computer terminals, cellular telephones and fax machines.

After the somewhat rudimentary precautions afforded to Steel I was intrigued by the awesome in-built security: two tons of armour plating and bullet-proof glass. My interest in the level of protection being provided for the Prime Minister was not appreciated by the Tory party chairman Chris Patten. A terrorist attack was a constant threat: 'Don't you realise the IRA are trying to kill one of us?' I should have known better: Patten's curt dismissal of my inquiry reminded me that Margaret Thatcher had always favoured travelling by road in an election battle bus rather going by train because railway bridges were thought to be an easier target for the IRA.

Steel would have given his right arm for the sophistication of Major's mobile communications centre during the 1987 general election when he and David Owen criss-crossed the country in matching yellow coaches in support of the alliance formed by the Liberals and Social Democratic Party. Mobile phones were a rarity and political correspondents on the two battle buses took delight in playing off one David against the other. The shared but troubled leadership of the SDP-Liberal Alliance by the 'Two Davids' had been satirised relentlessly by *Spitting Image*; a squeaky-voiced Steel sat in the pocket of Owen.

As the campaign progressed the relationship soured. Journalists on the rival buses spent the day hunting for contradictions. Whenever there was a stop, they rang their offices so they could compare and contrast what Steel and Owen were saying. Conflicting statements on defence and the possibility of a hung parliament only served to damage still further the credibility and electoral prospects of the Alliance, resulting a year later in a merger to form the Liberal Democrats. If the 'Two Davids' had been able to keep in touch with each other by mobile phone they would have had a greater chance of thwarting the news media and perhaps there might have been fewer headlines about splits in the Alliance.

A seat on a Prime Minister's battle bus used to be a sure sign of seniority and experience. An ability to brief key political correspondents while out on the road saved precious time, but shortly before the 2005 general election journalists heard that there would be no campaign coach for the Labour leader. Tony Blair intended to scale back media access. He no longer had any wish to have journalists travelling with him in such close proximity. However, his opponent Michael Howard did take to the road despite one embarrassing news story to the effect that the Conservative leader was about to tour the country in a battle bus that was failing to display an up-to-date tax disc. Howard's press secretary Jonathan Collett remembered travelling 15,000 miles in five weeks. The bus was a centre of attraction whenever it stopped in towns and villages. 'Our arrival created an event, giving the leader's tour a sense of urgency, in a highly visible form of brand messaging, perfect fodder for the television crews.'

Clocking up thousands of miles crisscrossing the country for campaign stops in marginal constituencies was no longer an option for the 2010 election once the broadcasters managed to end years of stalemate and secure the party leaders' agreement for three televised debates. Election planners realised that spending all day travelling was hardly be the best preparation for a series of head-to-head confrontations that were certain to attract a mass television audience and might have the greatest impact on the result. David Cameron's refusal to participate in a second round of head-to-debates in the 2015 election heralded a comeback for the battle bus. His decision to opt for an extended six-week campaign to allow more time to debate policy, and to visit swing seats, meant that he and his opponents would be back on the road. Campaign staff needed a travelling headquarters that would make an impact on campaign stops, and double up as a mobile studio and briefing area for journalists.

Nick Clegg's was considered the most sophisticated of the three executive coaches hired for the election. Nicknamed the 'yellow peril', it had a satellite transmitter to allow Clegg to conduct radio interviews on the move. Journalists had to pay £750 to spend a day on board whereas Labour charged £100 a day for a ride in a silver coach that carried the slogan, 'A better plan, a better future'. Unlike Clegg, who was often filmed in his battle bus, Ed Miliband travelled more frequently by train. Of the three leaders, David Cameron clocked up the most miles travelling by road. His battle bus was decorated with union flags and sported leather seats and plasma television screens, but a ticket to ride was by invitation only.

The Greens won the prize for innovation: a double-decker bus fuelled by recycled chip fat and vegetable oil that provided a perfect environmentally-friendly back drop for their leader Natalie Bennett. A pink minibus emblazoned with the words 'woman to woman' attracted the most publicity after it was unveiled three months before polling day by Labour's deputy leader Harriet Harman. Her aim was to get the party's women MPs out into winnable seats talking to women 'around the kitchen table' about the issues that affected their lives. Labour was accused by the tabloid press of being patronising and sexist. Ms Harman was mocked by the headline writers: 'Harriet's pink Barbie bus' (*Daily Mail*) and 'Hattie's batty battle bus' (*Sun*). A host of Twitter spoofs portrayed Barbie dolls driving an array of pink vehicles. On its first outing to Stevenage, Ms Harman and two fellow MPs, Caroline Flint and Gloria de Piero, made light of the online jokes and parodies. Their target was the nine million women who failed to vote in 2010. As the campaign progressed, and the pro-Tory press found other targets, Labour had the satisfaction of securing plenty of photographs and column inches in local newspapers only too keen to report the arrival of the controversial pink minibus in marginal constituencies across the country.

The battle buses of 2015 more than met David Steel's objective of 1979: they helped meet the media's demand for photo-opportunities, while at the same time providing a travelling base for the party leaders, aides and journalists. The length of the campaign, and the distances that were travelled, justified the investment. If the Conservative government survives the full five years of a second fixed Parliament the likelihood is that another drawn-out campaign will again see battle buses back on the road in 2020.

constituents

If the outcome of a general election is on a knife-edge MPs always like to think that years of diligent work on behalf of their **constituents** might be a decisive factor in their favour. Being seen regularly out and about in their constituencies, attending local events and supporting neighbourhood groups, helps to build up their reputation and secure the recognition they hope will see them survive a severe swing against their party. More than half the 650 seats in the House of Commons rarely if ever change hands, but if a landslide is in the offing even the safest constituencies can be at risk. In a closely-fought contest MPs calculate that personal loyalty is likely to be worth possibly 1,000 votes or more, perhaps enough to ensure their safe return to Westminster. Over many years reporting national and local affairs I have had countless conversations about what it means to be rated a good constituency MP, and whether that local record counts for as much as politicians hope and expect.

In some MPs' offices at Westminster their parliamentary staff spend countless hours trying to sort out complex problems, doing everything they possibly can to chivvy local authorities and government departments, seemingly never taking 'no' for answer. In other offices the workload seems nowhere near as intense. Long-suffering constituents complain that their MPs are nothing more than glorified post boxes, simply forwarding letters having marked them for the attention of the relevant authority. There is no real analysis of what has gone wrong, or what could be done to help, little of the added input that might have been expected from having sought the assistance of their elected representatives. MPs held in such low esteem present such a sharp contrast with those that attract nothing but praise for their tenacity and perseverance in obtaining answers and remedying problems. They are regarded as ideal constituency MPs, constantly reassured that they will be able to count on a loyal, local following.

Bitter experience has shown that in some general elections the swing of the political pendulum is so great that the track record of an MP counts for nothing. For those that have devoted themselves to tireless constituency work their rejection by the electorate is a terrible, personal setback, just as is the case with high-flying ministers or celebrated parliamentarians who think their achievements will surely be acknowledged at the ballot box. Conservative and Labour politicians have grown accustomed to the rollercoaster ride of a duopoly sharing power, of having either high expectations or of fearing the worst, a sense that possibly their fate is sealed once the mood of the country is seen to be swinging violently for or against the opposition or government of the day.

Two sensational shifts in political allegiance that had such a devastating effect in the 2015 general election were exceptional in that they were the result of a dramatic rise and fall in support for two of the smaller parties. In both cases the swings were so great they took no account of local loyalties and the many personal associations that went with years of dedicated constituency effort. A tidal wave of support for the Scottish National party left Labour MPs in Scotland as defenceless as the Liberal Democrats who were ousted from their cherished strongholds by a larger than expected swing to the Conservatives.

Rarely has there been an election when so many well-established MPs from two different persuasions have been subjected to the political equivalent of sudden death, a wipe-out in regional strongholds that had seemed so impregnable for so long. However conscientious each of the defeated MPs might have been in caring for the needs of their constituents, their party label mattered most of all on polling day. In Scotland, Labour MPs were no longer considered capable of matching the authority and vision of the SNP. Liberal Democrats in the south-west of England, and in other established seats across the country, had to pay a heavy price for joining the 2010 coalition government. Right up to polling day there were confident predictions that the loyalty built up over decades would ensure the re-election of at least half of Nick Clegg's parliamentary party. In Scotland there remained until the very last the hope that allegiances that went back for generations would be sufficient to counter the SNP's take-over of what had always been one of Labour's most dependable heartlands. The loss of all but one of the party's 41 Scottish seats, and the brutal ousting of 49 Liberal Democrats, is a salutary reminder to every newly-elected MP of the potential brevity of a career at Westminster.

New members have clear choices to make about the path they wish to follow in the House of Commons. They can at least make their plans with some certainty now that a five-year stint seems assured as a result of a second fixed term parliament that has set the date of the next general election as May 2020. As in previous elections the new intake will wish to become the jealous Guardians of their constituencies and the interests of their local electorates. Some MPs will want to go further than their colleagues in the hope of getting re-elected, prioritising the needs of their constituents at the expense of the chance to further a parliamentary role. Their time will be divided between duties at Westminster and demands back in their constituency. Others will aim for promotion to the front bench, or be seek to play a part in the expanding work of parliamentary select committees, perhaps intent on becoming an authority on controversial issues of the day. MPs with a busy workload at Westminster, or outside parliament, will almost certainly spend far less time in their constituencies. While they will make a point of attending weekly or fortnightly surgeries for constituents, their personal commitment and presence in the locality will hardly bear comparison with some of their colleagues. Much of course will depend on whether an MP has a safe or marginal seat, a factor that will probably have the greatest influence on their days at Westminster, and the judgement of their constituents.

Having lived in the same constituency for over forty years, while at the same time working at Westminster, I have witnessed at first hand a marked difference in approach. Chipping Barnet in north London is a safe Conservative seat, and over the course of 11 general elections there have been only three MPs in the period that I have been a constituent. Reginald Maudling, Chancellor of the Exchequer in the 1960s, was MP for my first six years, followed by the late Sir Sydney Chapman, who represented Chipping Barnet for 26 years, and then most recently by Theresa Villiers, Secretary of State for Northern Ireland. Maudling and Chapman each spent well over two decades as the local MP, but they presented a sharp contrast in their attitude towards the constituency. Maudling, tipped at one point is his career to be a future Prime Minister, was a household name, who commanded loyalty from constituents on the strength of high office in successive Conservative governments. He was rarely seen in the constituency, and his occasional visits to events held by his local Conservative association became even less frequent during his final, troubled years as an MP, and his death shortly before the 1979 general election.

Chapman ended his political career in 2005 reassured by the knowledge that he had earned the accolade of being considered a good constituency MP, respected even by his political opponents for his dedication to the needs of the local electorate. After four years representing Birmingham Handsworth, he was elected for Chipping Barnet where he established his family home, and became a well-known local figure in High Barnet town centre and surrounding streets. His children went to local schools; he supported numerous groups in the constituency; and became a great defender of the Green Belt around London's northern suburbs. At Westminster he served diligently in the whips' office of John Major's government and had the unenviable task of trying to keep troublesome Conservative Euro-sceptic MPs in line whenever they threatened yet another rebellion against their embattled Prime Minister. His reward was to be appointed Vice-chamberlain and he took on the task of writing a note to the Queen each evening to report on the day's proceedings in parliament.

Given his duty in the whips' office, Chapman disliked the grandstanding of some his colleagues and was never tempted to become a rent-a-quote MP. Indeed he used to tell me that he made a point of not answering journalists' questions whenever they tried to trap him into making provocative comments about unemployment or the state of the economy. He much preferred briefing local newspapers on his many constituency activities and various local initiatives. His refusal to get drawn into political dog-fights paid off in the 1997 general election, when Tony Blair's landslide victory unseated Conservative MPs from a large swathe of north London and south Hertfordshire. Chapman held his seat by the narrow margin of 1,035 votes, and next day's election maps on television and in newspapers showed that Chipping Barnet was the one remaining blue spot in what was otherwise a sea of red. One nearby Conservative MP who lost his seat was Michael Portillo in Enfield Southgate.

In subsequent conversations Chapman acknowledged that his tactic of keeping a low profile had probably been a factor in helping him retain his seat. As a result he had not been targeted by the left, as had been the case with Portillo and other neighbouring Tory MPs. He thought that being a local resident, and having spent so much time helping and getting to know his constituents, had also played a part in allowing him to hang on. Nonetheless he was in doubt from exchanges on the doorstep that he had been abandoned by many of his usual supporters. Most of them said that after 18 years under the Conservatives the country needed a change of government, and they could not bring themselves to vote for him. I was reminded of Chapman's lucky escape in a seat that had been solidly blue since 1950 when Scotland's political map went almost completely yellow leaving a single red spot marking the constituency where a solitary Labour MP escaped annihilation.

D

deposits

Having to forfeit the £500 that has to be paid for the privilege of standing in a parliamentary election is not always a source of disappointment. For a candidate from a mainstream party a lost **deposit** is a perpetual reminder of being rejected by the electorate, an embarrassing setback that opponents try to exploit for political advantage. Many of those who stand in by-elections and general elections know they have not the slightest chance of ever getting elected to the House of Commons. They regard the deposit as the necessary price for an opportunity to campaign for what they believe is a vital cause or principle; perhaps their aim is to publicise a local or national grievance. Some candidates on the fringe are there simply to enjoy a moment in the public spotlight, happy to stump up £500 in return for free publicity. Cheap at the price is the verdict of fancy-dressed attention seekers who push their way to the front of the picture as the count is being announced live on television.

Deposits are forfeited if a candidate fails to secure at least 5 per cent of the valid votes cast. In declaring the result a returning officer gives the figure for each of the candidates, but they are spared the indignity at the count of being singled out by name as having lost their deposit. Candidates obtaining no more than perhaps a hundred or so votes know instantly that their money will not be returned. Higher up the list there may be greater uncertainty, and a rapid calculation has to be made. Journalists are desperate to know because confirmation of a lost deposit by a candidate from one or other of the established parties is news in itself, a dramatic pointer to declining political fortunes.

A catastrophic slump in the Liberal Democrats' popularity, and their near wipe-out across the country, was one of the many dramatic story lines in an astonishing run of events that gripped audiences for the results night programmes in the 2015 election. Seeing his parliamentary colleagues being decapitated by the Conservatives in all their strongholds in the south-west of England was torture in itself for Nick Clegg, but the momentous scale of their UK-wide defeat was laid bare in the early hours of the morning when the figures indicated that the party had already lost deposits in well over 300 seats, a tally that was still rising. On the final count the Liberal Democrats forfeited 341deposits, higher even than their previous worst result of 303 deposits lost in 1979, the year of Margaret Thatcher's victory. In the following election the SDP-Liberal Democrat Alliance forfeited 199 deposits, but in the six subsequent six elections the highest loss was 11, and none had to be forfeited in 2010, a record that underlined the sheer magnitude of the post-coalition collapse in the Liberal Democrats' vote. Losing deposits in more than half the seats the party contested incurred a hefty price tag of £170,500, admittedly far less than the £45,000 lost in 1979 when a deposit of only £150 was required.

By far largest financial loss was incurred by candidates for the Greens who together forfeited 444 deposits, at a cost of £222,000. Natalie Bennett, the party leader, finished in third place in Holborn and St Pancras, well clear of the danger zone, but the surge in her support was not repeated across the country. The Greens fielded their largest ever slate of candidates, standing in just over 90 per cent of the 650 seats at Westminster. Hopes were high of building on the advances made in the 2014 elections to the European Parliament. Opinion polls forecast their share of the vote might reach 8 per cent, but so many candidates failed to reach 5 per cent that the Greens accounted for just over half of all the deposits lost by the five biggest parties.

While the proportion of electors turning out to vote has been declining for several decades, the number of people standing for parliament has shown a sharp increase in recent years because of fragmenting political loyalties and the growth in smaller parties. A total of 3,971 candidates were nominated in 2015, the second highest figure since 1997, of whom 1,565 failed to reach the five per cent threshold and lost their deposit. Candidates with the lowest number of votes included Nathan Handley, an independent in David Cameron's constituency of Witney, who mustered only 12 votes, and two candidates standing against the Mayor of London, Boris Johnson, in Uxbridge and South Ruislip – Jane Lawrence (Realists' party) secured 18 votes and James Jackson (independent) 14 votes.

Of the fringe contenders who stood in 2015 the comedian Al Murray, in the guise of the Pub Landlord, was the only one who succeeded in gaining sustained national prominence after declaring himself a candidate in Thanet South, the constituency targeted by Nigel Farrage, leader of the United Kingdom Independence party. Murray launched his campaign under the banner Free United Kingdom party. His ability to mock Farrage, coupled with his flair for generating some eye-catching stunts, generated considerable publicity. For some weeks he had a regular column in the *Sun*, standing in for the *Top Gear* presenter Jeremy Clarkson. Murray failed to get his party's name listed on the ballot paper and received only 318 votes, finishing sixth in a field of 11 candidates. Nonetheless he did not miss a trick, knowing precisely where to stand when the result was declared. As Farrage stood grim faced listening to the declaration and the confirmation that he had failed to take the seat from the Conservatives, Murray was grinning at his shoulder, making the most of a live television appearance.

If there is a lengthy line-up, as is often the case in a hotly contested by-election, a publicity-seeking candidate might need some skilful footwork to push in at the last moment so as to make sure of getting into shot. For almost 30 years the late David Sutch, leader of the Official Monster Raving Loony party, was a class act in the art of managing to upstage his opponents so as to make sure he was always in a prime position when the declaration was made. Sutch, or Screaming Lord Sutch as he preferred to be known, fought well over 30 by-elections, the last in 1997, the year before his death. He was a close friend of another indefatigable by-election candidate Commander Bill Boaks who campaigned on the issue of road safety.

Sutch and Boaks both became well-known because in their day there was a requirement that candidates' names and political descriptions had to be either read out on air or appear on screen when radio or television news bulletins carried reports from a by-election or high-profile constituency in a general election. Listeners and viewers are now told that a full list is available on line, on the websites of the BBC and other networks. Newsworthy contests remain popular with fringe candidates, but there is far less chance of getting mentioned on radio or television, which previously used to be an added draw. Presenters were sometimes heard struggling with whacky labels such as Monster Raving Loony, National Teenage (Sutch's first party) or Boaks' Trains, Boats and Planes party. Ludicrous political titles are a boon for satirists, and they were deployed to great effect in skits on *Monty Python's Flying Circus* and *The Goodies*. Hearing them pop up in news bulletins was always an added source of amusement.

A vast array of fringe candidates was again on offer in 2015: 27 Monster Raving Loonies had a combined haul of 3,898 votes; Doris Osen, thought to be the oldest candidate at the age of 84, secured 87 votes for the Elderly Persons' Independent party in Ilford North; Bez Berry, standing for Reality in Salford and Eccles pulled in 703 votes; Jonathan Dzon of the Pluralist party attracted 23 votes in Liverpool Walton; and Mark Flanagan finished bottom of the poll on 24 votes in Leeds North West having stood for the Above and Beyond party offering electors the option of voting for 'none of the above'.

Although the fringe might be losing out in terms of publicity, candidates are able to exercise the right to promote their cause to electors within their chosen constituency. If those contesting a seat have sufficient funds of their own to meet printing costs, an election addresses will be delivered free of charge on their behalf by the Royal Mail. A freepost allowance, in some cases worth tens of thousands of pounds, is a much valued concession for serious minded but hard-pressed activists who might already have struggled to stump up a deposit.

Activists from the left, disaffected by the policies of the Labour party and its affiliated trade unions, are becoming increasingly focused in their attempts to win representation. The Trade Unionist and Socialist Coalition fielded 135 candidates in the 2015 election, sufficient to secure its first-ever party election broadcast for transmission across England, Scotland and Wales. Bob Crow, the late general secretary of the transport union RMT, established the coalition in 2010, bringing together the Socialist party, the Socialist Workers' party, and other socialist groups. TUSC's national chair, the former Labour MP Dave Nellist, gained 1,769 votes in Coventry North West, the highest figure polled by its candidates who all lost their deposits. An end to austerity, abolition of student tuition fees and a return of the railways to public ownership were high in the party's list of demands. Re-nationalisation of the coal and steel industries were two key priorities of the former miners' leader Arthur Scargill, founder of Socialist Labour, when he launched his party's campaign to contest eight seats in Wales.

Dedicated socialists are among those who are determined, whatever the cost in lost deposits, to go on exercising their right to seek election to parliament. Having spoken over the years to candidates who have tried and tried again to win a seat, often campaigning with persuasion on local grievances, I know how gratified they are to find even the smallest increase in their share of the vote. Remote though it may seem to think they might ever win popular support, there is always the example of Dr Richard Taylor who stood as the Kidderminster Hospital Health Concern candidate and pulled off a sensational personal victory in 2001 when he secured a majority of 17,630 in the Wyre Forest constituency. He was campaigning for the restoration of an accident and emergency department and proved with ease that it is possible to connect with the public on a single issue.

When the deposit was raised from £150 to £500 in 1985 the threshold was reduced from 12.5 per cent to 5 per cent of votes cast. The reduction was agreed because of the damaging impact the threshold was having on the finances of the smaller parties. In the 1983 election 1,000 candidates lost their deposits, but once the change was made there was a dramatic fall in the number being forfeited. Due to the rapid rise since 1997 in the number of candidates being fielded by smaller parties, and a corresponding increase in lost deposits, there is renewed concern over a disproportionately heavy financial penalty. A report published in 2013 by Democratic Audit UK highlighted the damaging consequences of an 'uneven playing field' that 'protected the interests of the larger parties'. In nine elections between 1974 and 2010, the Greens paid out over £800,000 in lost deposits (measured in 2009-10 prices), a bill that topped £1 million as a result of losses incurred by a lower than expected turnout in 2015. UKIP had forfeited £900,000 over the same period but its vastly improved share of the vote had cut the number of lost deposits to 77.

Shortly before the 2015 election the Electoral Commission recommended that the £500 deposit should be scrapped because smaller parties and independent candidates were finding the cost of participating in elections was becoming unaffordable. Jenny Watson, the commission's chairwoman, acknowledged the argument of the larger parties that a threshold was needed to deter 'non-serious candidates', but a £500 deposit was an unreasonable restriction if the aim was to make it easier for candidates of minor parties to seek election. When Ms Watson issued her warning she had no way of knowing how costly the system would be for the casualties of May 2015.

election timing

Generations of political correspondents have spent countless hours writing and broadcasting about the likely choice of polling day. Speculating about the timing of an **election** used to be one of the mainstays of a journalist's life at Westminster – that is until the 2010 coalition government broke with tradition, and opted for the stability of a fixed term Parliament, deciding that Thursday 7 May would be the date of the 2015 general election. At a stroke David Cameron and Nick Clegg deprived reporters of the great unknown, the one overriding uncertainty that could be relied upon by the news media to sustain months of pre-election reportage. But journalists and political pundits can never be accused of lacking inventiveness, and although we had lost the opportunity to deliberate on perhaps the loneliest decision facing any Prime Minister, we were soon busily engaged in exploiting another imponderable, the unpredictability of multi-party politics.

Fragmentation became a buzz word in a political journalist's A-Z for 2015: the closer to polling day, and the greater the likelihood of another hung parliament, the more varied the forecasts. Pundits hedged their bets as they had to contend with a fall in the predicted share of the vote for the Conservatives, Labour and Liberal Democrats; the emergence of UKIP as a fourth major party; the unprecedented strength of the Scottish National Party; and indications of a surge in support for the Greens. Given the vagaries of first-past-the-post voting in 650 separate constituencies, the pollsters projected endless permutations for the future make-up of what they were convinced would most probably have to be another coalition government, or perhaps even a minority administration. To add further drama to the guessing game the news media made a collective decision in mid-January 2015 to start a 100-day countdown to polling day. As the date of the election was no longer news, and the tradition of a short, sharp three- to four-week campaign had been pre-empted, political journalists knew they had to inject a sense of excitement into their coverage, and what better way than to manufacture a timetable that would help generate interest and headlines for both newspapers and broadcasters alike.

Our previous pre-occupation with election timing had not been misplaced: until the 2010 election, Prime Ministers had jealously guarded their right to decide the moment they would go to the country and seek a new mandate from the electorate. British political history has often turned on the timing of elections and several post-war Premiers have rued their choice of polling day. Some of the most absorbing periods in my career have been spent observing the downfall and defeat of an ailing government, and contrasting that with the bravado of a Prime Minister prepared to face an early contest, assured of securing another healthy Parliamentary majority. James Callaghan, John Major and Gordon Brown, three Prime Ministers that chose to hang on, each had sound reasons for wishing to complete a full term but they were dogged by the 'will he, won't he' speculation that accompanied the slow, lingering deaths of their administrations.

My first taste of reporters' addiction to the 'great unknown' story line was at the 1978 Trades Union Congress at Brighton. Callaghan's speech had been eagerly awaited by the delegates, and among trade union leaders and journalists alike there was an expectation that the Prime Minister would go early and announce that Labour would opt for an autumn election. Callaghan, at ease on a conference platform, rose to the occasion, but then confounded the pundits with a rendition of the music-hall song 'There was I, waiting at the church'. Like the bride jilted by the non-appearance of the groom, I could see from my seat at the press table that the assembled union presidents and general secretaries were dumbfounded. They could not believe that Callaghan had rejected their advice to hold a general election that October, and later they made little secret of the private warnings they had given his government that public sector workers would not accept another year of pay restraint. In the late 1970s I had switched from political to industrial reporting. Little did I know it then but Callaghan's miscalculation in paving the way for Margaret Thatcher's victory in the 1979 general election would also go on to give me the opportunity to report the momentous strikes of her decade in power?

In later years Callaghan acknowledged that it had been an error of judgment, but from his perspective the decision was entirely understandable. He had been in Downing Street for only two and a half years, having taken over from Harold Wilson midterm in 1976, and he had every reason for wishing to complete Labour's programme. Although the Lib-Lab pact that had sustained his government had collapsed in the summer of 1978, inflation and unemployment were falling and the opinion polls were suggesting that Labour might soon be ahead. Even so, reporters on the labour and industrial beat understood why the union hierarchy were advising Callaghan to call a snap election rather than wait a year until October 1979. There had already been four years of pay restraint for public sector workers, and one of the factors influencing the Prime Minister's timing was whether to gamble on struggling on for a fifth year by attempting to hold wage increases to 5 per cent.

Within a matter of weeks, as the autumn pay demands of the rival unions escalated, so did the threats of industrial action, the very warnings that the Prime Minister had chosen to ignore. Disputes broke out across the public sector involving local councils, schools and hospitals, and the widespread strikes and disruption of the so-called 'Winter of Discontent' sealed Labour's fate. The following March, Callaghan lost a House of Commons motion of no confidence by one vote 311-310, after he had been deserted by Scottish nationalists, and he was forced to announce a general election for early May 1979, five months before he needed to. The humiliation of having no alternative but to go to the country was a humiliation Margaret Thatcher was always anxious to avoid on becoming Prime Minister. To reinforce her political authority she went to the country twice, in 1983 and 1987, on a date of her choosing, after only four years in office. By casting off the constraint over having to serve a full five-year Parliament she intended to signal to voters the smack of firm government.

Her successor John Major led the Conservatives to a fourth general election victory in 1992 but just as Callaghan was brought down by his failure to curb industrial militancy, Major's second term would be beset by internal party dissent over Britain's relationship with Europe. My return to political reporting could not have been more opportune. As the threat of industrial action receded, and there were few if any wildcat strikes, most trade union leaders backed Neil Kinnock's attempts to modernise the Labour movement, and a change of government seemed highly likely after the ousting of Mrs Thatcher in the wake of debacles such as the poll tax. Kinnock fought the 1992 election on a platform that incorporated the party's final acceptance of the employment and trade union laws that the Conservatives had introduced. In the months leading up to polling day, the two main parties were neck and neck in the opinion polls, and victory appeared to be within Labour's grasp.

Major had kept the country guessing about the likely date but the expectation was that he would seek the dissolution of parliament in early March, immediately after the final budget had been delivered by the Chancellor Norman Lamont. Reporters had known for some days that Major had an audience with the Queen later that week, and the announcement, when it came, ran like clockwork. Gus O'Donnell, the Prime Minister's press secretary, had worked in great secrecy to provide the best possible lift-off for Major, who was then an untried election campaigner. In a break with tradition, Downing Street set up a conference telephone call with the leading news agencies at 11 am to tell them simultaneously that Major would be leaving for Buckingham Palace within the hour. It had been essential to prevent the news leaking out in advance as confirmation that the Prime Minister was on his way to see the Queen was considered price sensitive information that could affect the stock market.

Giving broadcasting organisations two hours' notice of an announcement at 1 pm on the steps of No. 10 gave them ample time to deploy teams of reporters, camera crews and technicians. Split-second timing is needed for live coverage, so Major was careful not to walk out to the waiting microphones too soon, otherwise he might have clashed with the opening titles of the lunchtime news bulletins or failed to allow sufficient time for programme presenters to hand over to the reporters stationed in Downing Street. By holding Major back until exactly four minutes past one, No. 10 guaranteed the smoothest possible presentation. O'Donnell prided himself on arranging orderly doorstep appearances, and Major went on to confound the pollsters and faint hearts in his own party by achieving an overall majority of 21 after a short four-week campaign. His re-election did little to lessen the turmoil within his own party; his Euro-sceptic tormentors were about to spend the next five years devising ever more daring guerrilla tactics at Westminster.

The final demise of an ailing government is always unpredictable. Events move so fast that life for political correspondents is often a hand-to-mouth existence. Even before finishing one story, reporters are sent off to the next assignment. Adding to Major's woes were allegations of financial 'sleaze' that inflicted further damage to the standing of Conservative MPs, but despite having in effect lost control of his party, he was determined, like Callaghan, to go the distance and serve the full five years rather than take a chance on an early election. Such was the speculation that he might be forced at some point to go to the country that correspondents had to make constant checks. I was regularly being reassured by one ministerial adviser that Major would definitely not announce polling day until after his government had completed the process of privatising British Rail, so that it could not be taken back into public ownership should Tony Blair win the 1997 election.

Rail privatisation, as with the break-up of the coal industry, was one of the all-important Thatcherite objectives that could not be left to chance. British Coal, the National Coal Board's successor, was wound up early in 1997, but establishing a privatised rail network was taking Major longer than expected. Awarding franchises to competing train operating companies was a complicated process and when completed it would achieve a result dear to Mrs Thatcher's heart. In the early 1980s her government had struggled in the face of frequent strikes by train drivers and other rail staff. Privatisation would make it virtually impossible for the rail unions to organise future national strikes, as they would be required to negotiate with the individual operating companies. Drivers' wages have increased considerably as a result of private ownership but without the industrial conflict of the past. National pay bargaining is no longer conducted by British Rail and instead there are separate negotiations with 22 train operators. As a consequence the Conservatives believe they have all but eliminated the chances of the unions staging another UK-wide rail strike.

If fears about a failure to complete parliamentary business and deliver long-held promises had been factors that influenced Callaghan and Major, Tony Blair had to contend with the uncertainty of a national emergency when deciding the date of the 2001 general election. Like Mrs Thatcher, he too was all set to go a year early, confident of repeating his 1997 victory. Political journalists and pundits had all been predicting that polling day would be in May, to coincide with the council elections, but Britain had been overtaken by a crippling outbreak of foot and mouth disease. By early April, seven weeks into the epidemic, there had been well over 800 confirmed cases of the disease on farms up and down the country, from Cornwall to southern Scotland.

Television crews and photographers had begun assembling in Downing Street long before the expected announcement from the Prime Minister that the elections would have to be delayed. By the time I arrived there was hardly any room left; the crush behind the barriers was such that it was almost impossible to move. The first sign of action was the arrival of a civil service broadcasting engineer whose job it is to place a microphone on a stand a few paces away from the front door of No. 10. 'Testing … one, two, three … testing … one, two, three …'   Checking the Prime Minister's microphone is an essential precaution because government publicity staff are responsible for supplying the sound feed to competing radio and television outlets – a function over which Downing Street insists on taking control in order to ensure a clean picture of the Prime Minister standing in front of No. 10, without the clutter of a dozen or so separate microphones, sometimes bearing the logos of rival networks.

Blair duly announced that the council elections would be delayed from May to June but he made no reference whatsoever to the likelihood of a general election being held on the same day, or indeed any other. Once Blair finished his statement, political correspondents trooped across the road to a side door in Downing Street for a lobby briefing by his director of communications, Alastair Campbell. He seemed to share our irritation that there might be another month's uncertainty but I remember his being in a combative mood: 'I am not saying anything about the general election beyond what the Prime Minister has not said.' Blair had taken great care to avoid giving any hint that he would eventually opt for the same day in June as the postponed council elections because once he indicated the date of the election, Parliament would have to be dissolved, the civil service would be unable to implement any further changes in government policy, and No. 10 would lose the services of Campbell and the other politically-appointed special advisers who were expected to resign once the campaign was announced.

The sheer finality of naming the date helps explain the indecision of Blair's successor Gordon Brown, who in the autumn of 2007 faced a dilemma comparable to that experienced by Jim Callaghan. Having had only three months in No. 10 after Blair's long-promised handover the previous June, Brown was truly facing the loneliest decision. To his credit he had been dubbed an 'action man' by the tabloid press for the authoritative way he had responded to a terrorist attack at Glasgow airport and summer floods in Gloucestershire; Labour's opinion poll ratings had improved; and his agility in meeting the media's deadlines had allowed him to discard some of the political baggage of the past and to start reinventing himself in the eyes of the public.

Labour's annual conference that autumn was dominated by runaway speculation that the party was indeed gearing up for a snap election in November. Having had a ringside seat at Labour's 1978 debacle I had my doubts; I thought Brown, like Callaghan, would want above all else to complete the five-year mandate that the party had secured. Lord Kinnock was one of the few Labour voices ruling out an autumn poll: 'Brown's instinct is not to go for a snap election.' Then, without warning, Brown's commanding position was challenged by the shadow chancellor George Osborne who told his party's annual conference that a future Conservative government would increase the threshold for inheritance tax to £1 million.

As events would later prove Brown was a Premier easily buffeted by negative headlines, and once the opinion polls suggested that Labour and the Conservatives were neck and neck in the wake of the Tories' promise to remove 98 per cent of family homes from inheritance tax – a pledge that the coalition government subsequently failed to agree upon – he found he had boxed himself in, plagued by conflicting advice. Just as Callaghan had been warned by trade union leaders that a snap election might help pre-empt uncontrollable strike action, Brown was being advised that if he were elected Prime Minister in his own right, he would be in a stronger position to deal with potential turbulence in the financial markets following the Treasury's belated decision to guarantee the savings of Northern Rock's depositors.

Increasingly I felt I was a witnessing a replay of Callaghan's fateful lack of clarity. In his autobiography *Time and Chance* (1987), he admitted he had only himself to blame for allowing his supporters and journalists to fuel runaway expectations of a snap election in the autumn of 1978: 'I made a mistake in allowing the speculation to build up to an almost feverish crescendo without uttering a word to cool it.' But at Labour headquarters there was such certainty that Brown would indeed opt for a quick four-week campaign that party officials had been drafting in extra staff; desks, chairs and other office equipment had been hired in readiness.

An announcement had to be made that Sunday if polling day was to be on either 1 or 8 November, the last two possible dates. There was to be none of the precision of Thatcher or Blair but instead a self-inflicted own goal from which Brown would fail to recover. By Friday evening there was no going back: editors and political correspondents on Sunday newspapers were told that early on Saturday afternoon Brown would pre-record an interview with Andrew Marr for transmission on Sunday morning. Once Brown's aides confirmed to journalists that the Prime Minister had abandoned the idea of a November election the news spread like wildfire that Saturday afternoon. During a gap in a rugby commentary, the BBC's political editor Nick Robinson told listeners to Radio 5 Live that the election was off; word soon reached Conservative campaign headquarters, and the Tory blogosphere buzzed with jibes about 'bottler Brown'.

No wonder after the indecisive result in 2010 that David Cameron and Nick Clegg were so eager to lock Conservative and Liberal Democrat MPs into a fixed Parliament that would end five years later with a general election. Across the party political spectrum there seemed to be a general acceptance that the twin task of rebuilding the economy after the financial crash of 2008, and addressing the deep distrust of politicians at Westminster, required an unprecedented degree of certainty rather the customary speculation about possible dates for a general election. After the Conservatives stunned opinion pollsters and opponents alike with their unexpected victory in May 2015, Cameron embarked on another five-year term giving every indication that he believed a fixed Parliament would again work to his advantage. At last he had been able to form a majority Conservative government, albeit with a majority of only twelve. After the vagaries of coalition he seemed confident that his party would definitely want to go the distance, a goal that he had outlined for himself in a surprise pre-election interview saying it would be his intention to serve a second fixed term but not a third. Taking into account the devastating consequences of defeat for both Labour and the Liberal Democrats, the Prime Minister had every justification for assuming that the opposition too would be content to work towards a general election in May 2020.

fragmentation

After five years' experience of coalition government there seemed every prospect that the United Kingdom might be on the brink of multi-party politics, perhaps a rainbow parliament emerging from the 2015 general election that would match the predictions of the pollsters. Failure by either Labour or the Conservatives to win an outright majority in 2010 forced David Cameron to share power with the Liberal Democrats, a scenario that looked like being repeated if the opinion polls were correct in forecasting that neither of the two main parties was within reach of a commanding lead. Further **fragmentation** of the established order, and another hung parliament, looked the most probable outcome given the rapid advance of both the United Kingdom Independence party and the Scottish National party, plus a strengthening in support for the Greens. Those who doubted that further change was in the offing must have had second thoughts five weeks from polling day when seven party leaders took their places for the first televised debate of the 2015 campaign. Three women were in the line-up, adding another visual manifestation of the multi-hued nature of the multi-party choice on offer.

Britain's electoral arrangements have rarely favoured political insurgencies. Down the years numerous smaller parties have been snuffed out by a first-past-the-post voting system that has almost always delivered a majority for alternating Labour or Conservative governments. But their share of the overall vote has been in remorseless decline, a far cry from the 1951election when the two parties commanded almost 97 per cent of votes cast. A steady resurgence in support for the Liberal Democrats that began in the 1970s, and gathered pace in the 1990s, finally broke the two-party dominance of the House of Commons. Their 57 MPs held the balance of power in 2010, the party's chance to join the first coalition government since the Second World War. Further inroads by the SNP and UKIP, and their spectacular run of success in elections to the Scottish Parliament and the European Parliament, suggested that even greater fragmentation of the electorate was imminent.

Nigel Farrage could take much of the credit for having created an unprecedented opportunity for minor parties to reach out to a mass UK-wide television audience. Under his leadership UKIP had pulled off the equivalent of an electoral smash and grab raid. Given the size of its share of the vote in elections during the two preceding years, UKIP was deemed by television and radio to have 'major party' status for the six weeks of the campaign, a passport to a greater allocation of air time. Much to the chagrin of his three main opponents the guidance of the broadcasting regulator Ofcom, already put into effect by the BBC, was a further complication to tortuous negotiations with the main parties as the broadcasters tried to secure approval for a repeat of the three televised leaders' debates held in 2010.

After weeks of bad tempered exchanges, and threats that his podium might be left empty, the Prime Minister finally agreed to take part in one single head-to-head encounter, but only on condition that the line-up was extended to include other party leaders. Conservative strategists blamed Cameron's failure to win an outright majority in 2010 on his initial miscalculation in encouraging the previous round of debates, which were a first for a British election. The advice of his campaign team was blunt: another series of head-to-heads would give the Labour leader Ed Miliband an opportunity to repeat the breakthrough achieved five years earlier by the Liberal Democrat leader Nick Clegg. If Cameron did participate he should insist on the widest possible line-up so as to dilute the impact of those taking part. As UKIP could claim equal billing with the Liberal Democrats, and as Farrage was considered the greatest threat to the Conservatives' support, Cameron countered by suggesting that the Greens' leader Natalie Bennett should have an invitation, not least because Ofcom had ruled that her party did not need to be included. In her case the Conservatives' calculation was that she might attract votes from the left that might otherwise have gone to Labour.

Once the line-up was extended to include the SNP leader Nicola Sturgeon, there was no justification for excluding the Plaid Cymru leader Leanne Wood. At one point there was the possibility that an eighth podium might be required when Cameron indicated he would like to see the Democratic Unionists included as well, but the broadcasters argued successfully against their inclusion on the grounds that the parties of Northern Ireland were not contesting seats held by the Conservatives, Labour or Liberal Democrats.

Lynton Crosby, the Conservatives' election strategist, had achieved his twin aim of squeezing Miliband's exposure while at the same time diluting the impact of the one head-to-head confrontation that the Prime Minister had agreed to. Cameron's argument after the 2010 debates was that they attracted so much attention the leaders had insufficient opportunities to present their policies, but what he had not bargained for was that his intransigence had ushered in another innovation that in all probability appeared likely to weaken still further the appeal of the two-party system. On display for the first time was a glimpse of what of what multi-party politics could offer, an illustration of how the custom and practice of British politics might be reshaped through electoral reform and the introduction of a fairer system of voting.

Electors in England might have wondered why they were being addressed by two parties that they could not vote for and whose leaders were not even candidates, but the audience reaction was positive. Viewers welcomed a rare opportunity to hear the views of Scottish and Welsh nationalists, and the sight of three women arguing their point of view was applauded by feminist writers who found the usual all-male line-ups so off putting. 'Dawn of rainbow politics' was the front-page headline of the *I* newspaper above a picture of seven leaders standing behind their podiums for an 'epic television battle' that made political history.

Nicola Sturgeon, riding high on a surge in SNP support despite losing the 2014 referendum on independence, drew widespread praise for an impressive performance. She showed no hesitation when demanding an end to 'blind austerity', and while calling for the 'break up the old boys club' at Westminster, she insisted the SNP's aim in the House of Commons would be to push for 'progressive politics'. She was credited with giving the best defence of free university education since Scotland opted out of tuition fees, and was hailed on her return to Edinburgh as the new 'Queen of Scots' for upstaging her English rivals in a television triumph. She made the front page of the *Daily Mail* under the headline, 'Most dangerous woman in Britain', an epithet that other Tory newspapers adopted as the opinion polls strengthened their forecast of an SNP landslide.

Natalie Bennett was under the watchful eye of the news media in case of stage fright. Earlier in the campaign she was forced to apologise for an 'excruciating brain fade' during an LBC radio interview about the Greens' housing policy, but she was well prepared in her defence of public spending. She agreed with Ms Sturgeon that electors faced a choice between 'the austerity-heavy and the austerity light' of the two main parties, a line of attack followed through by Leanne Wood. She won the first applause of the evening from the studio audience for telling Nigel Farrage he 'ought to be ashamed' of himself for his scaremongering over HIV-positive foreigners seeking treatment from the National Health Service. Ms Bennett joined in, challenging the UKIP leader for his claims about the cost of health tourism.

Far from being able to reinforce his authority as Prime Minister as his advisers thought might be the outcome of a diffuse seven-way debate of Cameron v. the rest, he found himself facing a sustained assault from a trio of party leaders who on several issues had an agreed and co-ordinated approach. Ms Sturgeon's implacable opposition to the renewal of Trident nuclear submarines had been endorsed by Ms Wood and Ms Bennett at a meeting of the three party leaders the previous December. They continued their joint assault in a second five-way *Challengers' Debate* a fortnight later that excluded Cameron and Clegg. Miliband was the target, especially for Ms Sturgeon who promised the SNP would 'help Labour be bolder' as he was 'not strong enough' to defeat the Conservatives on his own.

Immediately after the debate finished the three women were photographed smiling together in a group hug on the platform, an image that drew immediate comparisons with Canova's statute The Three Graces. The trio's success in two peak-time television appearances generated further publicity, including online support for a petition to close the nuclear base at Faslane. Kitted out in mocked-up heroic outfits they were billed in the *People* as the 'three wonder women who've electrified opinion'. Few outside Wales had heard of Ms Wood before the election, but after the two debates she had been 'overwhelmed by the number of supportive messages from England'.

Farrage was keen to come across as the outsider in the first debate, the only party leader opposed to membership of the European Union and immigration, a stance he stiffened in the second encounter by portraying himself as the only voice of the right, entirely outnumbered by the left. His pitch seemed designed to motivate committed UKIP supporters. After being attacked again for intolerance, this time to cheers from the audience, he claimed he was being 'abused' by a panel that had lost the argument on immigration. He was jeered when claimed the audience was prejudiced 'even by the left-wing standards of the BBC'. Farrage renewed his criticism of the BBC after he was excluded from the leaders' last televised debate, a *Question Time* special for Cameron, Clegg and Miliband.

While lacking the sheer intensity of the three head-to-head jousts of 2010, the broadcasters' alternative offer of a wider range of debates, interviews and question-and-answer sessions had provided the smaller parties with an unparalleled opportunity to engage with the electorate. Ms Sturgeon emerged the undisputed star of the series, the leader who more than any other had enhanced her reputation. Her fluency, and the command of her arguments, when challenging Cameron and Miliband was not lost on the Scottish electorate. She had strengthened immeasurably her plea that by voting SNP her party's MPs could speak up for Scotland at Westminster with an authority that Labour could not match. Her contention that only the SNP could ensure that the voice of the Scottish electorate was heard in the House of Commons appeared to be irrefutable when compared with the record of the 'feeble fifty', the label that Ms Sturgeon's predecessor Alex Salmond attached to Scotland's Labour MPs in the 1980s for their inability to protect Scotland from Thatcherism.

The self-confidence of the SNP leadership was vindicated on polling day with a massive landslide that delivered historic swings that surprised even Ms Sturgeon: on a 50 per cent share of the vote, the SNP took 56 of 59 seats leaving Labour, the Conservatives and Liberal Democrats with one MP apiece. A night of wild celebration was topped by Salmond's ringing declaration: 'A Scottish lion has roared, and no government will be able to ignore it'.

Plaid Cymru had never laid claim to being able to pull off a rout of SNP proportions, but Ms Wood's party hardly benefited from her raised profile. While pleased Plaid retained its three seats in Wales, and had seen an increase in support, its 12 per cent share of the Welsh vote was less than that of UKIP. Farrage was doubly disappointed: he failed to get elected in Thanet South and the party lost Rochester and Strood, the seat where the defecting Conservative MP Mark Reckless had raised the UKIP flag in a by-election the previous December. Douglas Carswell, the first Conservative MP to defect to UKIP, retained his seat at Clacton leaving UKIP with only one seat to show for 3.8 million votes.

Within hours of the Thanet South declaration, Farrage announced that as promised he was standing down from the leadership, only to be back in post three days later after the party's national executive refused to accept his resignation. Farrage vowed to redouble his efforts to lead UKIP's preparations for the referendum on the UK's membership of the European Union that Cameron promised to hold before the end of 2017. Downcast though he was by UKIP's failure to win only one seat after securing not far short of 4 million votes, Farrage had the satisfaction of seeing UKIP become the third most popular party finishing second in more than 100 constituencies. Its 12.6 per cent share of the UK-wide vote pushed the Liberal Democrats on 7.9 per cent into fourth place. His anger with the dysfunctional lottery of a first-past-the-post voting system that left UKIP and the Greens with one MP each after winning nearly 5 million votes was shared by Ms Bennett. She failed to get elected in Holborn and St Pancras. Caroline Lucas, the Greens' sole MP, was re-elected in Brighton Pavilion, but despite winning more than 1.1 million votes, four times as many as in 2010, the party failed to secure any of its target seats.

Except for the SNP, and its phenomenal success in taking almost 100 per cent of the Scottish seats on 50 per cent of the vote, there was little to celebrate among for the political insurgents who had begun the 2015 campaign with such high hopes of making a breakthrough. They immediately united around a joint demand for proportional representation, more determined than ever to campaign against the absurdity of a voting system in which winner takes all. Their one consolation was that the broadcasters had taken advantage of Cameron's prevarication over the televised debates to introduce a series of innovative programmes that did acknowledge the fragmentation of the popular vote and the need to accommodate an expanding multi-party line-up.

Early on in the acrimonious argument over the various pre-conditions being imposed by the Prime Minister, Ed Miliband vowed that a future Labour government would make sure the rules for pre-election procedures enshrined the right of television and radio to hold debates whether or not all the party leaders wished to participate. One possibility was to expand the reach of the well-respected regime for determining the length and share out of party election broadcasts. Perhaps a lesson of 2015 was that the UK should follow the example of the USA and 25 other democracies around the world that have established independent commissions to determine the shape and timing of televised debates without taking orders from either politicians or broadcasters.

G

political gaffes

A spell of duty on **gaffe** watch can be great fun, a chance to prick the pomposity of overbearing ministers and self-important MPs. Political correspondents take great delight in their ability to spot and then exploit occasions when politicians slip up and lay themselves open to ridicule in the news media. Journalists and their editors are more than happy to be judge and jury in deciding what constitutes a gaffe, and if need be reporters are prepared to collude with each other as a pack to agree a version of events that a victim might find difficult to dispute. Story lines can be tweaked with such ingenuity that a politician might not have realised until reading a newspaper or hearing a news bulletin that a seemingly innocuous remark or stumble was even considered newsworthy in the first place. There is an endless appetite for fresh material which explains why rival politicians are only too pleased to get in on the act, keen to humiliate their opponents by tipping-off journalists to embarrassing blunders that might otherwise have gone unnoticed.

Gaffes are not always a media creation because sometimes a politician behaves so stupidly, or makes such a crass mistake, that their ineptitude immediately catches the public's attention, and becomes an instant talking point. Parliamentary reporters and sketch writers at the House of Commons are constantly on the lookout for an unfortunate statement or slip of the tongue. Some misguided remarks are simply amusing but others can have more serious consequences, require an apology, and if not remedied might conceivably threaten the reputation or career of a minister or MP. For the duration of a general election campaign the fear of going off message is one of the greatest restraints on party leaders and candidates when they speak in public or are interviewed by the media. Their behaviour on the campaign trail is under the same constant scrutiny, and the term gaffe has become so ubiquitous that it can be applied to almost any false move. Journalists cast their nets as wide as possible, waiting, watching and listening ready for the slightest indiscretion, an offensive comment, awkward photo-opportunity or any of the one hundred and one pitfalls that lie in wait during constituency visits or election events.

A simple slip-up like forgetting a name, or perhaps an inept mispronunciation, rarely lives on beyond the evening news bulletins or next day's newspapers. The far greater danger is a mistake that results from a misjudgement that raises questions about a politician's motives or competence. If a mishap is the result of a calculated attempt to gain publicity, and was ill conceived to begin with, any resulting press pictures or television footage will serve as a constant reminder of a foolhardy moment.

In a cynical age when politicians have struggled to win back public trust, election strategists must always consider how the actions of a party leader will be perceived and communicated to the electorate. They should have at the back of their minds the edict cited by the television presenter Jeremy Paxman,

'Why is this lying bastard lying to me?' and then reverse the question, 'Is this journalist about to stitch me up?' Every encounter with the news media has to be treated with a degree of suspicion, as does contact with members of the public given the ease with which pictures can be taken and commentary recorded on camera phones. Politicians need to be self-confident, impervious to the brickbats that they attract, but they can be arrogant and insensitive, architects of their own humiliation.

Elections are often remembered for their gaffes, whether it was Kenny Everett's 1983 entreaty to Young Conservatives, 'Let's kick Michael Foot's stick away' or Neil Kinnock punching his fists together in the air and shouting, 'We're all right' at Labour's 1992 Sheffield rally. Both were illustrations of the exuberance of earlier campaigns before they became so rigidly controlled. A lack of spontaneity and free expression has reduced the chances of politicians engaging with the electorate, but the campaign teams say that when so many innocent-looking by-standers like to think of themselves as would-be citizen journalists, they have no alternative but to insist on a disciplined approach. Gordon Brown's calamitous confrontation with Gillian Duffy while on a walk-about in Rochdale in 2010 prompted an even greater insistence on the need for caution. Dreading that another casual conversation might end in disaster, the three party leaders, David Cameron, Ed Miliband and Nick Clegg were steered by their minders well away from chance encounters with passers-by. The 2015 campaign had its fair share of unscripted remarks, embarrassing snatched photographs and the odd stumble, but the gaffe hunters were disappointed with their haul when compared with the turbulence and dramas of previous elections.

Cameron's unexpected revelation in the kitchen of his constituency home that he intended to serve for only a second term as Prime Minister was probably the biggest surprise, and despite denials to the contrary was considered a tactical mistake only weeks before polling day. Easily the most humiliating photo-call was the invitation to watch Miliband unveil a large limestone tablet on which had been engraved Labour's six election pledges, a photograph that would capture the misjudgements of his leadership and become an abiding image of the party's doomed election campaign.

A comparable failure to have an inkling of the potential for hubris was the miscalculation that lay at the root of a gaffe that occurred in the aftermath of Labour's defeat in 2010, a political clanger that was about to be given a new lease of life as an invaluable prop in Cameron's bid for re-election. Liam Byrne, formerly the Labour chief secretary at the Treasury, was 'burnt with shame' every time he saw the Prime Minister pull from his pocket a letter he had left on the office desk for his successor saying, 'I'm afraid there is no money. Kind regards – and good luck.' Byrne thought he was being a good sport leaving a cheery note that played to the customary banter among Treasury ministers that the next government will have to pick up the tab. His mistake was to put his jolly aside in writing. He was handing over to a political opponent a letter that could so easily be misconstrued. He seemed oblivious to the fact that he had been part of a government that had all but institutionalised the art of leaking official documents, or that he was a member of a political party that had few scruples when it came to exploiting the private misfortunes of opponents.

In apologising for his 'crass, stupid mistake' in a post-defeat mea culpa in the *Observer*, Byrne explained that his friendly few words for the new Treasury chief secretary were in line with a tradition that went back to Winston Churchill of politicians telling their successors to clear up the mess. He quoted the advice that the former Conservative Chancellor of the Exchequer Reginald Maudling gave James Callaghan when he became Chancellor after Labour's 1964 election victory. What Byrne did not acknowledge was that Maudling had not been so foolish as to put his thoughts in writing. Callaghan described the occasion in his autobiography *Time & Chance*. He had just installed himself in the study of 11 Downing Street when Maudling put his head round the door and joked, 'Sorry, old cock, to leave it in this shape. I suggested to Alec (Douglas-Home) this morning that perhaps we should put up the bank rate but he thought he ought to leave it all to you. Good luck.'

Byrne's misfortune was that his jokey letter provided written justification for the expenditure reductions being introduced by the Conservative-Liberal Democrat coalition government, a cutback that was said to be all the more urgent because overspending by the outgoing Labour government had contributed to the debt mountain left after the 2008 financial crash. Instead of going to the intended recipient, Byrne's Conservative opposite number Philip Hammond, the letter was opened by the new chief secretary David Laws, one of the Liberal Democrats MPs who gained promotion to ministerial rank. A few days later, at his first joint news conference with the new Chancellor George Osborne, Laws read out the note and praised Byrne for his honesty. The letter was put to regular use in helping to buttress the new government's attack on Labour's past profligacy, although Laws claimed subsequently that he had mentioned it 'almost by accident' not expecting, 'rather naively', the huge reaction when 'the whole story suddenly went stratospheric'.

Cameron's ploy five years later of keeping a copy of the letter in his inside pocket, ready to be flourished at an appropriate moment at campaign events, was a cruel and constant flashback to Byrne's original gaffe. He had already performed the same routine on numerous occasions, but photographs of the Prime Minister reading from the note during the final BBC *Question Time* special made next morning's newspapers. Every time the letter made a fresh appearance Byrne said he 'burnt with the shame of it', filled with anger and remorse for having 'made it easy for our opponents to bash our economic record by bashing me'.

Byrne's misjudgement in overlooking the extent to which a politician's every move can be turned to an opponent's advantage was a basic mistake, yet the same miscalculation was made when Labour's campaign team gave the go ahead for what was instantly dubbed Miliband's 'Edstone', a tombstone-like monument that listed the party's six election pledges. Without his closest advisers appearing to have any comprehension of the mockery that he would attract, Miliband stood, hand outstretched, beside an 8ft. 6in. high slab of limestone that 'set in stone' the undertakings on the party's pledge card. If elected Prime Minister, he intended to install the carving in the Downing Street rose garden as a permanent reminder of the promises Labour had made to the electorate. Miliband was having to compete for the media's attention with the day old daughter of the Duke and Duchess of Cambridge, and if his aides harboured fears that the leader's photo-call at Hastings on the final Sunday of the election would be no match for a royal baby, they did not have long to wait. A Twitter hashtag EdStone, and a Biblical tide of online mock-ups depicting Miliband as Moses delivering the Ten Commandments, rendered his plan to erect a monolith symbolising Labour's trustworthiness a laughing stock, a gaffe of monumental proportions that would dog the final days of his campaign.

After a weekend when press coverage had been dominated by news of the royal baby, later named Princess Charlotte, Miliband's inept photo-opportunity had at last given political commentators the chance to get back to business, to inject some light relief into campaign reporting. Spoof versions of the six pledges competed with yet more mockery of Miliband cast as Moses. The *Guardian's* sketch writer John Grace was merciless: Miliband had 'raised the stupidity bar still higher'. Even the title at the top of the pledges, 'A Better plan. A Better Future.' was a hostage to fortune. The verdict of the media was a damming indictment of the ineptitude of the campaign team. Michael Foot was blamed by the MP Gerald Kaufman for taking Labour to defeat in 1983 with a manifesto that was the 'longest suicide note in history', and Miliband would remembered for having put his signature to a set of election promises engraved on a stone tablet that was being derided as the heaviest suicide note. From the moment the monument was unveiled, and online chatter gave the first indication that the story was about to go viral, the Conservatives had piled in. George Osborne compared the stunt to Kinnock's hubristic cry at the Sheffield rally, in the final week of the 1992 campaign.

Staff at party headquarters spend weeks planning a grid of election events and photo-calls for the leaders' campaign tours, always hoping to avoid the danger of producing a timetable that fails to take account of unexpected ups and downs. Opinion polls in the final week continued to predict the outcome was neck and neck, and the calculation, based on constituency boundaries, was that Labour would get more seats than the Conservatives, and that Miliband rather than Cameron would walk into 10 Downing Street. For the remaining few days the priority was to avoid Miliband getting dragged into stunts that might go awry, or risk creating the wrong impression as happened with the Sheffield rally. No British political party had previously attempted to stage such an ambitious event in the hope of equalling the razzmatazz of an American political convention. There was music for all ages and tastes, and Kinnock's arrival on stage was reminiscent of a 1960s pop concert. High up on one side of the enormous stage were six flags: the Union Jack, four flags of the UK and the flag of the European Union, all fluttering in a breeze created by a wind machine. On the other side of the stage was an enormous video screen which simultaneously relayed Kinnock's speech. Applause from the vast audience was powerful and moving as he presented Labour as the government in waiting.

Kinnock had an unshakeable belief in the power of such events to build up morale. Nothing could match the pictures from Sheffield, and they were in marked contrast to the two televised speeches that same evening by John Major and Paddy Ashdown. A night of excitement and emotion might have inspired party workers for the final week, but there was much disagreement about the rally's impact on the wider electorate. The issue that had be resolved was the same that Labour faced 23 years later: Miliband's personal ratings had improved, as had Kinnock's, and the priority for each of them was to stage events that enhanced their status as future Prime Ministers. Unveiling a massive limestone pledge card that might double up as a tombstone should Labour lose was hardly a risk free engagement.

Stories lampooning Miliband had been the daily fare of the Tory tabloids for months. Reporters had been on permanent gaffe watch, ready to exploit any incident that might sustain the weirdo image that he had been saddled with. The previous Thursday he lost his footing when leaving the platform after the BBC *Question Time* special at Leeds Town Hall, a minor stumble, but one which fed into the story line of the popular press that he had been stunned by hostile questions, and by the accusation that he was lying when he denied the previous Labour government had overspent.

Cameron and Clegg were also taken to task by the audience in Leeds, but it was the questioning of Miliband that was viewed as the most telling. Labour cried foul, claiming those who took him on were all Tory voters. One questioner, Simon Wilkinson, a barrister and Conservative supporter, told *The Times* that he stood by his complaint that Miliband had been 'misleading the country' when denying that Labour would link up with the Scottish National party in a coalition government. Wilkinson was proud to have been in an audience that had finally offered the electorate an exchange that was as enlightening as Brown's infamous ill-judged encounter in Rochdale. 'The politicians are doing everything they can to avoid another Gillian Duffy moment. They met 160 Gillian Duffys in Leeds, which is no bad thing.'

Miliband's performance in question-and-answer sessions attracted added scrutiny in case there was any hint he was following the advice on presentation revealed in personal notes that the *Sun on Sunday* claimed he had left in his dressing room after the first televised leaders' debate in early April. A ten page 'secret crib sheet' amounted to a motivational pep talk. In addition to a list of off-the-cuff answers and put downs, there were pertinent reminders of the demeanour he should adopt: 'Happy warrior, calm, never agitated, negative – positive'. Another list gave the attributes he should cite when challenging the Prime Minister: 'Me v DC – decency, principle, values'. Miliband's awkwardness when he appeared in public was lamented in the post-defeat analysis of the *Guardian* columnist Polly Toynbee. 'He never learned those essential thespian skills for the television age.' Miliband let slip his ambivalence towards the importance of a television persona when interviewed by the *Radio Times* at the start of the campaign. He admitted he always switched off political programmes and did not like to see himself on screen. 'I would never want to watch anything with me in it.' Alan Johnson, the former Labour Home Secretary, feared the 'die was cast' in Leeds when Miliband was assailed about Labour's overspending. The *Question Time* audience, and the public at large, remained convinced that 'Labour had indeed driven the car into the ditch and declined to return the key'.

Cameron's on-screen behaviour was in marked to that of Miliband, his ease in front of camera having always seemed so effortless. His easy-going nature and engaging repartee led to accusations from his critics that slick presentation was no substitute for political judgement, but he had a natural flair when responding to an audience and his aptitude for coming up with friendly put-downs helped him to fend off awkward questions. In the years following his election as Conservative leader in 2005, he so honed his presentational skills that he had no hesitation in agreeing from the outset to take part in the first-ever round of televised leaders' debates. His refusal to countenance a repeat of the three head-to-head confrontations in 2010, fearing that Miliband might be the beneficiary, was exploited ruthlessly by his opponents, but he emerged unscathed from the replacement series of televised encounters despite the difficulty of having to defend his record in government rather than having the freedom to go on the attack.

After another assured performance a snap opinion poll by ICM for the *Guardian* judged him the clear winner of *Question Time*. He did slip-up next day when addressing workers at the Leeds headquarters of the Asda supermarket group, and hastily had to correct himself. He urged them to make sure they voted. 'This is a real career-defining ... country-defining election.' An earlier more substantive gaffe was a telling illustration of a compulsion on the part of politicians to profess support for well-known football clubs and other popular sports teams. In a speech in south London, he celebrated the success of Britain's diverse allegiances, a 'shining example' of a country where multi identities work. He then paid a penalty for not having familiarised himself in advance with the text of his speech, a failure that emerged when he extended his praise to other aspects of everyday life. 'Where you can support Man United, the Windies and Team GB at the same time. Of course, I'd rather you supported West Ham.' He blamed forgetting his long-running claim to be an Aston Villa fan on the kind of 'brain fade' that had afflicted Natalie Bennett, leader of the Greens. 'These things sometimes happen when you are on the stump.' For Aston Villa fans his blunder was unforgivable, and was mocked by Gary Lineker on *Match Of The Day*, a reminder that the Prime Minister had probably connected with a part of the electorate that political news might not always reach.

Cameron's swift acknowledgement of his mistake was another illustration of his gift for amusing self-deprecation. When needled about his privileged education at Eton and Oxford he deployed an array of one-liners, which he delivered with a smile: 'Yes, I know I have this terrible CV ...' Nigel Farrage, leader of the United Kingdom Independence party, was an even more accomplished performer. He usually owned up straight away, apologised for a gaffe on his part or a mistake by a colleague, executed a swift U-turn, and then moved on. His cheeky chappie demeanour, his confidence in looking to camera, and a willingness to give a straight answer were characteristics which had helped him escape unscathed from countless embarrassments.

Farrage's stickiest wicket in the election was over his demand that 17,000 foreign nationals being treated for HIV on the National Health Service should pay for their care. Leanne Wood, leader of Plaid Cymru, stood up to him in the first televised debate, saying he should be 'ashamed of himself'. When viewers gave their verdict on the seven party line-up, Farrage was way out in front with the SNP leader Nicola Sturgeon. A YouGov opinion poll several days later indicated public support for his concern about the cost of anti-retroviral drugs for sufferers not born in Britain; 50 per cent of those questioned backed a five-year ban on treatment. While political opponents claimed that his attempt to discriminate against foreign HIV patients was a smear that would cost his party support, Farrage did not back down, and if his blunder was regarded a gaffe by his critics it had apparently done little to deter the 3.8 million voters who backed UKIP.

heckling

A casual conversation with a bystander during a constituency walk-about can be as hazardous for a prominent politician as an unexpected interruption at a campaign meeting. Like A-list celebrities forced to dress down to avoid being recognised and harassed when out shopping, the leading contenders know that once a general election is underway their everyday behaviour will be scrutinised as never before. Party minders now go to extra-ordinary lengths to guard their leaders against the ever-intrusive tactics of the news media. An even greater threat is an unseen army of internet-savvy would-be citizen journalists who are equipped with camera phones, able within an instant to upload and share their images on social networking sites. By opting for an extended six-week campaign, the longest since 1997, David Cameron gave the parties plenty of leeway, but the end result was that the 2015 election was the most tedious and repetitive that most commentators and pundits could remember, and also the most over protected. Journalists craved for a repeat of the memorable moments that had brought previous campaigns to life, the chance encounters that can finish up with those in power being administered their comeuppance by an aggrieved electorate.

Getting caught on camera, arguing with an angry voter, does sometimes work to a politician's advantage, but the risks are so great for a party leader that they have to be shielded from random contact with the public. **Heckling** on a campaign stop is no longer as easy as it once was. A phalanx of minders provides constant protection, working just ahead of the leader's entourage, checking out passers-by, guiding their charges away from potential trouble, towards the casual but sanitised conversations that the managers of the main parties are looking for. Each and every election gathering has to be viewed as a potential danger area, necessitating ever tighter controls to head off unforeseen outbursts.

Election meetings that were once open to the public have been replaced with ticket-only rallies for the party faithful, events designed to weed out potential troublemakers. If a heckler does manage to infiltrate the invited audience, stewards are ready to pounce and escort them to the door. At the hustings of yesteryear politicians such as Neil Kinnock, as with Harold Wilson and Jim Callaghan before him, had the platform presence and force of delivery to see off anyone who dared to interrupt them. Another Labour heavyweight who I reported in the 1960s was the former Secretary of State for Defence, Denis Healey, who was more than capable of taking on all comers when heckled by campaigners for nuclear disarmament.

To his great credit John Major broke free from the carefully crafted image building of Conservative Central Office during the 1992 election and reverted to a soapbox, a political prop from his days as a young political activist out electioneering in Brixton Market. At a campaign stop in Luton's shopping centre, where a crowd of demonstrators carrying banners of the Socialist Workers party had been lying in wait, Major's aides took a stout wooden document box out of his battle bus. Gripping a loud-hailer, the Prime Minister was ready at last to be himself: 'Can you hear? Don't let the people who take to the streets take your vote away.' Old fashioned street corner campaigning was like a tonic, wiping away wounding remarks about lacklustre speeches and Dalek-like delivery.

Election strategists have reined in the risk taking of Major's day because they realise they have scant hope of influencing let alone supervising the way events can be misrepresented and wholly distorted in an ever-expanding world of mass communications. Smart phones and social networking have revolutionised the public's ability to offer their own take on the day's events, and the resulting online free-for-all is a constant reminder of the perils of modern political life. An unfriendly intervention on a walk-about, or a noisy interruption at a campaign event, can be doubly dangerous. A heckler might well make a cogent argument that leaves a party leader floundering, providing revealing audio for radio and good pictures for television. In responding the speaker might over-react, perhaps make a mistake or be rude and unpleasant, inadvertently supplying an embarrassing soundbite that can be endlessly replayed. The fall-out from a surprise encounter that goes wrong is impossible to predict, which only adds to the nervousness of the campaign team.

Today's protesters are far more sophisticated than their predecessors. Their stock in trade is an ability to engineer provocative confrontations that can create potentially damaging photo-opportunities. Often they collude with the news media in advance by tipping off photographers and camera crews. Party minders and spin doctors, already at the mercy of the high-tech photographic and recording equipment of the mainstream media, face the additional threat of an incident that seemed entirely trivial when it happened developing a life of its own on the internet. Within a matter of hours a mildly humiliating lapse can become an online sensation, about to go viral, and very likely attract the attention of newspapers, radio and television.

In agreeing to a fixed five-year parliamentary term, the Conservative-Liberal Democrat coalition pre-determined not only the precise date of the election but also the nature of the campaign itself. Instead of being restricted to a short three- to four-week contest that a government seeking re-election usually prefers after the dissolution of parliament, the political parties knew from the start they would have much more time to play with. In fact they were on an election footing from the turn of the year, months away from polling day, but still determined to start the countdown to May 7. As so little parliamentary business remained for the final session, Cameron was able to plump for an extended six-week campaign, seemingly prepared to set aside the inherent danger of the longer the campaign lasting the greater the chance of being knocked off course by an unexpected event.

A desire to return to previous patterns of electioneering was part of the Prime Minister's justification for refusing to participate in a repeat series of the televised leaders' debates of the 2010 election. Three head-to-head confrontations between Cameron, Gordon Brown and Nick Clegg attracted a mass television audience and dominated proceedings, but each week the pre- and post-debate commentary and analysis upstaged the rest of the campaign, preventing what the Conservatives argued was an adequate opportunity to present and debate the competing policies on offer. If

Cameron's advisers were hoping that a less confrontational series of televised debates would prevent life being sucked out of the rest of the campaign, they failed to anticipate the deadening effect on the public of having known the 2015 election date so far in advance. Without an element of surprise, and supporters being fired up by a short, sharp campaign, the parties struggled to win voters' attention for what became an endlessly repetitive chain of well-rehearsed policy announcements.

As the weeks dragged by commentators longed for a repeat of Gordon Brown's unforgettable 2010 encounter with Rochdale housewife Gillian Duffy, the nightmare scenario that reminded every election strategist to avoid at all cost a maverick encounter that might slip out of control. An absence of the headline-grabbing upsets of previous campaigns frustrated journalists on gaffe watch, and while the avoidance of serious mistakes soothed the frayed nerves of election minders, voters tended to switch off. The collective view of the travelling correspondents was that the campaign tours of the three main parties were so tightly controlled that David Cameron, Nick Clegg and Ed Miliband had done themselves a dis-service by not encouraging a greater degree of access and spontaneity.

Seared in their collective memory were the calamities of the past, mishaps that occurred even at the height of the control freakery of New Labour. In the 2001 election, Tony Blair was ambushed and harangued in Birmingham by Sharron Storer, the anguished partner of a cancer patient, during what is always one of the most dangerous moments for a party leader, the short space of time it takes to get out of a car and walk across a pavement or along an approach path before entering the controlled environment of the location being visited. Television crews covering the Prime Minister's arrival managed to get in close enough to film and record her unstoppable onslaught about the failure of Blair's government to spend more on the NHS.

John Prescott's confrontation later that day with an egg-throwing protestor at Rhyl in north Wales was another example of the same phenomenon: an uncontrolled photo-opportunity which took place during the few moments it took the Deputy Prime Minister to walk from his coach towards the theatre where he was due to speak. Security for Prescott was not as heavy as for Blair and a cameraman from HTV, Sion Jones, had the foresight to pick the right spot from which to film the arrivals; in the process he captured Prescott's left jab and secured the most memorable footage of the entire campaign. These two unforeseen events all but obliterated news coverage of the launch of Labour's manifesto.

As part of their attempt to exercise even greater control over the stage management of Blair's campaign visits, his aides often clipped a personal microphone to his tie or to the lapel of his jacket, and placed a transmitter on his belt or in his back pocket. His conversations with party supporters or the public, or perhaps question and answer sessions, were relayed to a sound system. In this way it was possible to corral camera crews some distance from the action, too far away for their microphones to pick up what was being said. Instead they would be supplied with a sound feed for use in television and radio. If an event went off script, or a conversation was in danger of going awry, the sound could be cut. Blair's minders had succeeded in providing him freedom of movement for photo-opportunities while at the same time reducing the ability of the media to eavesdrop an off-message conversation. If camera crews refused to go to the agreed position for filming, or complained about not being allowed to install their own microphones, they were told they would be banned from future events.

Gordon Brown's infamous altercation with the redoubtable Mrs Duffy, and his subsequent tirade about her being 'a sort of bigoted woman', was for the Labour party an abject illustration of the perils of having relaxed the rigid controls of the Blair years. To help reduce pushing and shoving among camera crews and sound recordists as they tried to keep pace with him on his walk-about in Rochdale, Brown had agreed to wear a Sky News radio microphone so that there would at least be a decent audio feed of his conversations with shoppers and passers-by. Such recordings are made on a pooled basis and shared out between the broadcasters. His fatal mistake was to climb into his official car with the radio microphone still attached to his lapel. Brown was in a foul mood, having realised his conversation with Mrs Duffy had gone disastrously wrong. His intemperate, abusive description of a life-long Labour supporter was of such horrendous proportions that it instantly entered the annals of campaign howlers.

Rather than take their chance with a walk-about or casual informal gathering, the three main parties adopted a safety-first strategy for the 2015 election. Much favoured campaign stops for the leaders included visits to business parks, factories and especially nurseries or primary schools. A photo-opportunity chatting to small children while hand painting presented none of the risks inherent in random conversations with shoppers or bystanders. Usually only one camera crew was allowed to take close-up shots, working on a pooled basis. Such events are relatively easy to manage and provide plenty of friendly footage and amusing badinage, but were anathema to the gaffe hunters touring the country on the leaders' election battle buses. Exasperation at their continued failure to secure damaging images and audio was compounded by the ticket-only regime for meetings and rallies. If an event was being used to provide a platform for a policy announcement, accredited journalists were given the chance to ask questions, but always in a tightly-controlled environment. Usually only party workers and the invited audience knew the location, so there was little if any opportunity for inter-action with members of the public in each locality. Such visits, and especially stopping off points for battle buses, used to be advertised locally in advance, but the parties insist the practice is frowned upon by police protection officers, and an air of secrecy except for those in the know, suited election planners.

By the third week of the contest Cameron's campaign had been so uneventful that he created a minor stir during a visit to Berwick on Tweed when he briefly ventured outside the protective bubble around him and walked towards a busker with a ukulele who was urging him to 'fuck off back to Eton'. Aides were caught on camera remonstrating with the Prime Minister's tormentor, and their contretemps provided an amusing sequence for *Channel 4 News* and *Have I Got News For You*. Gaffe watchers were disappointed because Cameron had been careful to steer clear of the busker so he was not in vision at the vital moment, and without face-to-face contact or seeing him involved in the altercation, journalists could hardly suggest it ranked alongside Prescott's punch. Similarly when a heckler tried to interrupt Cameron by shouting 'come on the SNP' at a campaign gathering in a Twickenham garden centre, the protestor was quickly pushed out of the way.

North of the border the general election generated a bout of the full-on campaigning that England had not seen since the polarising years of Margaret Thatcher. Political street-fighting returned with a vengeance, a re-run of the noisy and sometimes violent confrontations that there had been the year before during clashes between activists from Labour and the Scottish National party in the build-up to the referendum on independence. When campaigning for a No vote the previous summer, Jim Murphy, leader of Scottish Labour, had been greeted with constant interruptions and abuse. Such was the intimidation that he was forced temporarily to suspend his 100-day tour of street speaking in 100 towns. In the final week of the election an embattled Murphy, up against predictions of an SNP landslide, was joined by the comedian Eddie Izzard for a meeting in St Enoch Square, Glasgow. They were forced to abandon the event after it was disrupted by jeering nationalists shouting 'Red Tories out'. Murphy accused the SNP of failing to control the 'ugly face of aggressive nationalism'. Two party members were later suspended.

Wherever she went during the election the SNP leader, Nicola Sturgeon, was mobbed by her supporters, greeted like a visiting rock star. Ever the astute political operator, she put the adulation to good use, taking full advantage of endless requests to pose with admirers for selfie photographs. If an eager bystander was seen struggling to work out what to do, the First Minister for Scotland took command and was said by her minders to know instantly how to operate every camera phone on the market. By the final day of the campaign the SNP said that 20,386 selfies taken with Ms Sturgeon had been uploaded and shared on Twitter.

Stopping for selfies became so time consuming for the party leaders that they sometimes felt they were missing out on a chance to answer questions or talk politics. The craze for selfies became a defining characteristic of the 2015 campaign trail: instead of meeting un-vetted passers-by or having to square up to a heckler with all the risks that might entail, there was the soft option of trading on the celebrity status that leading politicians can acquire. Boris Johnson, the Mayor of London and parliamentary candidate in Uxbridge, was said by the London *Evening Standard* to have posed for 164 selfies in one day alone. Johnson, like Nigel Farrage, leader of the United Kingdom Independence Party, was happy to josh with strangers or spar with journalists, and they both understood how to exploit their street credibility by stopping for photographs.

Another leading Conservative happy to endorse the selfie culture was the Chancellor of the Exchequer George Osborne. 'It is just a very human reaction: "Oh look, that person's off the telly."' So great is the thrill for people who want to be photographed with someone famous that the party leaders would have been foolish not to factor in sufficient time. They had also discovered a sure-fire way to defuse potentially difficult encounters. If by-standers in the vicinity were waving around their smart phones all it took was to beckon them over, and the rush for selfies soon put a smile back on the proceedings. Prominent politicians could hardly be criticised for taking advantage of people's vanity, and for going along with a fad that come polling day might have served as a personal reminder as to who to vote for.

I

interviews

O nce an election campaign gets into full swing and the political leaders start touring the country, the demand for radio and television **interviews** becomes intense. Journalists from local and regional programmes, as well the national networks, have to queue up for a slot, often being allocated no more than four or five minutes at the most. For the politician every interview probably blurs into the next, but each encounter is a moment of potential danger. A trick question is a favourite for presenters: the cost of a pint of milk or a loaf of bread is one of those everyday statistics that can trip up a British politician just as US Presidential candidates are told to remember the price of an American shopping basket equivalent, a pound of hamburger meat.

David Cameron was caught out in the first televised debate of the 2015 election when he was forced to admit to the veteran broadcaster Jeremy Paxman that he did not know how many food banks had been established during his Premiership. Labour politicians and campaigners against poverty had made great play of the extent to which welfare claimants and others on hard times were being forced to rely on donated groceries, so there was no excuse for not being prepared. After being told that the number had gone up from 66 to 421, and that 900,000 people received free food parcels in 2014, the Prime Minister replied meekly that he wanted to see 'fewer people' dependent of free food aid. Paxman drove home his advantage, and after being asked three times for an answer, Cameron was forced to admit that he could not live on a zero hours contract.

Gordon Brown's nightmare of a live lapel microphone picking up his remarks about that 'bigoted woman' Gillian Duffy during the 2010 general election campaign, was a stark reminder of the hazards of an election walkabout or the risks entailed in responding to reporters' questions on the doorstep or in the street. A set piece interview in a studio, office or home can be equally fraught: often there are tricky questions to answer, and every word has to be weighed carefully. A politician's demeanour might well be a critical factor and the presence of a cluster of nervous party advisers is usually a sign of hidden anxieties.

Broadcasters, unlike newspaper journalists, sometimes get a ring-side seat at these moments of high drama. Perhaps a news conference has just finished, awkward questions from newspaper reporters were batted away successfully, but now the politician has to remain calm and convincing in a probing one-to-one interview. Politicians are invariably anxious for feedback: 'Was the interview ok?', 'I hope that answer made the point?', 'Did I look ok?' Without realising it, an interviewee can give an unintended clue as to what was really at stake, a pointer perhaps being their skill in delivering a much-rehearsed soundbite intended to put a gloss on a multitude of sins.

Looking back on countless interviews, my most vivid memories tend to be about the occasion itself rather than what was said. I was always fascinated by a politician's deportment, perhaps their surroundings, and however brief an interview might have been, I often found such encounters far more revealing than the answers I was given. Studio presenters have a different role: their task is to interrogate a politician on behalf of their programme, perhaps to an agreed agenda, with sufficient time for some challenging supplementary questions. As a BBC Radio correspondent out on the road, my task was to secure an instant response, most probably reaction to an ongoing political debate; the answers I recorded would be incorporated later in news reports or features, so my interviews tended to be limited in their length and scope.

During Margaret Thatcher's decade in Downing Street, observing her unerring knack when challenged of putting broadcasters in their place, I would often have to pinch myself when thinking back to the few moments I sat beside her, with my Uher tape recorder on my knee, at the Young Conservatives' annual conference in Eastbourne early in 1975. She had challenged the former Prime Minister Edward Heath to the leadership of the Conservative Party and her visit was an opportunity to woo the news media. I was invited to sit next to her on a settee in the lounge of the conference hotel; I proceeded to ask what I accept were probably some pretty run-of-the-mill questions for my report for the *PM* programme. I remember being struck by the informality of the occasion, a degree of familiarity that was not to be repeated. On being elected leader, her presentation was overhauled under the guidance of the political strategist Gordon Reece and she became far more wary of fraternising with journalists. As Prime Minister she certainly kept her distance from most broadcasters and in my experience, did not engage in the gossipy exchanges with BBC correspondents that many other politicians enjoy.

Another departed politician who has become a source of vivid flashbacks is the late Sir Cyril Smith, who since his death in 2010 has been the subject of sustained allegations of child sexual abuse. Although I was never aware at any stage in my career of improper conduct on his part, the occasions that I interviewed him have stuck in my memory. Smith, MP for Rochdale for twenty years, was a truly larger-than-life presence, one of the most recognisable figures not only in the Liberal Party as it then was but also among the politicians of his day. I found him overbearing, often bombastic when being questioned, but with a cutting edge to his political repartee. Some of my encounters with him in the 1979 general election were rather troubling because of their contrived nature.

In the 1970s the Liberals were lucky if they had a dozen MPs at Westminster and consequently their resources were stretched. In the 1979 election I was assigned to follow the Liberal leader David Steel and I had to crisscross the country to report on his campaign stops in far-flung constituencies. BBC Radio 4 had expanded its election coverage to include a late-night sequence of extracts from the day's speeches and the producers regularly had difficulty finding sufficient Liberal voices to ensure the output was balanced politically. I was asked to record relevant contributions whenever possible and Smith was an obvious candidate. He assured me that when I stopped off in Rochdale he would deliver an impromptu ten-minute speech. He insisted that there was no need for an audience; I should simply report to the address I had been given and he would deliver his remarks there and then.

True to his word, I remember being shown into a rear room and told to start my recording. Without notes and hardly pausing for breath, he launched into his speech, even adding the odd chuckle in response to an imaginary audience.

Standing beside him for ten minutes, holding my microphone, under the intensity of his delivery, was to say the least an unnerving experience; he was 6ft. 2in. and said to weigh over 29 stone. Needless to say my producers were delighted with the audio, happy to turn a blind eye even after I had the explained the potential deception. While alone with him I was conscious of people and movement in other rooms around us but I did not meet anyone else, my access was clearly being limited and I was left with the clear impression that this was not a moment for introductions, small talk or cups of tea, especially on the MP's home turf.

Of all the Prime Ministers and party leaders I dealt with at close quarters, Tony Blair was easily the most accomplished in understanding the demands of political interviews and then in applying the techniques that he had observed and mastered. Initially he had an easy going, if not always effective approach, but there was a rapid transformation in his presentation as he rose to prominence in the early 1990s as a Labour Party front bench spokesman on employment, education and home affairs. The more he came under the influence of Peter Mandelson, and later Alastair Campbell, the sharper his delivery became and the greater his command over the way each interview proceeded.

My first experience of his determination to try to exercise control over the way he delivered his answers was after his appointment as employment spokesman. During repeated interviews about the Labour's relationship with trade unions he did his best to ignore my questions and instead give answers that restated Labour's commitment to youth training. During one encounter in the run-up to the 1992 general election he again dictated the outcome of our exchange. Blair had been put forward by the party to respond to the results of the latest opinion poll and he arrived at College Green, not far from the BBC's studios at Millbank, armed with his pre-prepared soundbite, which he duly delivered.

I persisted in asking some supplementary questions, challenging him on issues thrown up during the election campaign. Blair would have none of it; he just laughed and said it would be a ridiculous waste of time for him to answer such questions when the BBC would only broadcast a fifteen-second soundbite. When I stood my ground, he refused to budge and had clearly thought through his position. He explained that if he was being invited to appear in a lengthy interview in a current affairs programme he was quite prepared to undertake the necessary preparation but if all a news bulletin wanted was a quick quote then it was unreasonable to expect a politician to think through replies to a host of potentially difficult questions.

I refrained from reminding him of his strictures on College Green when I was sent to his home in Islington in February 1996 to record his reaction to a fatal IRA bomb explosion at Canary Wharf. As the camera crew got into position in his sitting room, I was slightly taken aback when he politely asked what sort of response the BBC was looking for. I explained that the usual reaction was an expression of sympathy for those killed and injured, coupled with support for the Police and the security services and a line to the effect that terrorism had to be defeated. My instant run-down had probably helped him think through a suitable response and needless to say he did not hesitate in giving his reaction.

My most awkward encounter with Blair was one summer Sunday afternoon in the late 1990s at the height Kosovo conflict when I was sent hurriedly to Chequers to conduct a pooled interview on behalf of BBC, ITN and Sky. I was ushered into what I took be the sitting room and the camera crew prepared for the Prime Minister to enter. Clearly there had been some kind of delay and at one point Cherie Blair, who was wearing tennis shorts, walked through without a glance, but giving the impression she resented our intrusion into precious family space and time. Blair eventually appeared, sat down, and gave his reaction to the latest development; there was no small talk and we made a swift departure.

My presence had clearly been an issue and the second volume of the *Alastair Campbell Diaries* explained all. Blair's former director of communications pulled no punches when he alluded to my malign influence as a journalist whose interest in the dark arts of the spin doctor had become a little too intense for his liking. Campbell's diary entry was succinct about his annoyance with the BBC: 'I was pissed off they sent that tick* Nick Jones who they claimed was the only one available.'

*Tick: 'parasitic insect...unpleasant or despicable person.' (Oxford English Dictionary)

J

journalists

E lection campaign strategists are constantly pre-occupied trying to work out how best to take advantage of social media, anxious about the danger of being upstaged by an opponent who they fear might have found an even smarter way to communicate with potential voters. The internet has opened up endless opportunities for political parties to promote their policies; to enlist local activists to spread the word to a wider electorate; and to turn out the vote on polling day. Leading politicians have also become increasingly prolific online, eager to exploit social networking services such as Twitter to publicise their work without having rely on traditional media outlets

Journalists too have experienced a transformation in the way they report the news. Gone are the days of newspaper reporters having to wait until the next edition to see the publication of their work, or of broadcasters being limited to a fixed schedule of radio and television news bulletins. Journalists are expected to start spreading the word via the internet the moment they are sure of their story. The edict of their editors is that social media is their friend, an all-important vehicle through which they can build up their reputation and authority in print, on air, or on screen. Ownership of an exclusive story has to be established immediately, and then ruthlessly promoted via social networking and a personal blog. Twitter, Facebook, YouTube, Instagram, BuzzFeed and a host of other online platforms must be harnessed to drive the audience; to encourage readers to buy the latest copy of a newspaper or magazine; to persuade viewers to tune in to the next programme; or click on to a website.

Since I started reporting general elections in the mid-1960s there have been many changes in the working practices of political journalists, but easily the most far reaching have been the competitive forces unleashed by the internet, pressures that have far exceeded even the initial impact of 24-hour television news channels in the late 1990s.

While there were differing views over the degree to which social media influenced the conduct of the 2010 election, there was no doubt about the impact in 2015. Inter action with an increasingly internet-savvy electorate had been a powerful force for the Scottish National Party in driving up the Yes vote in the 2014 referendum on independence. Once the parties readied themselves for the months of campaigning that lay ahead, there could have been no clearer indication of the extent to which the online terrain would become a new front line in the election battleground. In the event, the innovative use of social networking provided plenty of examples of how the parties learned from the experience of the SNP, and how they too succeeded in building up a momentum online.

Journalists had to contend with another reality of the internet age: politicians had found a way to bypass reporters and seize the agenda. A posting on Twitter could easily become a 'breaking news' item, beating the news agencies and upstaging the story lines that had previously been determined by the established media. Countless platforms provided what was in effect a vast digital market place for a continuous conversation between media outlets, political parties, pressure group and the like. Rather like the trading floors in the City of London, this online political arena was the point where election news was traded, influencing not the price of stocks and shares, but the headlines for that evening's news bulletins or next morning's newspapers.

Where the online world of instant reporting so differed from my day was that the journalists had themselves become players on the enlarged political stage that the internet had created. Instead of simply reporting and analysing what parties and politicians were saying for press reports and broadcasts, political correspondents were competing with each other on social media, jostling for personal attention. They gave their own comment and reaction, as well as providing hard news and factual information; competing story lines were being bounced around between them, and often changed quite dramatically as the day progressed.

The ebb and flow of the dialogue that took place did have an impact on the conduct of the campaign, perhaps requiring a change of tack by political spin doctors, or an attempt to engineer a fresh twist to the day's events. Newspapers, television and radio made constant reference in their news coverage to what had been happening on line, charting the way the campaign was being shaped by digital electioneering. If a party leader used a posting on Twitter or Facebook to issue a comment or make an announcement, the resulting news stories would more than likely reflect the online reaction, either positive or negative, and the extent of the instant response supplied an insight not previously available.

There was no way of knowing whether an off-beat item, be it a mobile phone photo or wacky photo-shopped image, might suddenly go viral.

Considerable effort was made by the parties to monitor the direction of online chatter, and perhaps find ways to encourage or counter unexpected issues that suddenly started trending on social networks. While election strategists were well aware that this digital conversation might be influencing the news agenda, and was certainly of great interest to party activists and many younger voters, they knew there were still vast swathes of the electorate whose lives were not ruled by the internet, perhaps older voters or those whose daily routines meant they were too busy to spend precious hours online.

Political correspondents were also conscious of this mismatch, often complaining to their colleagues that the constant pressure to update their Twitter feed, or write a new blog for a website, was eating into the time they had to search out new information and prepare a considered report on the day's events. The question they posed, was the same one that was raised by some SNP campaigners in 2014: were these online platforms no more than echo chambers, offering a conversation with the like-minded rather than a means of reaching out to the wider electorate.

I had experienced precisely the same sense of frustration in the early years of rolling news, when the 24-hour channels of BBC, Sky, and also for a short time ITV, were regarded as a game changer in election coverage. We were all drilled to regard the news channels as our priority, the first outlet for breaking news. But the insatiable demand for updates on the hour, meant that correspondents out on location could not spend as much time as they would have liked on news gathering, and as has happened subsequently to a generation of journalists facing incessant online demands, we realised that there was a limited television audience for our continuous news coverage from the campaign trail. We had no hope of matching the viewing figures recorded for disasters or major national events. Our fear was that much of our effort was perhaps misdirected, providing a running commentary for a tiny audience at the expense considered analysis for the main bulletins.

Nonetheless the news channels have had a lasting impact on the way events are reported on television and radio. Instead of relying on pre-recorded reports as in the past, presenters spend far more time talking directly to correspondents. These live exchanges provide the sense of immediacy that editors demand. Two-way conversations have become the norm, and while producers insist they offer a more engaging format for most viewers and listeners, I mourn the loss of a more thoughtful style of reporting. When I joined BBC Radio in 1972, I would have estimated that 90 per cent of what I said on air was scripted; when I left in 2002 the reverse was the case, and 90 per cent of my output was live conversation, responding to questions put by radio and television presenters. Conversational reporting is engaging and does have its strengths, but can lack the authority of a well-written script, and does not always have the impact that might be achieved with a punchy pay-off, especially on those occasions when a presenter's questions may have diverted attention from the point a reporter was trying to make.

During a long-running event like an election campaign the output of the news channels is valued greatly across the media waterfront. Editorial and production staff in newspapers, radio and television can watch events as they unfold, enabling newsrooms to chart the way a story is developinh, and plan their own coverage. Likewise at party headquarters, campaign staff can see instantly how their own side is doing, and also what their opponents are up to.

Activity online has to be monitored just as intently given the great unpredictability of social media. Each of the parties went to great lengths to engage with online audiences. Their ability to post news alerts on Twitter and other networking sites had the additional advantage of enhancing their control over the timing and release of information about policy developments and election events. Communication with the media via the internet is so instant and so comprehensive that it was used by the parties as yet another justification for their decision to abandon the well-established practice of holding campaign news conferences.

A daily round of early morning jousts between the press pack and the leading contenders was one of the great traditions of reporting general elections. Their demise was one of the consequences of the fallout from the dramatic impact of the three televised leaders' debates of the 2010 campaign. Each debate dominated the news coverage for almost an entire week, so unsettling for election strategists that they had no hesitation in arguing there was no need to subject the leaders to the added hazard of a daily grilling by journalists. In truth campaign planners had felt for some time that the press conferences worked to their disadvantage. Political correspondents were well attuned to each party's weak spots, and despite the rivalries of their competing news outlets, the journalists could on occasion work as highly-effective pack, driving a story line to the politicians' disadvantage.

Tony Blair was the last Prime Minister to put himself and his ministers on parade for these early-morning rituals. By starting the day's campaigning with a news conference, the three main parties hoped to set the agenda, a chance to launch a policy announcement that could hopefully put their opponents on the defensive, and be developed further during campaign tours and constituency visits. Fleet-footed political journalists could get to all three briefings, and within the space of a couple hours or less, correspondents and commentators were abreast of what each party was offering. Each news conference was televised, available for instant use on news channels or the main bulletins and programmes. For radio and television producers they provided an invaluable resource, a stock of on-the-record answers that could be used to illustrate reports on controversial issues.

Journalists had most to gain from the willingness of the party leaders and their front bench teams to subject themselves to the challenge of taking on all comers at a crowded daily news conference, where they could be forced without notice to respond to an initiative that might have been announced minutes earlier by one of their opponents, or perhaps find themselves on the back foot trying to explain away an unexpected embarrassment or gaffe. However much political journalists might miss these early morning jousts, and what for many was their one and only opportunity to make a stab at holding party leaders to account, there was a collective sigh of relief at campaign headquarters when the introduction of televised leaders' debates gave the parties the chance to re-organise their campaign programmes.

Instead of being locked into a routine that obliged them to compete with each other every morning, strategists for the three main parties were free to plan their own individual grid of events. The removal of the straightjacket of a fixed timetable that suited the journalists but not necessarily the politicians, allowed them to exercise even greater control over media access to the party leaders, all but eliminating the chance of them being wrong footed in what could sometimes be the bear pit of a daily news conference.

Most political editors used to make a point of attending all three news conferences. Not only was there the likelihood that party leaders and their entourages might be present, but so too were the leading campaign staff. Here was an unrivalled opportunity to witness how each of the parties were faring during what in those days was usually a compact, three- to four-week campaign; a chance for a word in the margins with a minister, or a face-to-face chat with a top spin doctor or policy supremo.

I always leapt at the prospect of being able to attend all three news conferences in the correct sequence. In my diary for the 2001 election (*Campaign 2001*) I described hot footing it between the three venues at the mid-point of the campaign, eager not to miss the full glory of the morning's claim and counter-claim, or the noises off that so rattled the press officers. Anxious not to be the tail-enders, the Liberal Democrats had no choice but to go first at 8 a.m. in the hope they might be able to set the agenda. Their conference was held in Smith Square, in what was formerly Transport House, and before taking questions the party leader Charles Kennedy delivered a pre-prepared soundbite on the economy, 'We reject Tory stealth cuts or Labour stealth tax increases'.

There was no time to linger as Labour were kicking off at 8.30 a.m. at Millbank Tower, quite a step away. I remember being overtaken by Jon Snow, the bicycling presenter of *Channel 4 News*. In the unexpected absence of the Chancellor of the Exchequer Gordon Brown, Alistair Darling fielded questions, accusing some of the journalists of raising points planted by the Conservatives. By the time we had all trooped back to Smith Square for the Conservatives' news conference at 9.15 a.m., William Hague had the edge on his opponents because the war room in Central Office had been monitoring the coverage of the two earlier news conferences.

Hague, who was joined on the platform by Michael Portillo to launch the party's business manifesto, made much of having seen Darling as he struggled to avoid giving a straight answer on whether Labour might increase national insurance. Afterwards I managed to have a brief word with Hague's head of media, Amanda Platell, who was explaining how the Conservatives had tried to take advantage of the fracas at Rhyl, when John Prescott's left jab at an egg-throwing protestor delivered the most enduring the image of the 2001 election.

So much effort went into the build-up to each of the three televised debates of the 2010 campaign – and such was the extent of the aftermath – that party managers had every reason to limit the number of formal news conferences, so as to avoid at all cost getting trapped again by an inflexible programme that pitted them against both their opponents and the media. Having collectively eliminated the threat of a daily grilling by hostile journalists, the parties had far greater freedom to pick and choose the most opportune moment and location for policy launches.

Campaign teams were able to go one step further in the 2015 election in their manipulation of the release of news and information in the hope influencing the daily headlines. Almost every government announcement is now trailed in advance, the aim being to grab the news agenda, a practice that was formalised within the Whitehall information service after Alastair Campbell became Tony Blair's director of communications in Downing Street in 1997.

An over-long six-week campaign in 2015 tested almost to destruction the patience of an electorate that grew increasingly weary of a daily auction of competing and often contradictory policy proposals. Each announcement followed the same pattern: newspapers were briefed for next day's editions; there was a taster of what was afoot for the late-evening news bulletins; and these initiatives were then explained in greater detail during television and radio programmes the following morning. The aim was to prepare the ground for a party leader who would make a campaign stop to expand further on the policy being proposed.

All too often these launches would be in front invited audiences of party workers and supporters. Selected journalists usually had the chance to ask questions, but access was restricted, and these tightly-controlled events lacked the rigour of the daily news conferences of previous years. The party machines had succeeded in their twin aim of imposing message discipline and reducing the risk of hostilities with the media, but by dispensing with so much of the cut and thrust there had once been with journalists, potential voters could be forgiven for tuning the page or tuning out of election coverage, thinking they had read or heard it all before.

K

kitchens

General election campaigns force politicians to submit themselves to a well-established ritual of having to co-operate in filming set-up shots, a sequence of pictures that is used to illustrate a television news report. An interview alone does not suffice because a reporter needs a series of images to show a party leader or candidate at work, canvassing in the street, or perhaps with their family, out and about or at home. In the thirty years I spent trying to conjure up imaginative footage for the BBC, television editors became ever more demanding as did party press officers, who attempted to exercise ever tighter restraints on the access they would permit. But despite the reservations of spin doctors and their ilk, politicians realise they must embrace the opportunities offered by television, and more recently by video and online reporting, and as a result they are far more co-operative than their predecessors.

Archive footage from previous elections shows how candidates have become ever more confident of their ability to perform in front of camera, keen to demonstrate to the electorate that their family life is no different from that of the average voter, whatever the risks such exposure might entail.

Reality television has transformed the public's expectations. While some politicians do still go to extraordinary lengths to guard their family's privacy, others believe that a degree of intrusion is an inevitable consequence of modern electioneering, and that the best advice is to consider how best to manage the access that has been granted.

Camera crews are invited across the threshold far more readily than in my day; a variety of domestic chores provide the kind of action that will sustain a far greater range of set-up shots; and a favourite setting, not just for establishing footage but also for the interview itself is today's live-in **kitchen**, regarded by many as the hub of a modern family home. Indeed out of all the possible domestic locations, the once humble kitchen has, at least in television terms, undergone by far the greatest makeover.

Set-up sequences are essential in order provide footage under which a correspondent has the time to voice a few sentences of commentary or supply background information. Woe betide a producer who fails to think ahead of what might be required by the picture editor. Rolling news has only added to the pressure for a constant supply of fresh images of politicians in the headlines, otherwise a correspondent is forced to rely on using shots from the news library, but these might well be out of date or inappropriate. Given the limited choice that is often available viewers have rightly grown weary over the years of much of the conventional footage such as the greatly over-used walking shot, a visual cliché of television news, which all too often remains the only image that might be available. When deadlines are pressing and new pictures are needed camera crews have to rely on filming MPs hurrying along outside the Palace of Westminster, or perhaps climbing the stairs to the BBC's studios in Millbank.

As most interviews are conducted under considerable time constraints producers might have no alternative but to fall back on a rather predictable repertoire: asking ministers to open their red boxes and peruse their documents; suggesting MPs look at a House of Commons order paper; or perhaps walk up to bookshelf and pull down a book. A task has to appear convincing and one establishing sequence that became fashionable for a time but is no longer thought as trendy as it once was, is requesting the interviewee to walk into a room, sit down at a computer, use the keyboard and look at the screen.

If the weather is fine, a garden or local park might provide a suitable venue. Pruning roses, clipping a hedge or mowing the lawn are just some of the tasks that an MP might be asked to perform. By and large politicians will co-operate with these well-established routines. My most memorable put down in the early 1990s was from Beryl Goldsmith, a doyenne among MPs' secretaries, who took my call requesting an interview with the former Conservative cabinet minister, Norman Tebbit, who by then had returned to the back benches. I assured Miss Goldsmith there would be a television crew on College Green within an instant. Her reply was withering: 'Mr Tebbit does not do interviews on the Green. He is not one of those rent-a-quote MPs who pops up outside the House of Commons with Big Ben sticking out from the top of his head. His interviews are done in studios.'

The popularity of the kitchen dates from the 1960s because it provided a neutral but everyday location where a serious politician could be asked to carry out a simple, straightforward task for the benefit of photographers and camera crews. Harold Wilson was the first Leader of the Opposition, and then Prime Minister, to exploit the news media's insatiable desire to learn more about a party leader's home life.

After 13 years of Conservative government led by Winston Churchill, Sir Anthony Eden, Harold Macmillan and Sir Alec Douglas-Home, Tory fortunes had plummeted, and the 1964 general election was a chance for Labour to offer the country a change of direction.

Wilson promoted himself as a man of the people, a future Prime Minister with the common touch, whose domestic circumstances were far removed from the wealth and privilege of his aristocratic predecessors. He was photographed with his wife Mary in the kitchen, helping to dry the dishes. Macmillan had won the 1959 election in an era when he famously declared that rising prosperity meant the British people had 'never had it so good', but at the following election Wilson rather than Douglas-Home was able to take advantage of the way the gadgets and appliances of mass consumerism were transforming the appearance of the average kitchen. Another image from the 1964 campaign was of the fiery Labour MP Barbara Castle in the kitchen of her London home, one hand on the tap and the other on the sink. As Prime Minister, Wilson was photographed regularly on family holidays in the Isles of Scilly, sitting in a deck chair or walking round the harbour in shorts with his pipe and knapsack.

While campaigning for the Conservative leadership in 1975, Margaret Thatcher was photographed peeling potatoes at the sink in the kitchen of her Chelsea home. In the lead-up to the 1997 general election, Tony Blair, wearing an open-necked shirt, posed for the cameras making a cup of tea in the kitchen of his family home in Islington. Although he was not seen performing domestic chores, Gordon Brown was photographed in shirt sleeves, but wearing a tie, standing in the Downing Street kitchen in 2008, cup in hand, reading a document.

When informal filming is possible at a politician's home the preferred location for an interview is usually a sitting room, lounge or sometimes a study to give an added touch of authority. But just as a kitchen probably needs to be tidied up, care also has to be taken with regard to whatever else might be visible in the background. There is more than likely to be a carefully positioned standard lamp or vase of flowers, perhaps a coffee table or bookcase, but family photographs and other personal items may well have been removed and kept out of shot at an interviewee's request; most camera crews do check when setting up. Compared with images from the archives, today's footage has become ever more revealing about the interior of politicians' homes, as well as many other aspects of their family life.

In response to the open-door approach that David Cameron adopted from the start, there has been a step change in the willingness of party leaders to allow more photo-opportunities at home, or when out and about with the rest of the family. Cameron relaxed the boundaries on media access to his private life once he began campaigning for the Conservative leadership in 2005, happy to be photographed and filmed with his wife Samantha and their children at their home in Notting Hill. On becoming Prime Minister in 2010, he understood full well the political value of press and television reportage of the Camerons en famille, and while keen to guard against intrusive publicity, he again had no qualms about offering controlled photo-opportunities at either the family flat in Downing Street or their home in his Witney constituency. Initially, on being promoted to the front bench, Cameron had been photographed caring for his disabled son Ivan, who died in 2009, but as the years went by he extended his in-vision repertoire of domestic duties, and was often photographed or filmed preparing breakfast for the children, helping them get ready for school or checking their homework.

After Ed Miliband was elected Labour leader in 2010, he followed Cameron's example in allowing media access to his family. He was regularly photographed and filmed with his wife Justine and occasionally their two sons, Daniel and Samuel, sometimes being held in the couple's arms, taking their first steps as toddlers and later playing or walking along with their parents. When in March 2015 the BBC commissioned pre-election television profiles of each of the three main party leaders, he had no hesitation in allowing James Landale and his camera crew access to the family home in north London.

Over the previous decade the Camerons had been willing participants in what could only be described as a *Hello*-style of journalism that entailed scrutiny not just of David and Samantha's clothes and appearance, but also the very fixtures and fittings of each room that had been visited. They had traded on the insatiable appetite of newspapers and magazines for access to the favourite rooms of celebrities, or the kitchens of celebrity chefs, and the Camerons' regular at-home photo-opportunities had provided a succession of homely images that had been pored over by feature writers determined to put a purchase price on every item on view.

In fairness to Miliband, he had repeatedly made a point of telling journalists that he rarely read newspapers or magazines so he could perhaps have been forgiven for not anticipating the potential pit falls of the chez nous filming that he had agreed to, but his media handlers should have been on their guard. Cameron had effectively turned the kitchen into a must-see location, a setting where a family-orientated party leader should be seen hard at work, sharing the household chores. As it transpired, when discussing their domestic arrangements with Landale, Miliband joked that Justine had said their kitchen was precisely where she would like him to spend more time. In order to find a location for an establishing shot close to the sitting room where he was interviewed, the couple were filmed, mugs in hand, leaning on a work surface in a narrow, austere kitchen, that contained none of the stylish furniture or expensive appliances so evident in both the Camerons' Downing Street flat and constituency home.

When the *Daily Mail* columnist Sarah Vine, wife of Conservative chief whip Michael Gove, mocked the Milibands' 'forlorn' kitchen for being 'devoid of colour or character,' a friend of the Milibands, *The Times'* columnist Jenni Russell sprang to their defence saying in a tweet that this was simply a 'functional kitchenette' used for 'tea and quick snacks', and the family had a 'lovely' kitchen downstairs. Tory-supporting tabloids had a field day ridiculing 'two kitchens' Miliband, yet another headline that played to the agenda that the Labour leader was from a rich North London elite that was remote from the lives of 'ordinary working people'.

Miliband's discomfort provided Cameron with an opportunity to upstage his rival, and this time, under the influence of his culinary prowess, the Prime Minister's kitchens were about to morph into sets that could just as easily have accommodated the celebrity chef Jamie Oliver. For a feature in the *Sun*, Cameron was photographed in his Downing Street kitchen rustling up a quick lunch of sardines and mayonnaise on toast, and for his BBC profile the action switched to Cameron's constituency home. Yet again he demonstrated his ease in front of camera, and also an unerring ability to multi-task in the kitchen, as he readily answered Landale's questions while preparing lunch. Instead of busying himself with something as mundane as making a cup tea or washing up, Cameron was shown chopping tomatoes and mixing a salad, while at the same time offering his interviewer an exclusive story on a plate. A year after her resignation as a junior health minister following the 1988 controversy over salmonella in eggs, Edwina Currie had shown a similar degree of dexterity, fielding questions in her kitchen while tasting soup, but here was the Prime Minister in an open neck shirt giving every appearance of being a contestant in a party leaders' round of *MasterChef* or the *Great British Bake Off*.

An engaging informality was always a hallmark Cameron's set-up shots, his small talk with Samantha and the children only added to their appeal, but interviews were usually conducted in a rather more conventional setting. Never before had a kitchen been the location for an epic Prime Ministerial pronouncement. To Landale's great surprise, when asked if he intended to serve a third term, instead of dodging the question, Cameron opened up: "No ... I am standing for a full second term. I am not saying all Prime Ministers definitely go mad ... The third term is not something I'm contemplating. Terms are like Shredded Wheat – two are wonderful, three might just be too many."

Cameron's frankness caused amazement in Whitehall and Westminster. Six weeks from polling day was hardly thought to be a sensible moment for a Prime Minister seeking re-election to start speculating about who might succeed him, and thereby raise doubts as to whether or not he would be able to see out a full term. Nonetheless there were plaudits from cabinet colleagues who praised the Prime Minister for having made it clear that 'unlike Margaret Thatcher, he did not want to go on and on'. In justifying his 'very reasonable, sensible' response to Landale, Cameron called in aid the informal nature of their conversation: 'What I did in my kitchen was give a very straight answer to a very straight question.'

When Nick and Miriam Clegg were filmed for a profile for ITV, they had clearly had no intention of competing with the Camerons. After his election as leader of the Liberal Democrats in 2007, the couple imposed strict conditions on access: they said they would never allow pictures of their children to appear in the news media. Miriam had warned off photographers and camera crews in no uncertain terms: 'I'm like a tigress when it comes to my kids'. For ITV's profile, political editor Tom Bradby filmed the couple standing in the kitchen of their London home, glass of white wine in hand, beside a kitchen range where a paella was cooking on the hob. Next day a report in *The Times* had priced most appliances and utensils and agreed with the verdict of an interior designer in the *Daily Mail* that the kitchen was 'quite middle of the road' and needed refreshing.

By now no pre-election profile was complete without an establishing shot in the kitchen, and although she admitted she rarely cooked, Nicola Sturgeon, leader of the Scottish National party, did agree to be photographed standing beside her top-of-the-range coffee machine. Even so the appearance of the kitchen had not escaped the attention of the *Daily Mail's* columnist Quentin Letts who said it resembled a 'sparse wee scullery' that looked about 'as warm and inviting as the sea off Aberdeen'.

There was no holding back the tabloids when Tom Bradby revisited the Milibands' small upstairs kitchen for an ITV profile. Justine looked on as Ed prepared scrambled eggs and joked about their 'infamous' kitchen. 'This is the kitchen we use, I mean there's a kitchen downstairs. Our nanny lives downstairs and it's sort of a basement area … She uses the kitchen downstairs'. Miliband remark about an 'Upstairs, Downstairs' lifestyle had this time handed the *Sun* a story on a plate. 'We DO have two kitchens … nanny uses the one downstairs,' was the front-page headline over a mocked-up photograph of Miliband in tails and a white tie, looking as if he had just stepped from the set of the television drama *Downton Abbey*. The curse of kitchengate had entered the spin doctors' lexicon, another in a long list of locations where there was always a danger that mischievous journalists and photographers might serve up a tasty political gaffe.

L

Liberal Democrats

For a general election to deliver the near decapitation of not one but two political parties has propelled 2015 straight into the record books. A virtual wipe-out of both Scottish Labour and the **Liberal Democrats** was the devastating result that the opinion polls had forecast with great accuracy, unlike the overall outcome. Labour's all but obliteration in Scotland was a sudden death, an execution at the hands of the Scottish National party that had been only a matter of months in the making, whereas the Liberal Democrats' blood bath was of a far different order, a calamity that had its roots in a brave but risky decision to put party politics aside in the national interest in order to work with the Conservatives to form the first coalition government of the post-war years, an already dicey step that became toxic after a string of strategic errors.

I winced as the declarations were announced, watching with sadness as the slaughter continued almost unabated. The clear-out of Liberal Democrat MPs from their strongholds in southern England, the south-west and Scotland was personal: at some point or other in my career I had reported from most of the seats that were lost, either at general elections or sometimes during the by-elections that in previous years had provided the party with their ever-expanding power base. In the fifty years I had spent reporting politics I had seen the party grow from a parliamentary group that was down to six in the 1970s, able just about to squeeze into a London taxi, to become the third force in British politics, with ten times as many MPs.

Dogged determination and the fast footwork needed to exploit the tactical mistakes of alternating Conservative and Labour governments were the key to the Liberal Democrats' success. I had seen at first-hand how with limited resources successive leaders had built up and sustained a much feared election machine, capable of exploiting local grievances while at the same time attracting and holding a national protest vote. In 1979 I travelled from Cornwall to the northern tip of Scotland following David Steel as he did his best to fight off Margaret Thatcher's advance after the collapse of the Lib-Lab pact, and then watched in the 1980s how he managed an often troubled relationship with the Social Democrats which by dint of his own perseverance led to the merger in 1988 that established the Liberal Democrats. In the 1990s I could not help but admire the audacity of Paddy Ashdown, who with the military mind-set and endurance of a former marine commando, pulled off a string of sensational by-election victories that added to the woes of John Major's government. He built the foundations for a doubling in the haul of Liberal Democrat MPs in the 1997 election, the best result by a third party since 1929. Charles Kennedy led his troops to fresh heights in the 2005 election winning 62 seats, the largest contingent since the old Liberals under Lloyd George.

Nick Clegg was one of the 2005 intake and his future, and that of his party, seemed assured after his election as leader in 2007, despite the turbulence that had resulted from Kennedy's messy resignation the year before and Sir Menzies Campbell's brief stint at the helm. A young, fresh face at the top had raised morale, and there were high hopes given his previous experience as an MEP, and his earlier brief home affairs brief arguing against identity cards and excessive anti-terror legislation, but he struggled to make an impression in the two and half years leading up to the 2010 election.

Almost without warning Clegg was about to become the beneficiary of the solid advance that it had taken his predecessors decades to achieve. A steadily increasing parliamentary presence had strengthened the Liberal Democrats' claim to be third party of British politics, a status that the broadcasters had been prepared to acknowledge. Since the start of the televising of election campaigns in the 1950s there had been a requirement for balance, and the guarantee of air time for smaller parties had been a significant factor in the post-war revival of Liberal fortunes. The game changer of 2010 was the last-minute decision by a beleaguered Gordon Brown to agree to join David Cameron in the first-ever series of televised leaders' debates. An even greater surprise was that Labour and the Conservatives accepted without hesitation that there should be a three-way split with the Liberal Democrats. Equal billing with the Prime Minister and Conservative leader in front of millions of television viewers offered Clegg the national recognition that Steel, Ashdown and Kennedy had spent a life time establishing. 'I agree with Nick' was about to become the unlikely catchphrase of the 2010 campaign.

Broadcasters had been trying for almost fifty years to persuade the two main party leaders to agree to pre-election debates, and the assumption had always been that they would wish to follow the Republican-v.-Democrat format of the US Presidential elections. In giving their approval to a three-way split, Brown and Cameron had overlooked the fact that their greatest vulnerability was that they could be portrayed as the leaders of the 'two old parties', the embodiment of a failed political system. Clegg's tactics could not be faulted. An anti-politics mood was there to be exploited, and he seemed to know intuitively how to harness the electorate's deep-seated scepticism with his call for an era of 'fairer politics'. Clegg was the undisputed winner of the first debate, and the Liberal Democrats' opinion poll rating advanced by 10 to 12 points within the space of a week, the largest leap ever recorded during the course of an election campaign.

'Cleggmania' failed to deliver the breakthrough which the Liberal Democrats' hoped for. They secured nearly a million extra votes, but ended up with five fewer seats. Nonetheless the prominence that Clegg had gained strengthened his negotiating hand once Cameron and then Brown came to terms with consequences of a hung parliament and began to bargain for the Liberal Democrats' support. Clegg was the 'kingmaker', the leader holding the balance of power, and after five days of political theatre his party agreed to accept Cameron's 'big, open and comprehensive offer' to share power in the national interest. In dividing up the spoils of coalition Clegg became Deputy Prime Minister and his party accepted five cabinet posts and fifteen other ministerial jobs. I had expected Clegg to demand one of the top offices of state for himself, perhaps the role of Home Secretary, or at least education or health, a department and area of government that the Liberal Democrats would be able to declare their own, where he would be able to make a distinct contribution and have an impact that would be identifiable to the electorate.

Instead he took on the additional role of Lord President of the Council and had responsibility for political and constitutional reform, but after the first flush of Conservative-Liberal Democrat co-operation he came to be viewed by the public as no more than a glorified trouble shooter, stepping in whenever needed to keep the coalition on track. John Prescott, who had served for ten years as Tony Blair's indefatigable Deputy Prime Minister, regarded the job as secondary to his principal role heading a newly-created department for environment, transport and the regions. He was broad shouldered, more than capable of withstanding the brickbats that he attracted on the occasions he stood in for Blair. Having direct responsibility for a wide, specific brief meant Prescott could speak with unquestioned authority on the policy areas he was in charge of. Clegg relished the chance to present himself as an authoritative voice across government departments, second only to the Prime Minister, seemingly oblivious to the danger that he might come to be viewed as nothing more than a rent-a-quote deputy, whose eagerness to talk the talk would only encourage the news media to treat him as Cameron's aunt sally.

The warning lights should have started flashing as soon as Clegg saw there was no chance of forgiveness after the Liberal Democrats broke their 2010 election pledge to vote against any increase in tuition fees. Lifting the cap to allow universities to charge up to £9,000 a year was said by Clegg to be an unavoidable consequence of spending restraints that the coalition had been forced to impose in the wake of the 2008 financial crash. Two years later, after finally apologising for having made a promise the party had not been 'absolutely sure' it could deliver, he suffered the humiliation of finding his words had gone viral at the hands of internet satirists.

His party political broadcast explaining his U-turn in sombre tones was put to music, repeating 'I'm sorry, I'm sorry, I'm so, so sorry' over and over again.

Within months of that indignity he re-affirmed his belief in the phrase 'there is no such thing as bad publicity' by readily accepting an invitation to take listeners' questions on a weekly phone-in on LBC Radio. In the lead-up the following year to the 2014 elections to the European Parliament, he was still so confident of his ability to take on all comers that he agreed to two televised debates with Nigel Farrage, leader of the United Kingdom Independence party. The strength of Clegg's commitment to the European Union was no match for the populist line that UKIP intended to 'get our country back'. Farrage was delighted to have been afforded such a valuable platform, and the post-debate surveys suggested viewers thought he was the winner by a margin more than two to one. UKIP went on to secure 4.3 million votes and 24 MEPS, the first time for over a century that a political party other than Labour or the Conservatives had won both the popular vote (since 1906) and the largest number of seats (since 1910),

In some ways I was not surprised that Clegg never seemed to say no to an interview because that was a response deeply embedded in the Liberal Democrat psyche. In my many years at Westminster and out on the road I can think of no more than perhaps a handful occasions when an invitation to appear on radio or television went unanswered. If the Liberal Democrats were ever going to succeed in breaking the mould of two-party politics, each and every opportunity had to be seized, an approach that Paddy Ashdown applied with great vigour. In the 1990-91 Gulf War Labour's shadow foreign secretary Gerald Kaufman tried to starve his party's anti-war MPs of publicity by refusing to appear alongside them, not realising that Ashdown was only too ready to step forward. His frequent appearances prompted a telling line in a *Spitting Image* sketch: 'Over now to our assembled experts … and Mr Ashdown.' Indeed, on the morning the land offensive began, he had already given three live interviews before John Major emerged to make his statement on the steps of No.10. On one occasion the Prime Minister telephoned to compliment him on an interview in which he had correctly predicted the government's next move.

Ashdown spoke with authority: he was after all receiving daily briefings from a team of military and diplomatic advisers pulled together by the Liberal Democrats. Given his long experience, and his role chairing the party's campaign team for the 2015 election, I wondered whether he would seek to rein in Clegg, force him to concentrate on a few key themes and impose tight message control. The Liberal Democrats' unique selling point was that they had, as Clegg had said himself, made 'a brave and plucky decision' to join the coalition and put 'country before party'. They could stand on their record of serving the national interest: there had been stable government for a full five-year term and the economy was recovering.

In opting for an extended election David Cameron had piled on the pressure. The longer the campaign the greater the danger the Conservatives could blame Liberal Democrats for the coalition's failings. Would squabbling between rival ministers drive away even more supporters who thought Clegg sold out to the enemy by joining the 2010 coalition? Would a future coalition with Labour seem a better option offer? How would Clegg's fellow MPs react once they realised they were being targeted for decapitation by the Tories?

In response to repeated opinion poll forecasts of a hung parliament, and the indication that he might again be the kingmaker, Clegg spent the campaign promoting the Liberal

Democrats' role in either a coalition or minority government to be led by either the Conservatives or Labour. Instead of focusing relentlessly on their own policy proposals, he indulged himself in endless conjecture about the 'red lines' that would apply in any coalition negotiations. Launching their manifesto, he said his aim was to 'add heart to a Conservative government and a brain to Labour'. Clegg's response to Cameron's warning that the country faced 'competence or chaos' was to fuel the uncertainty, pile on the permutations. He left open the door to supporting a Labour-led coalition even if it was on 'life support' from the Scottish National party; he feared a 'panicky' Cameron was about to do a deal with the United Kingdom Independence party; and late in the day he predicted a second a general election by Christmas if either of the two parties tried to 'stagger through with a messy and unstable minority government'. Rather than defend their achievements and stick to a clear set of values, Clegg talked up the possibility of disarray. His campaign team had not contemplated the possibility that far too many voters, already feeling misled by the broken pledge on tuition fees, might simply have stopped listening to what he was saying.

On the strength of YouGov's final poll forecasting the Liberal Democrats would retain 31 of their 57 MPs on a 10 per cent share of the vote, Ashdown ridiculed the exit poll prediction that they would win only ten seats. In one of the most memorable lines from the BBC's election night coverage he laughed off the figures when challenged by presenter Andrew Neil: 'If this exit poll is right I will publicly eat my hat on your programme.' After reflecting on a final result that left the Liberal Democrats with only eight MPs on a 7.9 per cent share of the vote, Ashdown admitted that he had been 'absolutely blindsided' throughout by the opinion polls. He told the *Guardian* their inaccuracy had 'killed' their strategy: 'If the polls had shown the real situation – the Tories with a clear lead over Labour – then the argument that we had to be there to moderate them would have had far greater traction.'

Ashdown's former press secretary Miranda Green thought the root of their problem was the fundamental conflict of having moved from being an anti-establishment party to pragmatic partners in government. Liberal Democrats were ambivalent about being in coalition. Clegg and his colleagues had reflected that ambiguity when trying to communicate their justification for a partnership with the Conservatives: 'First thick-as-thieves, then pulling away, falling out with other ministers, and all the while trying to sell the ideal of co-operative politics. Towards the end, Clegg talked about what he and ministers had achieved, but it was too late.'

Clegg's resignation speech was judged the most thoughtful of three delivered within hours of the return a Conservative majority government. His frank assessment of why their defeat was 'immeasurably more crushing and unkind' than he could ever have feared, re-asserted the depth of their contribution to the coalition. They had left government with 'Britain a far stronger, fairer, greener, and more liberal country than it was five years ago'. Here were the themes that had got lost in the Liberal Democrats' campaign. As I watched him take responsibility for this 'most crushing blow' to liberalism, I could not help but reflect on one of his many pre-election interviews. He was asked by the *Independent's* correspondent Donald Macintyre why he had accepted the 'nebulous job of Deputy Prime Minister' rather than have taken a great department of state. While gearing himself up for another bout of coalition building, he had 'hardened considerably' his view that he had no other option as the leader of a smaller party. 'You've got to keep your hands free … to bash heads together, thump tables, stamp feet and make sure that coalition decisions are taken in a balanced way.' I could not fault the logic of his conclusion, but the job description he outlined was for an insider working within the cabinet office and the corridors of Whitehall, a role that necessitated the lowest possible public profile, and could not be squared with Clegg's wish to be a headline-grabbing, all-purpose voice of both the coalition and his party.

The Liberal Democrats' mauling at the hands of the Conservatives was a severe lesson for their activists and supporters: a minor party that participated in government had no protection whatsoever under first-past-the-post voting. They had been unable to repair their reputation for trustworthiness; the plausibility of their independence had been snuffed out; and there was little likelihood any time soon of another smaller party being tempted to join a coalition without the full protection of a tried and tested system of proportional representation. Should such an opportunity arise the chance to become Deputy Prime Minister might not always be considered the wisest option for the party leader.

the monstering of Miliband

Contenders for the Labour leadership have few inhibitions about the savaging they can usually expect from a majority of daily newspapers. From the outset, Ed Miliband was a target, accused by the Tory press of lurching to the left, reliant on his trade union paymasters. The pounding he would be subjected to, from his election as leader in September 2010, was as vicious as the treatment previously meted out to Gordon Brown, Neil Kinnock and Michael Foot, but the pre-election **monstering** of Miliband went further than simply the trashing of his personality and the ridiculing of his political credibility. Miliband found himself embroiled in what came to resemble a grudge match between himself and a handful of proprietors determined to use the political reporting of their newspapers to bolster their attempt to prevent the election of a Labour government that they feared would interfere with the conduct of their media interests.

Unlike some of his predecessors, Miliband did not hold back from combat at a personal level, repeatedly singling out Rupert Murdoch by name when reminding voters that as leader of the opposition he had stood up for the public against the scandal of phone hacking and the abuses of the big energy companies and bankers. Murdoch fought back through the *Sun*, his largest selling newspaper, which did not limit itself to a predictable mix of wounding personal attacks and Labour scare stories. Reportage to the effect that the Labour leader was a weirdo, ill-suited to high office, had long been a regular feature of the *Daily Mail* and *Daily Telegraph*, but the *Sun* went one step further in the lead-up to the 2015 general election, presenting news reports about Miliband as if they were appearing in the pages of a comic rather than a newspaper. Instead of using news photographs to illustrate its political stories, he appeared in the guise of a variety of cartoon characters, complete with fictitious speech bubbles.

The more extreme and outlandish the caricatures, the more they seemed to symbolise the *Sun's* declining circulation and fading influence. Murdoch's newspapers no longer packed the punch they once did, the political power they previously wielded having been dissipated in the wake of the 2011 revelations about phone hacking at the *News of the World,* the scandal that gave Miliband an unrivalled opportunity to stand up to the Murdoch press in a way that previous Labour leaders had so often fought shy of, but which he was ready to seize.

Popular newspapers thrive on denigration. Character assassination of politicians is a staple ingredient of much of their daily fare, and over the decades Prime Ministers and party leaders of every political hue have been scarred by the experience. Labour leaders expect to be demonised long before polling day, which was why Tony Blair and the architects of New Labour put so much effort into winning the approval of press proprietors ahead of the 1997 general election. Labour were finally abandoned by the Murdoch press in favour of David Cameron at the party's annual conference the year before Gordon Brown's defeat in the 2010 election. The message was clear: any newly-elected Labour leader would face business as usual, a return to the hostilities of the past. But the monstering of Miliband would have immediate traction because the leadership election had produced a narrative that would prove irresistible to Conservative-supporting newspapers.

His victory over the favourite, his brother David, was by the narrowest of margins and had depended on the votes of trade union members rather than MPs or the wider party membership. Not only was there the prospect of exploiting the ongoing fall-out from a family car crash, the tale of a younger brother depriving his older brother of his rightful political crown, but also the damaging scenario of newspapers portraying Miliband as being continually under the thumb of the trade union movement's chief bogeyman, the already demonised 'Red' Len McCluskey, general secretary of Unite, Labour's largest donor. Headline writers at the *Sun* were the first to adopt the tag 'Red Ed', a nickname which it claimed had instantly been picked up by 'newspapers round the globe'. Within months of Miliband's mauling events looked like turning the tables on his tormentors at the Murdoch press because suddenly they were on the defensive, although there was no way of knowing at the time how dramatic the consequences would be.

In support of a long-running investigation into phone hacking at the *News of the World*, and the circumstances surrounding the first convictions in 2007, the *Guardian* had consistently challenged the line of News International's management that it had all been the work of a single 'rogue' reporter. That defence, already under strain, started to collapse in January 2011 with the surprise departure from Downing Street of Andy Coulson, David Cameron's director of communications, who had been hired as the Conservatives' head of publicity following his earlier resignation as *News of the World* editor. The phone hacking scandal was about to explode, and even before the *Guardian's* sensational report in July 2011 that the *News of the World* had targeted the mobile phone of the murdered school girl Milly Dowler, Miliband had taken the initiative, urging the government to establish an independent review into press conduct. Such was the furore in the wake of the *Guardian's* claim, later much disputed, that voice mails left for Milly had been deleted, Cameron found that he too was in the firing line, having to explain his employment of Coulson and justify the prospect of the government's expected approval for Murdoch's bid to take full control of the highly-profitable BSkyB.

During the forty years that he had built up his British media holdings, Murdoch had had been ruthless in exploiting the political patronage of his newspapers, and for the first time a Labour leader had a chance, without fear of retribution, to shake off a press proprietor's deadly embrace. His moment to pounce was at Prime Minister's questions, the day after the *Guardian* broke the story: Cameron was dangerously exposed, his friendship with News International's chief executive Rebekah Books raising as many questions as the hiring of Coulson, and the imminent nodding through of the BskyB bid. Like Blair and Brown before him, Cameron had spent years courting and cultivating the Murdoch press, but Miliband was ready to turn his back on the fawning and collusion of the past. He called for Brooks' resignation and for the BSkyB bid to be referred to the Competition Commission. Of far greater personal danger to both Cameron and Murdoch was Miliband's renewed demand for an inquiry. There was no escape for the Prime Minister, who must have sensed that

MPs felt liberated, no longer frightened of the country's most powerful media proprietor. 'Yes, we do need to have an inquiry, possibly inquiries, into what has happened …'

In newspaper columns next morning, the verdict of Labour-supporting commentators was that they had witnessed Miliband's most effective performance at Prime Minister's questions since he became party leader. He had 'taken the momentous step of turning against Rupert Murdoch's empire' (*Guardian*); for the first time he had displayed 'authentic anger without fear of retribution from News International' (*Independent*); and had 'shamed Cameron into ordering an inquiry' (*Daily Mirror*). There was swift vindication of Miliband's judgement in toughening his stand, and especially the link that he had made between phone hacking and the need to re-examine Murdoch's attempted take-over of BskyB. First was the surprise announcement that Murdoch had decided to close the *News of the World*, and then within hours, news of Andy Coulson's imminent arrest.

Cameron remained on the defensive as events unfolded over the following four years, amid the cascade of revelations about the conduct of Murdoch's journalists that flowed from a lengthy inquiry conducted by Lord Justice Leveson and a succession of court cases. Leveson's report and recommendations in favour of statutory press regulation were eventually rejected by a majority of newspapers. They were determined to continue their own system of self-regulation, and in a show of defiance the industry said it would go ahead and establish an Independent Press Standards Organisation in place of the discredited Press Complaints Commission, a move that Labour opposed.

Although the coalition government eventually acquiesced in the face of the proprietors' intransigence, campaigners for media reform kept up the pressure, and Labour's 2015 manifesto called for the introduction of a Leveson-style system of independent self-regulation, as had been endorsed by Royal Charter. Another Labour commitment was a pledge to protect the 'principle of media plurality'. While no precise figure was given for the maximum share of the media market that a company should be allowed to control, the wording of the manifesto left little doubt that Murdoch's UK press and television holdings would be a target. 'No one media company should be able to exert undue influence on public opinion and policy makers…so much power that those who run it believe themselves above the rule of law.'

Once the 2015 election campaign began in earnest at the turn of the year, Miliband took every opportunity to remind audiences and interviewers of his track record in being able to reach a conclusion and then act: 'I have taken some big calls, on Rupert Murdoch and phone hacking.' By repeatedly making a point of mentioning the name 'Murdoch' in speeches and answers, he sent another signal: the hostility that he was facing in newspapers such as the *Sun*, *Daily Mail* and *Daily Telegraph* was not going to deflect him from introducing policies to curb the abuses of big business, whether energy companies, banks or major media outlets.

Battle lines for the monstering that would ensue were apparent from late 2013: press proprietors started to prepare for the launch the following year of their independent regulator, and Miliband made it clear that a future Labour government would enforce the Royal Charter. In the view of the *Daily Mail*, Labour had backed state-sponsored regulation that would 'end 300 years of press freedom'. From then on Miliband could expect no mercy; he and his family would have to endure the kind of onslaught that Fleet Street had inflicted on Labour and trade union leaders of the past.

His pledge at the 2013 party conference to introduce a two-year freeze on energy prices gave the tabloid headline writers a chance to turn up the heat. 'Back to the bad old days' was the *Daily Mail's* front-page take on what it said was Miliband's lurch back to Labour's price controls of the 1970s. That weekend a two-page spread under the infamous headline the 'Man who hated Britain' argued that 'Red Ed's pledge to bring back socialism is a homage to the Marxist father he idolised'. Miliband accused the *Mail* of 'besmirching and undermining' his father, a Jewish refugee, by suggesting that he had not merely been unpatriotic, but actively hated the country. 'It's a lie.' David Cameron and the Deputy Prime Minister Nick Clegg both said they would have defended their fathers if they had been attacked in that way. After what the *Mail's* editor Paul Dacre described as a week of 'collective hysteria' against his paper, he acknowledged that the headline might have seemed 'over the top', but when read with the article itself was 'justifiable'.

Equally wounding was the 'weirdo' agenda that the tabloids began to exploit with the tacit support of the Conservatives. Peter Brookes, *The Times'* cartoonist, had already taken to presenting the Labour leader and his shadow chancellor Ed Balls as *Wallace and Gromit*, the toothy, absent-minded inventor accompanied by his faithful dog. Miliband's teeth were a gift for the cartoonists. The depiction of him as a somewhat goofy geek had not gone unnoticed by the *Sunday Telegraph*, which had evidently read the mind of Conservative spin doctors. Alongside a cartoon of Miliband with tombstone teeth, its columnist Iain Martin could not resist posing the question: 'Is this the Tories' secret weapon?'

Britain's cartoonists are often credited with being the first to associate a politician with a particular facial characteristic, quirky gesture, prop or perhaps item of attire, and for the press photographers Miliband's protruding teeth were about to become an example of life imitating art. Shortly before a photo-call in May 2014, Miliband was happy for the press pack to join him as he popped into a café at the New Covent Garden flower market for an early-morning bacon sandwich, not realising that his troublesome teeth would also be on the menu. London *Evening Standard* photographer Jeremy Selwyn was one those invited to sit down a few metres away. As the Labour leader started struggling to eat his bacon butty, he captured a moment that politicians dread, an image that would come to be associated with any mention of their name. 'I do like taking photographs of politicians in off-guard moments,' was Selwyn's reply when explaining why photographers were always hunting for revealing pictures that hadn't been stage managed by the parties. Selwyn had form: he was responsible for the equally comic shot of Miliband's brother, David holding up a banana outside the 2008 Labour conference.

Having relied for months on a succession of alarmist stories about the policies of a future Labour government, the *Sun* changed tack in February 2015, alternating its scare tactics with the kind of lampooning that might have suited a satirical magazine. Instead of photographs of Miliband from the campaign trail, he appeared in political stories as a cartoon character, in marked contrast to the authoritative pictures of Cameron that were printed alongside. Initially he was depicted as Wallace, complete with goofy teeth plus mock quotations. Later images were of him as a school dunce and then, in a two-page spread about Labour's manifesto, in the guise of Homer Simpson delivering *The Simpsons'* catchphrase translated into *Sunspeak*: 'Manifest-D'oh!' Miliband morphed into a green tinted Frankenstein for a report on the dire consequences of a coalition between Labour and the Scottish National party, later re-emerging being called to heel as the poodle of the former SNP leader, Alex Salmond.

Rupert Murdoch was said by the *Independent* to have intervened personally to instruct the *Sun* to be more aggressive in attacking Miliband because of the threat that a future Labour government would impose a Leveson-style press regulator, and limit the size of News Corporation's share of UK's press and television. In a BBC interview in April 2015, the week before the *Independent's* report, the *Sun's* editor, David Dinsmore confirmed that a Murdoch-Miliband confrontation had been influencing the paper's coverage. 'Miliband is at pains at every stage to say he is the man who stood up to Rupert Murdoch … that makes it quite easy when it comes to choosing sides.'

A journalist was filmed preparing a report for the paper's website SunNation. Visible on her screen was a tiny image of Miliband popped into the cleavage of a Page 3 model, mimicking Conservative advertisements that showed a tiny Miliband tucked into the top pocket of Salmond and later Nicola Sturgeon, as the Tories stepped up their campaign warning that Labour would be under the control of the SNP. 'Yes it's cruel, but we quite enjoy it, being cruel.'

Ridiculing Miliband might have amused Murdoch's journalists, and helped to sustain the impression that the Labour leader was a weird and remote geek, but their mockery lacked the political bombast of the paper's heyday, under its legendary editor Kelvin MacKenzie. The *Sun's* shrinking circulation, having fallen over three decades from nearly four million to well under two million copies a day, was partly responsible, but so was the absence of the killer instinct of the past, a bravado that could stop other journalists in their tracks, and deliver a political knock-out blow. The *Sun's* 1992 election front page of Neil Kinnock's head superimposed on a light bulb alongside the headline, 'If Kinnock wins today, will the last person to leave please turn out the lights', was the one which made MacKenzie's name, but far more destructive was the 1983 the headline, 'Do you seriously want this old man to run Britain?' beside a photograph of Michael Foot wearing a duffel coat.

The *Sun's* savaging of Miliband intensified in the countdown to polling day and its eve-of-poll edition reprised the bacon sandwich photograph in a front-page that harked back to Kinnock's 'light-bulb' moment. 'Save our bacon' was the headline alongside the shot of Miliband awkwardly trying to gulp down his breakfast. The text was as partisan as MacKenzie's in 1992, but perhaps did not have quite the same bite: 'This is the pig's ear Ed made of a helpless sarnie. In 48 hours, he could be doing the same to Britain...don't swallow his porkies and keep him out'.

Miliband paid a heavy price for his bravery in taking on Murdoch so publicly, and especially for pressing ahead with a manifesto that threatened the interests of the other leading newspaper proprietors. As the campaign progressed he showed during the televised debates, as well as out on the stump, that he was far more authoritative and personable than his goofy caricature suggested. What he could not wipe away was the lingering suspicion in the minds of so many voters that he was rather weird, not up to being Prime Minister, doubts that had been reinforced so comprehensively in wounding press reportage that stretched back not months but years. While their influence is nowhere near what it was a decade or two ago, the UK's national newspapers do retain appreciable impact on the daily news agenda. Their story lines still have considerable influence over what is reported on radio and television; they help sustain the content of countless websites and blogs; and drive so much of the chatter on line.

Peter Mandelson began the task of trying to neutralise press hostility under Kinnock's leadership, a task that accelerated as soon as Blair was elected leader and Mandelson was joined by Alastair Campbell. Their aim was to kill off, or at least limit, damaging story lines, but the extent of their subsequent manipulation horrified the left and appalled the media reformers who subsequently applauded Miliband's stand against Murdoch and welcomed his refusal to go along with the collusion of the Blair years. Newspaper circulations are in rapid decline and the threat they pose to the Labour party is receding. During the 2015 election, Tory-supporting titles were estimated to have daily sales of 5.2 million copies, as against 1.6 million copies that were anti-Tory, a political share-out and level of circulation that might have changed dramatically by 2020.

N

nationalists

When historians reflect on the momentous political advance of Scottish **nationalism** they can hardly ignore the impact of unrelenting press hostility. Months of acrimonious reportage in the UK's national newspapers became a recruiting sergeant in building support for independence in the 2014 referendum, and then for the Scottish National party's remarkable landslide in the general election seven months later. Abuse was in effect an ally in a campaign to reinforce the Scots' sense of identity, and later in their determination to have Scotland's voice heard at Westminster and Whitehall. The SNP were not averse to goading their tormentors: they understood the potency of being able to traduce unelected newspaper proprietors in what was once Fleet Street for fostering divisive and uncalled for interference in the affairs of Scotland.

Comparable belligerence towards the workings of the European Union influenced the course of British politics for decades. Divisions within the Conservative party under both Margaret Thatcher and John Major were exacerbated by the undeviating negativity of the popular press, an anti-EU agenda that later thwarted Tony Blair, undermining his enthusiasm for

Britain to abandon the pound and join the euro. The threat posed by Scottish nationalism acquired a similar potency after David Cameron signed the 2012 agreement to give the Scottish Parliament the authority to stage a referendum.

Two years were to elapse before the vote took place, and as the months went by the greater the vilification of Alex Salmond, First Minister of Scotland, the more the Yes campaigners succeeded in driving up support for Scotland to go its own way. They insisted the Scots were not going to be browbeaten by newspaper editors in London. Salmond's successor Nicola Sturgeon would attract the same venom once she launched her campaign for the general election. Her plea that Labour should work together with the SNP to 'lock David Cameron out of Downing Street' provoked an all-too predictable response from newspapers such as the *Daily Mail* and *Daily Telegraph*: she had become the 'most dangerous woman in Britain'.

In the final run-up to polling day the alarmist predictions of the Prime Minister and his allies in the press were found to be having an increasing impact south of the border. Polling evidence suggested that the combined effect of the Conservatives' campaign tactics, amplified by frequent scare stories about Ms Sturgeon's ability to dictate terms to Ed Miliband in a Labour-SNP coalition, were strengthening the Tories' pitch to win over undecided English voters. They would have to choose not just between economic 'competence or chaos', but also between a government capable of preserving the union and a coalition that would have no alternative but to allow another referendum, leading to the possible break-up of the UK.

Political campaigning is in the DNA of Britain's media proprietors. It helped the press barons of earlier years establish the mass circulations that provided the editorial patronage that encouraged them to become formidable players on the political stage. When the tone and direction of the day's coverage can be determined at a publisher's whim, their collective influence can succeed in driving the political agenda. Nigel Farrage's early success in building support for the United Kingdom Independence party reflected the anger of voters whose disillusionment with the EU had been fuelled by an endless diet of stories about unelected bureaucrats in Brussels inflicting change after change on the British way of life. UKIP's stance of trying to win back control from Europe appealed to newspaper proprietors who were only too happy to use him as a foil to remind Conservative ministers that they too wanted to limit Brussels' interference and prevent the introduction of EU-wide regulations that might damage their media interests. Until a tide of favourable publicity turned against him closer to polling day, Tory-supporting tabloids had been only too happy to present Farrage as the friendly 'bloke next door', the one man prepared to speak up for the British public.

In the two years that UKIP campaigned in the local authority elections in 2013, and then the elections to the European Parliament the following year, Farrage was invariably photographed smiling, enjoying a glass of beer or having a quick smoke. By contrast Salmond was being demonised in the great tradition of a Fleet Street bogeyman. Cartoonists captured the zeitgeist of this political dichotomy: Salmond was a dejected Mickey Mouse character in a tatty kilt taking hit after hit, whereas a folksy Farrage, pint and cigarette in hand, was always celebrating success, his chastened rivals cowering in the distance.

A hardening in the tone of press coverage was noticeable after the publication in November 2013 of the Scottish

Government's white paper, *Scotland's Future*, setting out a 'once-in-a-generation' chance to create a fairer, more prosperous country by voting to leave the UK. Tabloid headlines dubbed the manifesto a 'fantasy wish list'; the nationalists had embarked on 'mission impossible'. Salmond faced a chorus of press criticism, his strategy doomed to failure as the SNP was battered by set back after set back: entry to the EU by an independent Scotland was 'almost impossible'; the verdict of the Bank of England and the Treasury was that Scotland could not 'go it alone and keep the pound'; the figures for North Sea oil revenues 'did not add up'; the rejection of Trident nuclear submarines would 'weaken Anglo-American relations'; and so it went on. Newspapers ratcheted up still further a run of scare stories in the final few weeks before the vote: shoppers in Scotland would pay for independence in 'higher prices'; Scottish banks were 'drawing up contingency plans to leave'; global investors were 'pulling out'; sterling would fall by '15 per cent'; money was already 'flooding' out of the UK.

Broadcasters were denounced for swallowing the hostile agenda of the London press, of parroting alarmist propaganda. Nick Robinson, the BBC's political editor, was one of those singled out for criticism after he challenged the First Minister over a report that the Royal Bank of Scotland might move its headquarters to London. Salmond accused the BBC of being 'absolutely' biased in its coverage. Nationalists waving Yes campaign flags marched on the BBC's studios in Glasgow holding aloft a large banner that rammed home the point: 'Sack Nick 'The liar' Robinson a totally corrupt journalist'. The 'Better Together' campaign deplored the intimidation of journalists which it blamed on the uncontrolled aggression of SNP activists, a fervour that Salmond had unleashed but failed to control.

Robinson's discomfort reminded me of the ability of another charismatic street fighter to whip up his supporters to treat the media as the enemy. At a rally at the height of the 1984-85 pit strike, I was standing among a small group of journalists holding up my microphone when we caught the attention of Arthur Scargill, President of the National Union of Mineworkers. To cheers from the crowd, he denounced us as 'vermin' promoting the lies of the National Coal Board. We were 'a bunch of piranha fish' who would always go on supporting Margaret Thatcher. During a friendly chat several weeks later I challenged him about his love-hate relationship with the media. Some reporters might wonder why they were being attacked, but Scargill said he could not separate guilty and innocent correspondents; he had to attack them all. Berating journalists at strike meetings invariably got a good audience response so whenever he spoke in public he purposely attacked them because he felt this made him 'more interesting' for the media at large. Salmond had grasped the same point: the London press might think they were the cheerleaders for the No campaign, but the virulence of their coverage was also strengthening the resolve of the SNP's most ardent followers.

Unlike the strikers involved in the industrial disputes of the 1980s, the SNP's dedicated activists had the benefit of the internet, an online world where supporters could communicate with each other, and also reach out to a wider audience, by-passing national newspapers, broadcasters and other established media outlets. A sense of alienation experienced by journalists from London when they were reporting events in Edinburgh or Glasgow was mirrored by online intimidation of celebrities who stood out against independence. After she donated £1 million to the Yes campaign, the Harry Potter author J K Rowling became a target for what came to be known as 'Tartan Trolls' or 'cybernats' who harried their opponents by posting abusive messages on Twitter. 'Tirade of hate that shames Salmond' was the headline on a *Daily Mail* splash that catalogued what it said was the bullying and intimidation of the SNP, followed on the eve of poll with a front-page headed with the words, 'The Seriously Nasty Party', each capital letter in red.

Ten days before the referendum the 'Better Together' campaign went into a tailspin after the *Sunday Times* published a YouGov opinion poll that forecast they would be defeated by the narrowest of margins: 51-49 per cent in favour of Yes. Such was the consternation on the No side that Cameron cancelled Prime Minister's questions to make an emotional appeal for Scotland to remain in the UK. Together with Nick Clegg and Ed Miliband, he signed a joint undertaking that was dubbed 'The Vow', a promise by the Conservatives, Liberal Democrats and Labour to 'guarantee more devolved powers to Scotland'.

Shy No voters were credited with saving the day for the union in a record-breaking turn-out of 84.6 per cent, just ahead of the previous best figure recorded in the 1950 general election, and the highest since the introduction of universal suffrage in 1918. The defeat of the Yes campaign by 55-45 per cent was followed almost immediately by Salmond's resignation. He praised the remarkable response of the Scottish people and urged the SNP to 'hold Westminster's feet to the fire on the "vow" to deliver further meaningful power to Scotland'. Within weeks Nicola Sturgeon had been elected leader and succeeded him as First Minister.

Far from being knocked back by their defeat Ms Sturgeon was able to ride a wave of post-referendum pride in Scottish identity, and a determination to use the 45 per cent Yes vote to power a general election campaign to push the SNP's representation at Westminster way beyond the six seats they won in 2010. Cameron had provided Ms Sturgeon with a ready-made argument for the SNP to become Scotland's voice in the House of Commons. In welcoming the No vote on the morning after the referendum, the Prime Minister said that reforms to strip Scottish MPs of voting powers over English issues would have to take place 'in tandem with and at the same pace as the settlement for Scotland'. His unexpected declaration of support for 'English-only votes for English laws' shattered any hope of maintaining the cross-party consensus of 'Better Together' because it favoured the Conservatives at the expense of Labour and the Liberal Democrats.

In playing to the gallery of his English MPs Cameron was having to acknowledge the potency of another grievance inflamed by Tory-supporting newspapers. They rarely missed an opportunity to remind readers that England was being short changed as a result of the long-standing Barnett formula for allocating resources. Public spending in Scotland was in excess of £10,000 per head per year, £1,600 more per head than in England. Cameron's attempt to try to capitalise on the divisive card of 'English votes for English laws' allowed Ms Sturgeon to seize the initiative north of the border. She had a fresh grievance to exploit. Recruitment of new members soared, as did the SNP's opinion poll ratings, in sharp contrast to the demoralisation in Scottish Labour, struggling to prepare for a desperate, all-out fight to retain its 41 seats at Westminster.

Ms Sturgeon presented a fresh face, a far less abrasive persona than Salmond, hardly capable her supporters might have thought of being demonised in the Tory press with the same ferocity as her predecessor. Her campaign theme was short and to point: the SNP were seeking an end to austerity by allowing a small rise in public spending, a message that cut right across the bows of the three main parties as they struggled to outline coherent figures to support their competing but rather confused undertakings to cut the deficit.

Cameron had bequeathed Ms Sturgeon another unparalleled opportunity to promote the SNP's bid to become the legitimate defender of Scottish interests at Westminster. By refusing to participate in a repeat series of the televised head-to-head confrontations of the 2010 campaign, and by agreeing instead to join a panel that included the leaders of the smaller parties, the Prime Minister had handed her the chance to take part in a seven-way debate on a UK-wide platform in an election in which she was not even a candidate. Nick Clegg, no longer the outsider, was among the also-rans as Ms Sturgeon and Nigel Farrage jostled for the top spot in the first set-piece televised event of the election. They both realised the potential impact of what had been billed the opening round of the campaign, five weeks from polling day. A YouGov sample for a post-debate opinion poll had Ms Sturgeon nosing comfortably ahead, most commentators agreeing that she outperformed the pack, displaying a deft political touch in her rejection of 'blind austerity' in favour of a progressive approach to public spending.

Her assured performance drew praise from the *Sun*: 'a smiling assassin whose skills on the podium shone through'. In the view of the *Daily Mail* she had left Ed Miliband 'squirming as she attacked him from the left on tax and spending'. A tweet from the Conservative campaign headquarters claimed her domination of their exchanges was 'a glimpse of what life would be like under a Miliband-SNP deal'. To underline the point the Tories rushed out an online version of a poster depicting a miniature Miliband peeping out of Ms Sturgeon's top pocket, replacing an earlier version that had the Labour leader tucked into Salmond's top pocket. Miliband was about to find himself boxed into a corner from which there would be no escape. However hard he tried to deny the accusation that a future Labour government would only survive at the behest of the SNP, he struggled to present a convincing defence given the pollsters' consistent prediction that his party would lose almost all its seats in Scotland.

At the launch of the SNP's manifesto Ms Sturgeon outlined her vision of an alliance with Labour that would deliver 'a new era of progressive politics'. She insisted her party would exercise influence at Westminster responsibly and constructively for the benefit of Britain. Cameron's rejoinder was that it would be 'a match made in hell' for the UK economy, a line of attack reinforced next day in a speech by the former Prime Minister Sir John Major, who argued that a Miliband government propped up by the SNP would be 'a daily dose of political blackmail'. Again Miliband tried his best to dispel the notion that the SNP would be 'calling the shots' if he was Prime Minister, telling the BBC, 'That ain't gonna happen'.

Labour's repeated rebuttals were having to compete against a story line that increasingly dominated the news agenda: Ms Sturgeon would be the power behind the throne in a Labour-led minority government. The *Daily Mail's* front-page headline accentuated the threat: 'How I'll blackmail England for £148 billion by the most dangerous woman in Britain'. A two-page profile in the *Sun* had the menacing headline, 'The Scotweiler – the ruthless woman who would split the UK'. An analysis of Treasury figures was used by the *Daily Telegraph* to support a claim that 'every working family in Britain' would be £350 a year worse off under a Labour government propped up by the SNP.

Keeping Miliband on the defensive, dogged by constant questions about the vulnerability of a minority Labour administration, suited both Prime Minister and First Minister. Backed by soundings from English marginal constituencies that the threat of a Labour-SNP coalition was the issue that was resonating most of all on the doorstep, Cameron readied himself for the final push telling *The Times* that he had only 'ten days to save the United Kingdom'. If Labour had enough MPs to try to form a government, they would have to rely on 'a bunch of people' who did not want the country to succeed. Miliband stood his ground in the leaders' last televised joust, a BBC *Question Time* special from Leeds: he would not share power with the SNP even if it meant giving up the chance to become Prime Minister. 'I'm not going to sacrifice the future of our country, the unity of our country, I'm not going to give in to SNP demands'. Ms Sturgeon upped the stakes in her final televised debate by warning that the SNP would be prepared to vote down a Labour budget that continued with austerity. Backed by an endorsement from the *Sun's* Scottish edition, she kept up the pressure until last moment, promising 48 hours from polling day that immediately the result was known she and leading members of her cabinet would be ready to fly to London to negotiate a formal deal with Labour.

Post-election analysis of the reasons why voters switched sides in the 34 seats taken by the Conservatives from both Labour and the Liberal Democrats vindicated the attack strategy pursued by the party's Australian election strategist Lynton Crosby. He won the unanimous praise of Tory tacticians for having used the fear of a SNP-dominated coalition as a wedge to peel off enough waverers from the two other main parties to secure Cameron an overall majority of 12. Crosby's legendary status within the party had seemed in doubt when the opinion polls predicted a dead heat, but his colleagues said he resolutely held his nerve and was always in control of the campaign. In the final week of the election he was convinced the Conservatives win from 306 to 333 seats, and he was only two short of his target.

Crosby told the *Daily Telegraph* he was bemused by Miliband's failure to find a convincing way of denying the claim that Labour could only get into government with the support of the SNP. 'When it became clear Scotland was a serious problem, they should have completely reshaped their campaign in the rest of the country.' Labour's plight was acknowledged by Tony Blair's former press secretary, Alastair Campbell, who reflected on Labour's plight in the *Daily Mirror*. Crosby had run a 'brutally efficient' campaign that turned the election into a referendum on whether the country wanted a Labour-SNP government rather than another five years of Cameron. Miliband's senior press secretary Tom Baldwin told the *Guardian* that much of the blame lay with the pollsters for having generated a scare story based on a false premise. A deal with the SNP was 'never on the cards', yet the BBC had been 'too easily swayed' by the agenda of the Tory press. All too often its coverage had provided an 'echo chamber' for the *Sun*, *Daily Mail*, *Daily Telegraph* and *The Times*.

Like most political journalists I thought the opinion polls must be right in their prediction that the overall result would be neck-and-neck. On the other hand there was nothing to doubt their forecast of sweeping gains for Nicola Sturgeon. Nonetheless I had not envisaged that Scottish Labour would lose all but one seat. For an old Westminster hand the sight of 56 SNP MPs assembling for a photo-opportunity outside the House of Commons is my abiding image of the 2015 election. On countless occasions in my years with the BBC I included in my reports an SNP response to the major issues of the day, perhaps on the Budget or a major industrial or constitutional story. Their reaction was required in order to ensure political balance, not necessarily for its newsworthiness. The nationalists' historic breakthrough has reshaped the political map of the UK, and re-ordered the news agenda. Scottish politics are no longer the regional news story they once were, thanks to the nationalists' canny knack of capturing the headlines.

opinion polls

After weeks of constant electioneering the release of
the first survey revealing how people actually voted is
invariably the most nerve wracking moment of a campaign,
provoking whoops of excitement or perhaps utter despair.
Against all expectations the exit poll for the 2015 general
election gave the Conservatives a commanding lead, sending
Labour and the Liberal Democrats into an immediate tailspin,
a downward spiral of defeat that shattered the credibility
of **opinion** pollsters who for so long had been calling the
shots during an extended build-up to polling day. They had
been consistent in their prediction that the result would be
close, probably a dead heat between David Cameron and
Ed Miliband, a forecast that had dictated the course of the
campaign, influencing tactics to a far greater extent than had
ever previously been the case.

Election strategists said subsequently that if they had only
known the opinion polls were so misleading, they would have
changed their approach and adjusted their daily programme
of events. A second hung parliament seemed so certain on the
strength of the pollsters' findings that speculation about the

formation of another coalition government had dominated the news agenda for weeks, prompting endless theorising about how the rival parties might line up and their likely terms for a deal. An edifice built entirely on conjecture was about to collapse within hours of the exit poll being announced in the opening sequence of the election night programmes. Early declarations soon confirmed the accuracy of the exit figures: the Conservatives would easily be the largest party, and they were on their way to an overall majority. If, there and then, there had been an instant opinion poll among politicians, party workers and journalists, asking for views on the veracity of opinion polls, the polling companies and their array of pundits would have had a rude awakening, and found their reputation for reliability was on the floor.

There had not been such a momentous misreading of voting intentions since 1992 when pre-election opinion polls gave the Labour leader Neil Kinnock a two-point lead over John Major, followed by an exit poll that predicted a hung parliament, only for the Conservatives to be re-elected with a majority of 21. Grave though their failure had been the pollsters promised to review their techniques, their track record improved, and so too did the accuracy of exit polls. The drubbing of 2015 was a far greater calamity than the debacle of 1992 because of the rapid growth in the number of polling companies, and their ability to command a level of news coverage that the parties found difficult to ignore. Instead of the 50 or so opinion polls that were conducted during the 1992 campaign, and four on the eve of the election, there were literally hundreds of surveys published in the course of the 100-day countdown to polling day in May 2015, including 11 on the eve of poll, of which ten suggested there was only one point between Cameron and Miliband, a far cry from the eventual result and the Conservatives' 6.6 per cent margin over Labour.

Such was the outrage over the inaccuracy of their findings that the leading companies issued a rapid apology, and agreed to co-operate with an inquiry to be conducted by the British Polling Council. In response to much ridicule the pollsters' advanced numerous theories to explain why their systems failed to predict a sizeable swing to the Conservatives. Their self-justification did little to silence either those politicians demanding that polls should be banned prior to polling day or in countering the avowed reluctance of some editors to spend anything like as much again on commissioning opinion surveys.

Rapid advances in polling techniques had opened up opportunities for the companies to benefit from the determined efforts of national newspapers to maintain their competitive edge, despite steadily declining circulations. Costly face-to-face surveys in high streets and shopping centres that once took several days to complete were being replaced first by telephone canvassing and then by online surveys, allowing pollsters to offer editors a constant supply of up-to-the-minute results. For a relatively modest outlay of around £5,000 per survey editors had the ability to create their own headlines in a crowded market place. A switch from weekly to daily polls transformed news reporting of the 2010 election campaign. The *Sun* started publishing a YouGov daily tracker poll three months ahead of polling day. As soon the go-ahead was given for the first-ever series of live televised leaders' debates, other newspapers rushed to hire pollsters who were able to supply surveys of viewers' opinions within minutes of the end of each programme. YouGov, established in 2000, pioneered online polling, confident that its computer programmes could take account of different statistical weightings so as to produce accurate predictions. Its president Peter Kellner promised that the *Sun's* innovation of publishing day-by-day results would 'follow the fortunes of the parties in real time', and reflect the 'trends that will shape the final outcome'.

Opinion polls had been a staple of the national press for decades because they gave editors and proprietors considerable clout when attempting to influence the politics of the day. Newspapers could frame the scope of a survey, and then choose the date of publication to suit their own news agendas. Timing was always considered a matter of critical importance, a moment perhaps to pile on the pressure facing an unpopular government or boost the fortunes of the opposition. Polls could be used by newspapers to test public reaction to new policies and gauge opinion on a host of controversial issues. Newspapers were in control: they commissioned the polls; approved the line of questioning; and the timing of publication was always at an editor's discretion, a powerful weapon in the battle for headlines.

When I started reporting politics at Westminster in the 1960s far fewer opinion polls were being commissioned, and there were only a handful of companies, including established names such as Gallup, NOP, Marplan and ORC. A newcomer to the scene was MORI, under the chairmanship of the ebullient Robert Worcester, which was soon generating a flow of news stories from polls conducted for the *Sunday Times*, London *Evening Standard* and other newspapers. Worcester was the first pollster to promote himself as a political commentator, a role that Kellner undertook once YouGov introduced online polling. Throughout the 1970s and 1980s there was a steady expansion in the number of polls appearing in daily papers, and also in the extent to which they had in effect become highly politicised due to the way questions could be framed and publication of the contents so easily manipulated.

By the 1992 election the influence of the polls was greater than I had previously experienced. Wide variations in the predicted size of Labour's lead were causing considerable confusion and uncertainty. Kinnock was forecast to be ahead but short of an outright victory, a degree of volatility that encouraged the Conservatives to think that Major still had every chance of being re-elected. Fluctuations in the polls featured regularly in the BBC's reporting of the election. At one point in the lead-up to polling day, when Labour had a five-point, I was asked to seek the reaction of Tony Blair, then a rising front bencher, who while pleased by the prediction seemed annoyed by the BBC's focus on opinion polls rather than Labour policy.

Politicians' irritation at the impact the polls were having on the BBC's coverage led to the introduction of new editorial guidelines that reflected the influence of John Birt, who became director general in 1992 after serving five years as deputy. Birt instigated far-reaching changes in the way political news was reported. Opinion polls had to be subjected to greater editorial scrutiny; news stories had to indicate how many people had been questioned, and also the period over which a survey was conducted. Correspondents often lacked the space in tightly-written voice reports to include all the data that was required. Editors and producers became increasingly reluctant to quote opinion poll findings in bulletins and programmes, and within a few years they were rarely being afforded anything like the same prominence. Instead the BBC compiled a regular poll of polls that gave an indication of overall trends, a practice that avoided previous criticism that broadcasters were paying undue attention to newspaper-inspired surveys.

While polls that continued to command press headlines rarely formed the sole basis for radio or television reports, their impact on the political parties was inescapable, and so was their influence on the wider news agenda. So dominant was the thrust of their leverage on events in the 2015 election that they inevitably became the prism through which the campaign was reported. The surveys were so comprehensive, and so consistent in their forecasts that they could not be ignored. Kellner was one of an array of pollsters called upon to interpret their findings, elevated to a new political commentariat that was soon writing newspapers columns and supplying regular punditry for radio and television programmes. Not content with simply conducting surveys and analysing the information they had obtained, the pollsters had morphed into players on the political stage exploiting their predictions to help float competing scenarios for a future coalition government.

As polling day approached in what was being billed the most unpredictable election since the Second World War, the focus shifted towards the exit poll, which was again a joint undertaking by BBC, ITV and Sky News. Surveys of voters leaving polling stations had become so extensive, as had the breadth of the expertise among those crunching the figures that they had succeeded in re-establishing a reputation for accuracy in their on-the-day assessments of the electorate's verdict. Exit poll credibility began to recover at the close of the 1997 election. In the lead-up to polling day, the pollsters were predicting that Major would go down to a hefty defeat, a forecast that caused consternation in Tory high command. At one news conference, MORI's chairman was challenged on his claim that Major did not have 'a prayer' of catching up with Blair. Andrew Cooper, the Conservatives' deputy head of research, was convinced undecided voters would return, as they had in 1992. 'If Bob Worcester goes on predicting a landslide for Labour right up to polling day, he'll lose in spades.' Worcester and his colleagues had the satisfaction of being proved right by an exit poll commissioned by the BBC and ITN which put Labour ahead by 18 per cent, only a couple of points below MORI's forecast.

By the 2010 election the exit poll had been extended to 130 polling stations and a canvass of 18,000 voters. It suggested a hung parliament with the Conservatives 19 seats short of an overall majority, an assessment that proved to be entirely correct. Under the continued leadership of Professor John Curtice of Strathclyde University, preparations were made for an even larger exit poll in 2015. A team of around 400 researchers from Ipsos MORI and GfK NOP stood outside 141 polling stations in 133 constituencies across the UK. As they left 22,000 voters were approached at random and asked to fill up in secret an exit poll ballot paper. Three quarters of those stopped agreed to take part, far higher than average response rates that were sometimes as low as one in ten for telephone and online surveys. Professor Curtice headed a team of eight leading pollsters in a BBC basement that spent the day analysing responses from around the country. When the election night programmes released the results at 10 p.m. there was amazement: the Conservatives were predicted to be the largest party with 316 seats, well ahead of Labour on 238, the Scottish National party's tally was forecast to be 58 seats and Liberal Democrats to retain only ten seats.

Kellner, who was one of the pundits on the BBC's results programme *Election 2015*, expressed disbelief. All 11 eve-of-poll surveys had shown Labour and the Conservatives were neck and neck. YouGov had questioned 6,000 people online and found 'no sign of an on-the-day shift'. Another guest, Blair's former press secretary Alastair Campbell, shared Kellner's scepticism. He had been at Labour headquarters all day and the exit poll did not 'feel right' to him. After Labour failed to take its first target seat of Nuneaton, Kellner conceded that all 11 pre-election polls had obviously made the 'same mistake'. In an early bid to pre-empt the criticism he knew the pollsters were bound to attract, he said the lesson of the exit poll was that politicians should always campaign for they what believed in; they should stand on their principles rather than be swayed by opinion poll numbers.

Cameron had enhanced his reputation by confounding not only the pollsters' predictions but also the expectations of the exit poll. Gaining 331 seats, an outright majority of 12, was so out of step with the polling companies that they had to act swiftly to limit damage to their reputations in the highly-profitable sector of commercial and consumer brand polling. Stephan Shakespeare, founder of YouGov, was among the first to apologise. 'The first thing we have to do is say we got it wrong. There is no point in saying it wasn't that bad.'

Rather shamefacedly the *Sun* reprinted its election-day front page which had carried the words, 'Well Hung' in capital letters over YouGov's 'knife-edge' prediction of a 34-34 per cent dead heat. 'Probe as pollsters say sorry for fiasco', was the headline over a report that the British Polling Council, supported by the Market Research Society, was to hold an inquiry to discover why 'all the pollsters underestimated the Conservative lead over Labour'. In his weekly column in the *Sun*, Kelvin Mackenzie advised the paper he once edited, and other titles, not to pay for polls that had each cost between £8,000 and £10,000. Due to their 'almost criminal ineptitude' the pollsters had misled readers and viewers. 'It would make a great court case and the polling companies would go thousands of miles to avoid bad publicity.'

One theory that attracted much comment was the polling companies' failure to reflect the significance of 'shy Tories', voters who were not prepared to reveal their support for the Conservatives, and whose importance was first identified by Rob Hayward, a political analyst and former Conservative MP. In the 1992 election he advised Major to ignore polls suggesting Labour was ahead because his research showed there were voters who would come out on polling day, but 'felt too awkward to tell anyone'. The Conservatives were re-elected with over 14 million votes, the 'highest popular vote for any party in Britain'. Hayward told the *Daily Telegraph* he had detected the same phenomenon in 2015, but the pollsters still had not learned from their mistakes in 1992. 'Basically they were fooled by the soft Labour vote: those people who were initially tempted by Ed Miliband and then shied away from voting for him in the cold reality of the polling booth.'

Hayward's thesis was endorsed by Kellner who thought the Conservatives had suffered from a similar problem in 1992 and 2015. In both elections the party had a 'difficult brand image', but those who were critical and reluctant to give their support did in fact vote Tory on the day. Ben Page of Ipsos MORI agreed that his company had over-estimated the Labour vote, more a case he believed of 'lazy Labour' than 'shy Tories', a group of voters who had suggested they would vote but failed to do so. Damian Lyons Lowe, founder of Survation, was one of the few pollsters to claim that his company had detected a late swing. An eve-of-poll telephone canvass had indicated a 6 per cent lead for the Conservatives, but he sat on the figure because he thought it was a 'rogue' poll. He would always regret not offering the data to the *Daily Mirror* which published Survation polls.

Another point of criticism was based on evidence that suggested online polls tended to favour Labour whereas telephone canvassing did not show the same bias. Sir David Spiegelhalter, a leading statistician at Cambridge University, argued that the root of the problem was a basic design fault in the 'cheap and cheerful' polls that the newspapers published. Less than a third of those approached in telephone surveys and online panels were prepared to give an answer, so the initial data was really poor. 'The pollsters make lots of adjustments to patch them up, but they are still unreliable, and then the BBC puts them together in a poll of polls that produces an even more confident but biased opinion.' James Morris of the American pollsters GQR, who had been working for Labour, thought the refusal to respond was probably as high 20 per cent. Pollsters in the USA were experiencing even greater difficulty in canvassing opinion. Only 9 per cent of those approached by telephone in the 2012 US Presidential election had responded.

Undue reliance on unrepresentative samples was a criticism that had echoes of the complaints made by the former Deputy Prime Minister Michael Heseltine when he challenged the pollsters' pro-Labour predictions during the 1997 election. He claimed that of 2,000 people asked to take part in a telephone canvass, only 1,000 agreed and a quarter of them would not say how they would vote, so on his calculation such a survey was based on only 36 per cent of those originally approached. 'The public don't take the polls as seriously as the media do. For most people they're a great big joke.' Almost two decades later the Conservative election strategist Lynton Crosby compared a pollster relying on an online survey to a doctor who recorded a patient's daily temperature but gave no diagnosis of what was going on. A database at party headquarters built up on the results of internal polls contained details of 'tens of thousands of potential Tory voters who had been quietly monitored', and who helped Cameron return to Downing Street.'

Crosby added his weight to the contention that the media had paid so much attention to what the pollsters were saying that it had distorted news coverage, a trend he thought 'quite dangerous'. Polls were no longer simply an assessment of what was going on, but had become part of the political process, and 'actually influence' what had happened. 'I would subscribe to the view there should be a stay on publishing polls publicly for two or three weeks before an election.'

Some journalists acknowledged that only when polls were shown to be so wrong did they understand the extent of their influence on reporting and commentary. Writing in the *Independent on Sunday*, John Rentoul said that once a story line had become established events continued to be seen through that same prism. Richard Sambrook, a former director of BBC News, admitted that the dominant narrative of a neck-and-neck election, although plain wrong, had determined much of the coverage, 'eclipsing policy analysis'. Having been distracted by inaccurate forecasts, news organisations such as the BBC would have to consider the role polls should play in reporting the 2020 election. The *Guardian* was the first newspaper to act, declaring that it would 'take a pause on reporting polls as political news'. Monthly opinion surveys would be continued, and maintained in 'a low key way', while methodologies were refined. Seven decades of regular polling had been 'right more often than wrong', but had the forecasts been different nightly news bulletins would 'surely have concentrated rather more' on spending cuts and rather less on the potential role of Scottish nationalists in a hung parliament.

Soul searching among journalists, and the willingness of pollsters to co-operate with the British Polling Council's investigation into the causes of possible bias, gave further impetus to a bill introduced in the House of Lords to establish an independent Ofcom-style regulator for the polling industry. Lord Foulkes, a former Labour Scottish Office minister, first proposed the bill in the aftermath of the referendum on Scottish independence. He was highly critical of a YouGov poll in the *Sunday Times* that predicted a 51-49 per cent lead for the Yes campaign, a forecast that triggered an 'over-reaction' by the Westminster parties and a huge devolution of powers to Scotland. Lord Foulkes blamed 'media moguls' who demanded snap opinions to support their vested interests. Restrictions on the publication of polls in the period immediately before an election were already in force in France, India, Italy and Spain, and he hoped a new regulator would work out the parameters for a similar limitation during UK elections. Kellner and his fellow pollsters vowed to oppose a pre-election ban, arguing that the public should have access to any data that was being collected, but their punditry had been found wanting and they would struggle to recover their previous standing in the political commentariat.

P

photo-opportunities

Competing demands for **photo-opportunities** presented a constant tug of war during the 2015 general election. Party leaders out on the campaign trail were forced to divide their time between contrived photo-shoots laid on for the news media, or finding themselves besieged by potential voters clutching camera phones, desperate to take selfies. Celebrity status has imposed a fresh demand on high-profile politicians in an era when smartphones and tablets are so popular, and when so many people have an insatiable desire to take a picture of themselves with 'someone famous.' For a team of election minders, who had to work against the clock to ensure the swift transfer of a party leader from one event to the next, a nightmare scenario was to see their charge disappearing in a sea of camera phones. At campaign stops there were usually two separate locations. Outside a venue, during a leader's arrival and departure, there would be party members and supporters crowding round, requesting selfies, and inside a tightly-controlled photo-opportunity where entry was permitted only to a strictly-vetted band of television crews and press photographers. A sharp contrast in the way political parties attempted to deal with these rival attractions pointed to one of the contradictions of the 2015 campaign. The unprecedented clamour to be photographed with a well-known politician necessitated at least some freedom of movement, but the parties had no intention of allowing unrestricted access where it mattered most of all to the news media.

Political journalists, photographers and camera crews were unanimous in declaring 2015 the most carefully controlled general election they had experienced. They accused the parties of avoiding direct engagement with voters in favour of a succession of stage-managed stunts with invited audiences that misled the public into thinking there was an open discourse with the electorate, a deception the media by and large had little alternative but to play along with. Campaign events attended by party leaders have to be covered, whether or not they produce a headline or newsworthy image. Television news bulletins must have on-the-day footage, just as a wide choice of the latest photographs is essential for next day's national newspapers, so no major news outlet can take the risk of not being represented. Spin doctors and strategists know full well that the media pack is a captive audience, and that however many complaints there might be, a tight limit on access is one of the conditions that applies in return for the privilege of reporting an election from the front line.

Morning news conferences that once dominated the start of each day's campaigning have been replaced with a limited number of set-piece occasions, such as manifesto launches, and also question-and-answer sessions that became an add-on at a succession of daily photo-opportunities, all tailored to the task of promoting the latest policy agenda. There was a regular, almost fixed routine to the daily programme in 2015. Labour and the Conservatives went to great lengths early each evening to brief the national newspapers about the policy initiatives they were launching next day. News releases issued in advance under an embargo would be timed for inclusion in the 10 p.m. news bulletins on BBC, ITV and Sky News. These were the stories the parties hoped would go on to dominate the morning output and feature in the newspapers, preparing the way for the photo-opportunities that would supply the visual backing for the daily campaign message.

Each publicity department always hopes to upstage their opponents by coming up with the most topical story lines, and then framing the photo-shoots to match. On occasion all their creative efforts barely get a mention, either because they were not considered as newsworthy as was originally hoped, or because of being overtaken by more important political developments. Equally there is no way of knowing whether a stunt will backfire and create headlines for all the wrong reasons. Bizarre poses run the danger of being mocked online or of supplying political cartoonists with the inspiration for a fresh caricature. Presenting an even greater challenge to the control-freak mind-set that tends to grip campaign headquarters is the threat of a snatched photograph or video that manages to capture a party leader off guard at an embarrassing moment.

Thinking up and then arranging locations for eye-catching pictures requires constant application by each media team. Margaret Thatcher's willingness to indulge the press pack by picking up a baby calf on a farm visit provided an enduring image from the 1979 general election. She had the support of some of the leading publicists of her era who led the way in creating events and photo-opportunities that exploited the news media's ceaseless demand for fresh material, a lesson that the Labour party still had not learned by the 1983 election when newspapers and television often had little alternative but to make do with shots of Michael Foot walking his Tibetan terrier Dizzie on Hampstead Heath.

Each election tends to throw up new concepts and ideas, perhaps a fresh interpretation of a well-worn routine or a chance to exploit a new fad or fashion. The overall aim is always to offer the media imagery that builds on campaign themes. David Cameron's perpetual refrain throughout the 2015 election was that the Conservatives were 'on the side of working people', and that if re-elected he would lead a government that would again be 'helping hard-working families'. These slogans were reinforced by repeated photo-shoots in workplaces and schools across the country. When visiting factories and building sites, Cameron and the Chancellor George Osborne were rarely seen unless wearing high-visibility jackets or vests. At each location, chatting to production line staff of construction workers, they stood out in their orange or yellow attire, usually wearing hard hats as well. On the occasions when the Prime Minister was joined by his wife Samantha, she was kitted out in similar fashion, happy to smile for photographers once she had donned her safety helmet.

While the press pack soon became bored by such repetitive photo-opportunities, the party's election strategists knew that their message was being reinforced every time the pictures were shown in television news bulletins or appeared in next day's newspapers. Presenting a positive emphasis on the world of work strengthened the hard sell of the Conservatives' campaign, a pitch that the party constantly returned to. Labour and the Liberal Democrats offered a competing range of photo opportunities, but their imagery lacked the consistency of the 'high-vis' approach adopted by the Tories. Rather than try to match Cameron's formula of a walk-about and chat inside a workplace environment, Ed Miliband steered clear of situations that might have given photographers the chance to picture him in awkward poses that played to the weirdo image that he had been burdened with by the tabloid press. Instead he chose to make his daily appearance standing in front of a lectern that he used at campaign stops around the country, ranging from a factory car park to the middle of a cricket pitch. His campaign aides wanted to present an image that enhanced his authority as a prime minister-in-waiting, anxious to avoid a repeat of the free-style, off-the-cuff delivery of his 2014 party conference speech when he spoke for 65 minutes largely from memory, only to be accused afterwards of having failed to mention either the deficit or immigration, two issues that were included in the advanced text. He did acknowledge later that one of the perils of delivering a speech without a script was 'not remembering every detail'.

Cameron's eagerness to get stuck in and put himself about during photo-opportunities was not risk free. During a visit to Dorset to meet local people who had benefited from tax and pension changes, he joined a family barbecue where he was offered a hot dog. Instead of picking it up to eat, he sat down and used a knife and fork, fearing no doubt that he might be snapped by photographers in a pose that suggested he was having the same difficulty that Miliband experienced when he was pictured struggling to eat a bacon sandwich. Locations were often chosen because they were considered a safe environment, where there was the least chance of an unplanned interruption or hostile questioning. Other popular venues that chimed with the Conservatives' campaign message of promising support for 'hard-working families' were play groups and schools. At a primary in Westhoughton, Bolton, the Prime Minister sat down and read an extract from *The Paper Bag Princess* only for the six-year-old pupil sitting beside him to look down, and then rest her head, face down on the table. 'She was bored … she had heard it all before', was a line from the caption for an image that earned its place in newspaper picture galleries of the 2015 campaign.

Cameron followed Mrs Thatcher's example of being happy to be photographed with animals. His visit to a farm near Chadlington in his Witney constituency produced another abiding but much lampooned image. He was photographed cuddling a newly-born, orphaned lamb, feeding it with a bottle of milk. At one point the lamb snuggled up so close, they almost nuzzled each other's faces. Cameron smiled so much he seemed as much at ease as Mrs Thatcher appeared in 1979 when she spent 13 minutes cuddling a calf on a farm in East Anglia, asking kindly if the photographers had all the pictures they needed. Lord Tim Bell, her public relations adviser at the time, told *Election Snapshots* on BBC Radio that the picture appeared so frequently during the campaign that it did become a distraction. Herbie Knott, a press photographer, recalled that Mrs Thatcher was less ambitious in the 1983 election, and on a farm visit in Cornwall simply patted a cow on its head.

By being agreeing to be adventurous in seeking publicity Mrs Thatcher helped to redefine the way campaigns were conducted, her advisers having realised that politicians had to be seen in everyday situations, and that imaginative photo-opportunities would engage the news media and help her reach out to voters. Some photo-shoots are more likely than others to be ridiculed, and cartoonists do find the association of politicians with animals an irresistible combination. Peter Brookes (*The Times)* had the headline, 'Nasty party photo-op' over Cameron with his hands round the lamb's throat and a slogan on his jacket that said, 'Vote Tory or the lamb gets it'. Steve Bell (*Guardian*) highlighted the Prime Minister's troubled relationship with Nicola Sturgeon, leader of the Scottish National party. They were shown nuzzling up to each other, Ms Sturgeon's head popping out from a woolly fleece, a wolf in sheep's clothing.

Animal photo-opportunities were also on the Liberal Democrats' agenda for Nick Clegg. After an audience with the Queen on the day of the dissolution of parliament, he went in his yellow battle bus to a nature reserve in Solihull and was photographed holding Humpty the hedgehog, so called because he had fallen off a wall. Clegg shared Cameron's confidence and ease in front of camera. On a visit to Newlyn fish market he had no hesitation in holding up a large, freshly caught cod, which prompted an array of comparable poses including one of Boris Johnson, the Mayor of London, cradling a gutted whole salmon. At one photo-opportunity Clegg whizzed off down a zip-wire, but did not have to endure a repeat of Johnson's mishap during the 2012 Olympic Games when he was left dangling 20 ft. in the air.

By the midpoint of the campaign the routine had become so predictable that reporters assigned to follow the party leaders began to expose the ploys that were being used and to criticise the absence of contact with un-vetted members of the public. A wide shot of Cameron hosting a rally in a large warehouse in Cornwall revealed that the building was empty except for the band of supporters grouped together in one corner. Conversations during an unannounced town centre walk-about were not spontaneous. When Cameron stopped to talk he was not engaging with casual by-standers but party members who produced Conservative placards once photographers were on the scene.

Requests for the leaders to appear in selfies became so incessant that the craze started to generate a rash of photo-opportunities over which the party minders had no control. Refusing to stop was not always an option, and the tabloids were soon competing with each other to assemble rogues' galleries of leaders pulling funny faces when they failed to smile at the appropriate moment. In the opening week of the campaign, Cameron blamed the 'curse of the selfie' for hindering his campaign. 'The picture is so important to them, you often don't get the conversation…I want to know what the party activists are finding on the doorstep.' But even the Prime Minister could not halt what was fast becoming the 'selfie election,' and when visiting Pirate FM in Penzance he held up a selfie stick for the first time so as to include the radio station's staff in the background.

Miliband had a stroke of good fortune when his battle bus, parked outside the Westminster Hotel in Chester, was gate-crashed by bride-to-be Nicola Braithwaite and her hen party of 25 friends. After negotiating with press spokesman Bob Roberts she climbed aboard and he took a picture of her with the Labour leader. On disembarking, her friends chanted 'selfie, selfie, selfie'. Miliband stood there smiling on the steps of his coach as they turned their backs to capture their image and his on their mobile phones. Within days a 17-year-old called Abby started a Twitter craze with the hashtag Milifandom protesting at Cameron's refusal to back votes at 16. Flower crowns were added to online pictures of Miliband, who told the London *Evening Standard* that his wife Justine 'rolled her eyes' in bemusement and disbelief when he owned up to having a fan club of teenage girls.

After all the criticism that he had faced for his geeky appearance, and the embarrassment of having to endure a *Daily Mail* series on 'Red Ed's very tangled love life' that identified former girlfriends, he had obviously been touched by the warmth of the reception he had received at campaign stops across the country. In his resignation speech, only hours after Labour's defeat had been confirmed, he paid tribute to a team that had run the 'most united, cohesive and enjoyable campaign' he had ever been involved in. 'Thank you for the selfies ... and the most unlikely cult of the 21st century, Milifandom.'

Nicola Sturgeon and her predecessor as First Minister of Scotland, Alex Salmond, were by comparison old hands when it came to understanding and exploiting the selfie craze. They had been inundated with requests for mobile phone photographs the previous year when besieged by SNP supporters during the Yes campaign in favour of Scottish independence. Salmond told *The Times* it could take him hours to get round the aisles of a supermarket because he kept having to pose for selfies. 'It's a compliment and I love it. Anybody who doesn't shouldn't be in politics.' Ms Sturgeon won the accolade queen of the selfies in a review of selfie images in the *Guardian* and a guide published on line by BBC Scotland which was entitled, 'The Art of the Sturgeon Selfie'. She was judged the most proficient exponent because she knew instinctively that the best picture was obtained by just touching her head against the person holding up the camera phone.

Ms Sturgeon was just as sure footed in her photo-opportunities. She walked with ease across a beam and parallel bars during a visit to a gym in Cumbernauld; looked quite demure travelling around key seats in a helicopter emblazoned with a larger-than-life portrait of herself emblazoned on the side; and tried her hand as a pastry cook at a cookery school in Kilmarnock. When the SNP's 56 MPs gathered for their first photo call she stood in front as they lined up beside the Firth of Forth with the vast sweep of the Forth rail bridge providing a dramatic backdrop. Her photo-opportunity captured an historic moment, an image that reflected the impact of a landslide for her party that had reshaped the political map of Scotland.

Queen

Resolute though she was to remain above the fray, an unholy alliance of journalists, politicians and constitutional theorists were determined to try to enlist the Queen as a pawn in a power play surrounding the result of what was being billed the most unpredictable general election since 1945. Five days of political theatre were required to resolve the hung parliament of 2010, a minor delay compared with up to three weeks of mayhem that was thought might be needed to sort out the multi-party muddle the pollsters were forecasting would be the outcome of the 2015 election. The Queen was facing the prospect of having to remain aloof at Windsor Castle from polling day until the Queen's Speech three weeks later while David Cameron and Ed Miliband haggled with as many as six smaller parties in an attempt to cobble together a coalition, or alternatively agree a pact to sustain a minority government. One alarmist scenario was that the sovereign might end up being ambushed into reading the speech on behalf a Prime Minister who might then be unable to command a majority in the House of Commons.

A tangled web of eventualities spun by an array of authoritative Whitehall watchers, eminent royal historians and commentators started to disintegrate the moment the early declarations began to confirm that the Conservatives would be not only the largest party but would actually go on to form a majority government. As had been the case in 2010 the Queen had taken up residence at Windsor Castle where she spent the night, but once the result was certain she left that morning for Buckingham Palace to prepare for the formality of inviting David Cameron to become Prime Minister and form a government. After he had received confirmation that his party had secured the 326 seats needed for a majority government, he left Downing Street at 12.30 p.m. with his wife Samantha for the short drive to Buckingham Palace for a brief audience with the Queen, a moment for him to savour what he had earlier told party workers was the 'sweetest victory of all'.

A strong expectation of another hung parliament, and the uncertainty being generated over the likelihood of difficult post-election negotiations, had forced the Queen to re-arrange her diary. She had to pull out of a service of remembrance to mark the 70th anniversary of VE Day that was to be held at Westminster Abbey on the day after the election. Palace advisers were concerned she might be photographed next to one or other of the party leaders. They feared that even a smile might be misinterpreted, possibly prompting speculation that she perhaps favoured one outcome or another. In the event there had been no need for a change of plan as her audience re-appointing Cameron as the 12th Prime Minister of her reign took place far sooner than anyone had envisaged. For the rest of the day events ran like clockwork, demolishing in one fell swoop a range of scenarios that had required preparations for all manner of contingencies. Across Westminster and Whitehall civil service manuals and memoranda on the monarch's role in a hung parliament were being safely replaced in bookshelves and filing cabinets.

Nonetheless the VE Day commemoration did provide compelling footage for live television coverage, as well as haunting images for next day's newspapers. On most front pages were pictures of the wreath laying at the Cenotaph in Whitehall. Graphic photographs captured the drama of the morning, symbolising the startling finality of the election result. Standing in a line, holding wreaths of poppies, were the newly re-elected Prime Minister and two unexpected casualties, Nick Clegg, Cameron's former deputy in the Conservative-Liberal Democrat coalition, and Ed Miliband, former leader of the Labour Party. Hours earlier they had both resigned in rapid succession. In fraught, emotional speeches they accepted responsibility for leading their parties to catastrophic defeats, and although no longer in office, the wreath laying was an engagement they had both been duty bound to fulfil.

While there was never any likelihood of a smile of the kind that Buckingham Palace had sought to guard against there was an encounter at the Cenotaph that caught the photographer's attention. During the official line-up Cameron was seen for a brief moment close to Nicola Sturgeon, the First Minister of Scotland, who hours earlier had been celebrating the SNP's landslide victory north of the border. She was photographed turning to look at Cameron in a brief act of acknowledgement. In the *Daily Mail's* opinion her glance seemed to be a hint of a power struggle to come: 'Look that says: I'll make your life hell, Dave'.

In confounding all expectations by sweeping back into power with a majority of 12, having won 331 seats to Labour's 232, Cameron had put an end to weeks of conjecture about coalition haggling and the possibility of a constitutional crisis that might have resulted in the Queen getting more deeply involved than royal protocol recommended. One scenario that emerged, and was then later dismissed by a clutch of Whitehall mandarins and academics, was that either Cameron or Miliband might attempt to form a coalition or minority administration that was inherently so unstable that the Queen herself should not be asked to conduct the state opening of parliament. Perhaps that duty could be performed by the Leader of the House of Lords. Columnists and commentators seized on the uncertainty, but the unanimous conclusion of various constitutional authorities was that come what may the Queen would attend in person, and would deliver her speech to both Houses of Parliament.

The Times claimed that it was Buckingham Palace where there had been a 'change of heart': 'Queen to take control of election aftermath' was the headline on its front-page exclusive. She was prepared to be 'thrust centre stage if Cameron tries to hang on to power without the backing of enough MPs'. In the *Daily Mail's* account of soundings among 'royal sources' there was the same certainty: the Queen was determined to remain 'a symbol of stability amid fears of a "Fallout Friday" in the City of London' if there was a hung parliament. A few days earlier 'royal sources' were reported as having told the *Sunday Times* they feared that the Queen's Speech might be used as 'a mechanism for testing a particular prime minister's control' of the House of Commons.

Sir Jeremy Heywood, cabinet secretary and the country's top civil servant, had been charged with the task of guiding the political parties through the complicated coalition negotiations that seemed inevitable given the pollsters' prediction of an election stalemate. If there was a hung parliament the news media was told his priority would be to observe royal protocol and keep the Queen well away from any political turmoil. However, his predecessor Lord (Gus) O'Donnell, who advised on the 2010 coalition talks, had added fuel to the speculation when he told *Today* that if the Conservatives were the largest party but 'well short on numbers' for a majority, Cameron could still go ahead with the Queen's Speech even if it was subsequently defeated in a motion of no confidence. Such a step, said Lord O'Donnell, would be a matter for the Prime Minister's 'political judgement', but he insisted the rules were clear: the ability of government 'to command the confidence of the elected House of Commons is central to its authority to govern', and the Queen would conduct the state opening because 'that's her job'.

Journalists were eager to explore the Queen's role in the hope they might discover a fresh twist to the storyline given the Conservatives' determination to ramp up the speculation that English voters would be reluctant to accept the legitimacy of a Labour government that relied on the support of the Scottish Nationalists. In a dramatic intervention, the Home Secretary Theresa May claimed that the prospect of a pact between Ed Miliband and Nicola Sturgeon would paralyse the country. In an interview with the *Mail on Sunday*, she gave a vivid warning of the tension that could arise: 'If we saw a Labour government propped up by SNP it could be the biggest constitutional crisis since the abdication.'

Calling in aid the constitutional paralysis after Edward VIII abdicated in 1936 was a link to the royal family that whetted the news media's appetite. The Queen's unprecedented intervention four days before the 2014 referendum on Scottish independence had stepped up the need for vigilance on the part of reporters. As she was about to leave after Sunday morning service the police had unexpectedly invited the press to move forward to observe her exchanges with well-wishers outside Crathie Kirk, near Balmoral Castle. When one onlooker joked about her silence in the referendum campaign her response topped the news bulletins: 'Well, I hope people will think very carefully about the future'. Royal 'insiders' insisted she had remained politically neutral, but she had broken her silence and her remarks were interpreted as an endorsement of the 'Better Together' campaign. The Sun's headline writers were in no doubt: 'Queen: Think before you've throne it all away.' The Daily Telegraph's cartoonist had some fun: The Queen was positioned standing in a glen beside a loch close to Balmoral. The speech bubble said, 'One couldn't possibly comment', but she was wearing a hat, jacket and skirt emblazoned with the Union Jack, and her two corgi had coats decorated with the Union flag.

A week after Scotland voted No to independence by 55 to 45 per cent Cameron inspired fresh puns in the headlines when he breached protocol by revealing the Queen's delight at the result. He disclosed her reaction during a private conversation at an event in New York with the city's former mayor Michael Bloomberg. His comments were picked up on a broadcaster's microphone: 'The definition of relief is being the Prime Minister of the United Kingdom and ringing the Queen and saying, "It's all right. It's okay". That was something. She purred down the line.' His boastful breach of etiquette was roundly criticised by royal watchers. 'Pussy Furore' was the Daily Mirror's headline, but the Sun mocked up a photograph of the Queen to look like a cat and beside it were the words, 'It's Purr Majesty'. Cameron telephoned immediately to apologise, and did so in person at his next audience with the Queen. His transgression in revealing her reaction to Bloomberg was a 'conversation he should never have had and won't happen again'.

Cameron's contrition was welcomed by newspaper diarists who noted that he had again been too deferential to repeat the suggestion made by both Tony Blair and Gordon Brown that an official photograph should be taken at the moment a new Prime Minister received the seals of office, a request the Palace had always turned down. As the only pictures that are allowed are of the Prime Minister stepping out of the car in an inner court yard, most attention in recent years has been on what the Premier's wife was wearing. Samantha Cameron's dress was said to look like the new electoral map of the United Kingdom, mostly blue but with large patches of yellow, the colour of the SNP.

Usually there is advance warning to the media about the timing of a Prime Minister's journey from Downing Street to the Palace and return to No.10. A fixed term parliament has added even more certainty to the arrangements. In the years that choosing a date for a general election was still at a Prime Minister's discretion, far greater care had to be taken. In 1992 Gus O'Donnell, then the Downing Street press secretary, gave news agencies two hours' notice of the time John Major intended to set off for the Palace. An advance warning was required in order to alert the Stock Market as confirmation the Prime Minister was on his way was considered price sensitive information. Occasionally a Prime Minister is at the mercy of events, well aware that the Queen might be getting impatient for the audience to take place. In 2010, after post-election coalition talks dragged on five days, Gordon Brown felt he could wait no longer. He wanted to be seen leaving No.10 while it was still daylight, for one final photo-opportunity in Downing Street. He and his wife Sarah, holding hands with their two sons, walked towards the car that would take him to see the Queen to resign his post and hand back the seals of office.

Amid the tortuous constitutional theorizing that dominated so much of the campaign reporting ahead of the 2015 election there was one brief interlude. Photographs of the Queen smiling in a pink outfit told their own story. Kensington Palace used Twitter to keep the country informed about the birth of the Duchess of Cambridge's daughter Charlotte. The first tweet said she was admitted to hospital at 6 a.m. and was in the early stages of labour, and a second tweet at 8.34 a.m. said the Duchess was 'safely delivered of a daughter'. Later that day the Queen, wearing a pink coat and hat, beamed happily as she celebrated the safe arrival of her new great-grandchild at a military parade at Richmond Castle in North Yorkshire.

News bulletins referred to the birth having taken place 100 hours before polling day, a cue to the programmes to discuss whether all the publicity surrounding the new princess might generate a feel good factor that could help the Conservatives. 'Cameron is set for a baby bounce' was the verdict of *Mail on Sunday* which devoted 35 pages to its coverage of William and Kate holding the baby princess together with pictures from earlier in the day of Prince George with his father. Political cartoonists joined in on the act: Cameron and Clegg were shown as the happy couple holding not a baby but a copy of the '2nd coalition agreement', and a smiling Nicola Sturgeon stood on the steps of No. 10 carrying in her arms a baby Ed Miliband wrapped in a shawl alongside the caption 'Labour pains'.

R

results evening

For the foot soldiers of political journalism the **results** night after a general election can bring mixed fortunes. Broadcasters always want to be at the newsiest location at precisely the right moment, but they can be unlucky. Just as results determined by a first-past-the-post electoral system can be something of a lottery, so is the timing and outcome of each declaration. Depending on their newsworthiness, correspondents will have been assigned to constituencies up and down the country. Reporters are also needed at the various party headquarters to wait for the first local or perhaps national pointers to the likely outcome, but again there is often great uncertainty as to whether a change of government is in the offing, and no telling where or what the story might be.

Election-night coverage has become so sophisticated, able to draw on such a vast array of live broadcasts from across the country that the results programmes are slick productions, far more adventurous than in the less frenetic era that existed before rapid expansion of television services in the 1980s. Increased competition across the air waves in the wake of non-stop 24-hour news, and latterly the explosion of communication on line, has speeded up the output, demanding an ever faster response from broadcasters at the newsiest declarations.

To help local authorities save money, counts are increasingly being combined on a city, borough or county-wide basis. They are usually conducted in large municipal halls or community centres containing row upon row of tables where the votes are sorted, checked and counted. For election-night television programmes, these mega-counts are great locations for live coverage offering close-up shots of the massed ranks of constituency workers and campaign aides wearing the rosettes of the rival parties, all watching impatiently as the votes are being counted. Tension increases once candidates prepare to mount the platform ready for a returning officer to declare each result, the cue to television producers to line up the shot and to alert the presenter, and for hand-overs to radio reporters to start their commentary.

An unexpected victory, or perhaps the sensational defeat of a prominent politician, can provide an electrifying moment for radio and television, great copy for newspapers and an opportunity for instant interaction on social media. But apart from swing seats and constituencies where there might be a high profile casualty, most of the individual counts are invariably a foregone conclusion. A far more demanding and longer-lasting assignment is reporting from one of the party headquarters, especially if a change of government is thought to be imminent. From late evening, through the early hours and on into the morning and much of the following day, there is always plenty of action.

Reporters, broadcasters and television crews are usually corralled together, either outside or in a media briefing area, latterly known as the spin room. Once declarations start being made there is a constant procession of party officials, spin doctors and the like, all determined to put the best possible gloss on the early results. Initially commentary and interviews from the various party headquarters can provide a break from studio discussions and the predictions of pollsters, but once a pattern emerges and the overall result becomes clearer the mood changes, perhaps elation at one location presenting a stark contrast to faces etched with the prospect of defeat at another.

My first taste of election night drama in and around party headquarters was in 1974, the year of two closely fought general elections that resulted first in a Labour-led minority government and then a narrow Labour majority that had to be reinforced later by the Lib-Lab pact. For a newly recruited radio correspondent there could hardly have been a better introduction to the world of doorstep reporting. Months of uncertainty generated frequent late-night assignments in and around Westminster. We reporters spent hour upon hour waiting for meetings to finish, hoping for a statement or interview.

In the 1970s broadcasters and reporters were not made as welcome as they are today. On results nights we were often forced to spend much of the time outside on the pavement seeking reaction as party officials went to and fro. Much later we would await the arrival of MPs and possibly ministers fresh from the declaration of their results, on their way to thank party workers, to celebrate or perhaps commiserate with defeated colleagues.

Smith Square, a short walk from the House of Commons, was then the location that mattered most of all: in one corner used to be Conservative Central Office and across the road, on the other side of the square, was what was then Transport House, headquarters of the mighty Transport and General

Workers' Union, where the Labour Party also had its offices. The two front doors were literally a short step away from each other and their close coexistence reflected what had always been seen as the durability of the two-party system. In the post-war years Labour and Conservatives had been accustomed to commanding the lion's share of the total vote, but the Liberal Party, under the dynamic leadership of Jeremy Thorpe, was about to challenge the established duopoly, and in 1974 a third location was added to our Westminster itinerary, the National Liberal Club in Whitehall Place.

There had been a dramatic build-up to what would be the first of the two elections that year. By December 1973 a work to rule in the pits had so reduced winter coal stocks that the Conservative government had been forced to impose a three-day working week to restrict the commercial use of electricity. After the National Union of Mineworkers rejected a 16.5 per cent pay increase, Edward Heath attempted to break the impasse by calling what became known as the 'Who governs Britain?' general election of February 1974. Heath said the country had to choose between a 'strong government' or give way to 'a powerful group of workers…the extremists, the militants'. But he misjudged the electorate, and for the first time since the Second World War there was a hung parliament as no party had an overall majority. Conservatives had gained the most votes but less seats than Labour, and eventually Heath was forced to resign.

Harold Wilson returned to Downing Street heading a minority government that promptly settled the miners' strike with a 35 per cent pay increase. In a second general election in October, Labour won by a majority of three. The closeness of the two results was a consequence of Thorpe's success in reducing to 75 per cent the combined share of the vote taken by Labour and Conservatives. Fourteen Liberal MPs were elected in the February election on 19.3 per cent of the total vote. The party's share fell to 18.3 per cent in October, and one seat was lost, but Thorpe had broken the mould of post-war British politics. Over the previous three decades Labour and Conservatives had between them regularly commanded well over 90 per cent of the votes cast, although sometimes a few percentage points below. From 1974 onwards the two-party system failed to exercise anything like the same hold over the British electorate.

BBC output had been increasing throughout the early 1970s following the introduction of colour television. I was one of a lucky generation of reporters recruited as a result of the extra income generated by the colour licence. Popular late-night viewing had been one of the many casualties of the 1974 three-day week, which did Heath no favours. Programmes were required to close down at 10.30 pm, although the late-night curfew was lifted for the election campaign. BBC Radio had seized the opportunity, putting extra effort went into its early morning output.

I spent the February results night outside Transport House. Once the last of the overnight counts had been declared, and it was clear that Wilson had been gaining seats at Heath's expense, I was ushered inside and headed to the office of Ron Hayward, the Labour Party general secretary. There was lots of clutter in his room, papers piled high on the desk; I sat beside him to record an interview for the *Today* programme. He was pleasant enough given the lateness of the hour and had made me welcome. I was after all the only broadcaster seeking his overnight reaction.

A decade later there would be much stricter controls on interviews and far tighter deadlines for broadcasters. LBC radio, launched in October 1973, was at the forefront of a rapid expansion in the commercial sector; Channel 4 was launched in 1982; and breakfast television started in 1983. Such was the impact of television that the political parties rapidly re-adjusted their approach to the news media, realising they could exploit the access and opportunities they were offering. Broadcasters had to start queueing up and competing with each other. Gone were the days when a radio reporter could sit down with a party general secretary on election night and record a leisurely interview.

I had to wait almost 20 years before returning to Smith Square for another chance to experience the drama of results night, and on this occasion I was in Conservative Central Office on the day of the 1992 election. Although John Major seemed to have surprised himself by the strength of his fight back against Neil Kinnock, the BBC's final poll of polls put Labour in the lead on 39 per cent, a point ahead of the Conservatives. Some pundits were hedging their bets arguing that the outcome was still too close to call and their uncertainty seemed justified by exit polls from the BBC and ITN predicted a hung parliament. When I arrived just before 11 p. m. crews from the competing television and radio stations were already staking out their own patch of territory in a conference room where television sets on one side of the room were tuned to the competing election night programmes.

The first result came through at 11.05 p.m. – Chris Mullin was returned as Labour MP in Sunderland South. Suddenly someone shouted: 'Basildon is being declared.' This was the first of the marginal constituencies where Labour had been hoping to beat the Conservatives. There were looks first of disbelief and then sheer joy on the faces of Central Office staff when it was clear David Amess was safely back. The swing against the Conservatives was only 1.3 per cent, nowhere near what Labour needed. I found myself being berated by a party worker who had joined the throng. 'You all thought Essex man had deserted us, didn't you? Well, he hasn't.' A procession of senior Tories lined up to give their reaction to the results programmes. We did not have long to wait. Within minutes of seeing Kinnock arrive for the declaration in his constituency, ITN predicted an overall Conservative majority of seven seats. Two reporters hurried in from Smith Square. They said Tory party workers were hanging up blue and white balloons outside Central Office. It was 1.31 a. m.

Just before Kinnock's result was announced at 1.55 a. m. newspaper correspondents started to hand around copies of their first editions. The *Sun* was still forecasting a possible Labour victory. Under the headline, 'It's a Neil Biter', the front page splash, by political editor Trevor Kavanagh, said: 'Neil Kinnock was on the brink of walking into Number 10 last night.' Ironic though it was, I thought that for once Kinnock would have approved of a *Sun* front page.

Major's triumphant return to Downing Street was a moment for the Conservatives to savour. Their fourth general election victory in a row was an achievement not matched for 150 years. An overall Tory majority of 21 seats secured Major the personal mandate he had craved, but his MPs were deeply divided over Britain's role in Europe; a string of by-election defeats would erode the Prime Minister's authority; and his party would prove incapable of matching New Labour's zeal and the rise of Tony Blair.

Five years later my results night posting for the 1997 general election gave me a chance to witness one of the most momentous nights in the history of the Labour Party. Instead of having to stand outside on the pavement, we were welcomed into a media room at Labour's glitzy campaign headquarters in Millbank Tower, a world away from the clutter of Transport House. I had rarely seen a media team looking so relaxed. Press officers who had experienced the harrowing defeat of 1992 were convinced Blair had won by a comfortable margin. The final opinion polls were unanimous in putting Labour way out in front, the largest ever lead enjoyed by an opposition party since serious polling began after the Second World War.

Once the results started coming in we crowded round the television sets. David Hill, the party's chief media spokesman, could not believe the gains Labour were making and the staggering size of the swings. Soon he could hardly contain himself: 'Look, these swings are now so high, we've got a world event on our hands.' Such was the carnage for the Conservatives that we broadcasters were feeling somewhat redundant. Events at counts around the country were so electrifying that the election programmes were not interested in round-ups from the media centre on a night when seven Conservative cabinet ministers were defeated.

The stupendous scale of Blair's victory took time to absorb. By the final count Labour had taken 418 seats and had secured a majority of 179 on a 44.4 per cent share of the vote. On revisiting the media centre in the short lull before Major and Blair had their audiences with the Queen, I spoke briefly to Peter Mandelson, one New Labour's key strategists. His grandfather, the former Labour Home Secretary Herbert Morrison had run the post-war campaign that produced the 1945 landslide and a Labour majority of 146. 'I never thought I would beat my grandfather. Everyone always said the 1945 result would never be revisited.'

Results programmes are addictive, hence my frustration at being forced to become a viewer rather than a contributor to election-night coverage. Armchair political anoraks are always on the edge of their seats at 10 p. m. ready for the exit poll. In place of the sometimes hit and miss forecasts of previous years there is now a massive effort by a team of pollsters working jointly for the BBC, ITV and Sky News to ensure the greatest possible accuracy. Party workers reacted with disbelief when the 2010 exit poll forecast a hung parliament, but hours later the prediction proved to be entirely correct as the Conservatives had fallen 19 seats short of an overall majority. Nonetheless despite an enviable track record and an even larger sample, the result of the 2015 exit poll was greeted with consternation by politicians, pundits and rival psephologists. For weeks on end the opinion polls had been suggesting the Conservatives and Labour were neck and neck. Such was the consistency of their findings that another hung parliament had seemed inevitable, prompting endless speculation that the two main parties would find themselves having to compete with each other to put together another coalition government. Initially it seemed the entire political establishment was struggling to accept that the exit poll figures were plausible: the Conservatives would be the largest party with 316 seats, well ahead of Labour on 238; and Scottish National Party would take 58 of the 59 seats in Scotland.

If the exit poll was accurate David Cameron was on course to remain Prime Minister as head of a minority government, without the need for a coalition, an outcome that his opponents had said for weeks was beyond his reach. Basildon was the 1992 result that confirmed John Major was heading back to Downing Street, and the declaration at Nuneaton, a seat targeted by Labour, was the first to offer the same comfort to Cameron. A swing to the Conservative MP Marcus Jones of just over 3 per cent was the reassurance the Prime Minister had been waiting to receive.

For the results programme aficionado the defeat of the shadow Chancellor Ed Balls at Morley and Outwood was as memorable as the ousting of Michael Portillo at Enfield Southgate in 1997. The shock on Balls' face when the returning officer declared that Andrea Jenkyns had taken the seat for the Conservatives by 422 votes matched the agonised reaction of the Business Secretary Vince Cable, who in a night of carnage for the Liberal Democrats, lost his seat in Twickenham to Tania Mathias on an 11 per cent swing to the Conservatives. The decimation of the Liberal Democrats, left with only eight out of 57 seats, and their brutal eviction from all their West Country strongholds, was as calamitous as Labour's virtual wipe-out in Scotland. Given the sensational events of 2015 the broadcasters will no doubt be hoping that the pollsters complete a hat trick in 2020 and deliver an exit poll that triggers another night of political shock and awe.

S

Scotland

On assignments north of the border, I was always struck by the almost tribal nature of politics in **Scotland**. My first encounter with the depth of loyalty shown by members of the Scottish National party was at the Glasgow Garscadden by-election in April 1978, at the height of the first significant surge in SNP support. Donald Dewar, who in 1999 became First Minister in the inaugural Scottish Executive, held the seat for the Labour party despite a strong showing by the nationalists, but his victory in the by-election had been far from certain. The discovery of North Sea oil fields in the early 1970s had given the nationalists a powerful political weapon, and their campaign slogan *It's Scotland's oil* had provided fresh impetus to the strengthening campaign for home rule.

Garscadden, like other deprived suburbs in around Glasgow, seemed pretty grim to me, with extensive, bleak housing estates and as I recall it, a rather brutal and windswept 1960s shopping centre. A knife-edge by-election had clearly gripped the local community, and as I walked round the constituency, compiling a report for the *PM* programme, I came across groups of children and youngsters with the black and yellow posters and flags of the SNP being challenged by opposing gatherings holding red banners for Labour, a degree of political rivalry that I had not experienced since my own childhood.

My first encounter with a comparable level of political tribalism was as a nine year old during the 1951 general election and the defeat of the Attlee government by Winston Churchill. We lived then in Bilston, near Wolverhampton, in the heart of the Black Country, and there was fierce rivalry between families in Labour-supporting council estates and the residents of nearby 1930s semi-detached houses where there was an occasional Conservative poster on display in a front window.

Walking to Ettingshall Primary School meant coming face to face with children from Labour families jeering from across the road at passers-by who they thought were Conservatives; one particular target was the family of a Tory local councillor who lived close by in Stow Heath Lane. Because of my father's job as a reporter for the local paper, the Wolverhampton *Express and Star*, I came from a politically aware household but I had learned early on that my parents kept their party affiliations to themselves, so I remember being taken aback by the divisiveness of electioneering among the families of the children I went to school with.

Donald Dewar held Garscadden for Labour with a 4,000-plus majority, and although the SNP increased their share of the vote, failure to take the seat had halted the 1970s advance of the nationalists. SNP politicians of that era were already household names: Winnie Ewing, the party's second MP, did lose her at Hamilton in the 1970 general election, but Donald Stewart had captured the Western Isles and Margo MacDonald had won the Glasgow Govan by-election in 1973.

In the general election of October 1974, the SNP polled almost a third of all votes in Scotland, returning to Westminster their best-ever tally of 11 MPs.

Given the importance of the 1978 Garscadden by-election, BBC Radio was anxious to report the outcome, and my task was to be ready for a live two-way from the count as soon as the result was announced. Radio and television output in the late 1970s was a fraction of what it is today; there were no breakfast shows, no rolling news programmes and indeed no all-night broadcasting at all on the domestic services. The last news bulletin of the day was the *Midnight Newsroom* on BBC Radio 2 and the only other potential slot was during *Round Midnight*, presented by the legendary disc jockey Brian Matthew, whose programme was on air until closedown on Radio 2 at 2 a.m.

Having to accommodate a political two-way conversation in the middle of his late-night arts and music programme must have been regarded by Matthew as something of a chore but when the result was announced, well after midnight, I remember how interested he was and his willingness to give me the time to describe the strength of the nationalists' campaign and the significance of the result.

During a much earlier foray into Scottish politics, I had witnessed an example of political tribalism of a far different political hue. I spent the 1970 general election reporting the speeches of the former Conservative Prime Minister Sir Alec Douglas-Home; much of my time was spent travelling around the lush farmland of the Scottish Lowlands and the dramatic countryside of the Highlands. Douglas-Home's priority was to shore up Conservative support in Scotland. In the early 1950s the Tories had a fifty per cent share of the vote but they had been under sustained attack from Labour and the SNP, and as a result their representation at Westminster had been cut from 36 MPs in the 1951 general election to 20 by 1966.

Each evening Sir Alec would speak at two or three meetings in village halls and meeting rooms. They were usually in the ultra-loyal heartlands of what had once been the Scottish Unionist party. Often a laird in his kilt would be seated on the front row with his family beside him, and on the chairs behind would be their estate workers and other villagers. Concerns about the future of the Commonwealth, Britain's relationship with the Ian Smith regime in Rhodesia, and doubts about the possibility of Britain joining the Common Market prompted most questions. Sir Alec, who had renounced his title as the Earl of Home to serve as Prime Minister, was on home territory, at ease with his audience. His constituency of Kinross and West Perthshire was a safe Conservative seat and the Hirsel, on the Scottish Borders, had been the family estate of the Earl of Home since 1611.

At the time I was a parliamentary correspondent for *The Times* but to my disappointment Douglas-Home rarely produced a worthwhile story. I was told by the newsroom that the editor William Rees-Mogg felt the *The Times* had not done enough to support him either during his brief Premiership or later in the 1964 general election, when the Conservatives were defeated by Harold Wilson. To make amends Rees-Mogg had insisted that Douglas-Home, then the shadow Foreign Secretary, should be accompanied by a reporter from *The Times*.

My only source of amusement was to see him struggle each evening to do justice to the text that he had been supplied by Conservative Central Office. The 1970 poll was dubbed the 'shopping basket' election and to keep up the pressure the shadow cabinet were supplied with details of the latest price increases for groceries and other household goods. Sir Alec would manfully include the shopping basket list in his speeches, trying desperately not to get the pounds and ounces muddled up with the pounds, shillings and pence. I could tell he did not have much faith in the strategy and that he most certainly did not have to do the weekly shop. Nonetheless the Tories' aim of appealing to housewives was an effective strategy and Edward Heath defeated Wilson.

Assigning a reporter to follow Sir Alec finally paid off for *The Times* the night he had to address a meeting at Aberdeen Girls' High School. On arriving in the city and checking out the location, I discovered that local police officers had searched the school hall and that plainclothes detectives had accompanied him throughout the 100-mile drive south from Inverness to Aberdeen. A threat had been made on his life by an anonymous telephone caller the day before; the call was from a public call box and the caller said an attempt would be made during Sir Alec's election campaign.

Little did I realise then that the easy-going days of electioneering were drawing to a close. Previously I had not been aware of a threat to politicians; there might have been the odd constable standing around if a prominent MP stopped to speak on the steps of a town hall or in a village square but I had never known of a hall or meeting room having to be searched in advance by the police. In writing up my report for *The Times*, I realised the police had taken the tip-off extremely seriously because of fears that the heightened civil rights campaign in Northern Ireland might have an impact in Scotland; the emergence of armed paramilitary groups had led to the first deployment of British troops the previous August.

My lack of any real insight into the security issues was compensated by my eyewitness account: Sir Alec was staying at the Station Hotel, Aberdeen, which had police officers on guard outside and plainclothes detectives inside who had kept watch at his pre-speech dinner with two Conservative candidates. Next evening, on my return to the Kinross and West Perthshire constituency, a telegram was waiting for me at my hotel, the Drummond Arms in Crieff. It had been written out by hand at Crieff Post Office: 'Best thanks for your well dug out exclusive on Douglas-Home this morning stop regards Colin Times.' My story had made the front page and my hero-gram from the home news editor Colin Webb is pinned to my yellowing newspaper cuttings for the 1970 general election.

Douglas-Home's diligence in criss-crossing Scotland paid off: the Conservatives clawed back three of the seats they had previously held, a valuable contribution to Heath's victory over Wilson. But the party's 1970 tally of 23 of seats in Scotland was only half that of Labour and fell away steadily in subsequent elections until finally, in the 1997 landslide of Tony Blair, the Conservatives ended up without a single MP north of the border.

Within months of taking office, Blair found that New Labour had become embroiled in allegations of sleaze surrounding political life in Paisley and Renfrewshire, to the west of Glasgow. After the Paisley South MP Gordon McMaster committed suicide, leaving a note that accused colleagues of running a smear campaign against him, a by-election was called. Along with other journalists, I spent the evening of the count on the steps of Paisley town hall, waiting for the result. Our presence was not welcome as party officials were desperate to prevent the new Prime Minister getting dragged into a corruption scandal. Nationalists had taken advantage of Blair's embarrassment, and although Labour's candidate

Douglas Alexander was elected by a comfortable margin there had been a swing of 11 per cent to the SNP. Alexander, a former parliamentary researcher for Gordon Brown, rose swiftly through the ranks, becoming Secretary of State for Scotland, and later for International Development. Ed Miliband appointed him shadow Foreign Secretary and he was campaign co-ordinator for the 2015 election.

Memories of a fraught evening came flooding back as I watched live coverage of Alexander's anguished reaction as the returning officer announced the result for the Paisley and Renfrewshire South constituency, one of the many Labour citadels that for so long had been a target for the nationalists. A majority of 16,600 was no protection against the SNP's momentous advance, and his defeat by Mhairi Black was one of many election-night headlines. Ms Black, a 20-year-old student yet to complete her final exams at the University of Glasgow, was elected Westminster's youngest MP since 1667. Her majority was more than 5,000, a swing from Labour of 27 per cent.

The SNP achieved almost a clean sweep of Scotland's 59 seats, leaving the Conservatives, Labour and Liberal Democrats retaining one seat each. In their landslide of 1997 Labour took 56 Scottish seats, an achievement that exactly matched the SNP's tally. Hanging on to a solitary seat was no consolation to Labour. Unlike the slow death that had faced the Conservatives north of the border, their annihilation had been inflicted in just one election with record-breaking swings to the SNP that in the Glasgow North East constituency hit 39 per cent, the biggest ever achieved in a British general election.

T

trade unions

Political point scoring between Labour and Conservatives has no surer target than tit for tat abuse about their respective paymasters, the barons of the **trade union** movement and the bosses of big business. Boom years in the City of London have ensured there is no shortage of hedge fund millionaires and other wealthy donors to help replenish Tory coffers, whereas a severe contraction in union membership has had profound consequences for Labour's finances and the party's structure and political outlook. A slow but steady uncoupling of the bonds that tied trade unionists to the party they established has accelerated the hollowing out of a relationship that could once be relied upon to deliver rock solid Labour seats in constituencies across the United Kingdom

A massive landslide for the Scottish National party in the 2015 general election exposed the frailty of that link. All but one of Scotland 41 Labour MPs were unseated by record-breaking swings to the SNP in a catastrophic wipe-out, a victory that far exceeded the 'wildest dreams' of the party leader and First Minister for Scotland, Nicola Sturgeon. Scotland's once dominant industrial belt, for so long a Labour heartland, had been a byword for trade union solidarity. They might not always have had the resources to match their political opponents, but the unions had the necessary feet on the ground to help organise and sustain a loyal Labour vote.

The shattering of the certainties of the past had its roots in the unprecedented turnout and support for the 2014 referendum on Scottish independence. I had assumed that union leaders would have been at the forefront of that debate, anxious to stress the advantages of UK-wide national pay bargaining. Safeguarding jobs in shipbuilding, defence and North Sea oil was of such importance, I was sure the union hierarchy would steer their members, along with the Labour party, into the No camp. But the prominent union voices that I had expected to hear were largely silent, and as the referendum debate intensified I came to understand the reasons for their reticence. Scottish independence had developed into such a heart-felt issue that it cut right across traditional loyalties and had split the membership. Their dilemma was understandable: from the left's perspective, the SNP's vision of an independent Scotland was far more attractive to many union activists than the status quo.

In the early months of the independence debate, as I waited in vain for a clear expression of opinion, I was convinced that the presidents and general secretaries I had known in the 1970s and 1980s would have been centre stage, determined to be heard, their views hardened by the feedback they would have been receiving from numerous union branches and constituency parties. No issue used to be off the agenda at a TUC or Labour conference; countless resolutions kept the leadership in touch with rank and file opinion. Hours were spent locally and nationally debating not only day-to-day concerns like employment and pay bargaining, but also highly-divisive issues such as defence spending and nuclear disarmament.

Defeat for the pro-independence Yes campaign, instead of being a setback, reinvigorated the SNP under the leadership of Ms Sturgeon, who had succeeded Alex Salmond as Scotland's First Minister. A recruitment drive attracted such a surge in applications from across Scottish society that union leaders who had been silent the year before were forced to recognise that their members were voting with their feet. In the seven months between the September referendum and polling day, the SNP's trade union group had increased its membership from 1,000 to 15,000. From across the labour movement there was evidence of growing support for the nationalists' anti-austerity agenda.

Len McCluskey, general secretary of Unite, Labour's largest financial backer, was the first to break ranks. Half of his Scottish members had switched their support to the SNP. Its election manifesto contained policies that reflected his union's policy and he urged the Labour leader Ed Miliband to be prepared to work with 'any progressive party' that backed the aims of the union movement. Unite, strong in manufacturing and engineering, and Unison, the second largest union, with members across the public sector, had both remained neutral in the independence debate, unlike smaller unions representing groups such as train drivers and postal workers that relied on national pay bargaining, pension schemes and employment conditions.

A haemorrhaging of union support was without doubt a factor in Labour's annihilation at the hands of the SNP, highlighting that wider failure to engage with activists who had moved much further to the left than the leadership. Opportunities for them to participate in a two-way dialogue were few and far between. A rapid dismantling of the policy-making role of Labour's annual conference that began under Tony Blair's leadership had all but neutered active participation at a local level. Constituency parties and affiliated union branches no longer had the direct input of previous year, and this absence of involvement from the bottom up had further marginalised the TUC, and isolated the union rank-and-file from the Labour leadership. This dis-connect between disillusioned trade unionists and their traditional structures was easily exploited by the SNP; nationalism was a cause that Scotland's left had embraced.

Blair had been so determined to curb the power of the party's policy-making procedures, and to free himself from troublesome relationships with trade union leaders and conference delegates, that he failed to appreciate the need to sustain meaningful participation. I had first-hand experience of his reluctance to recognise the value of the union movement's pioneering work. My card was marked after a speech at the 1995 TUC conference at Brighton when the newly-elected Labour leader told delegates there would be no repeal of the Conservatives' employment laws. Blair ridiculed the work of labour and industrial correspondents who liked 'living in a time warp', perpetuating their 'old rituals of winding up the issues' before annual conferences; there was, he said, no point in journalists 'dramatising each event as if the destiny of the nation hung on it'.

Alastair Campbell, Blair's press secretary, told me the day before that he had written much of the speech, and I suspected he had encouraged Blair to put us in our place. Next morning, after visiting a breakfast rally at the Grand Hotel, I thanked them for the name check. Blair laughed and then took me slightly to one side. 'Look, it must be very sad being a labour correspondent, reporting all those meaningless resolutions. I do wish you could find a different agenda.'

Blair seemed oblivious to the positive impact of union campaigns and their success, often years later, in changing government policy. Labour's 1997 manifesto included a commitment to introduce a 'sensibly set national minimum wage', which was the fruition of years of resolute campaigning by union leaders such as Rodney Bickerstaffe, former general secretary of Unison. In his first speech as the new general secretary of what was then the National Union of Public Employees, Bickerstaffe moved a composite motion at the 1982 TUC conference calling for a 'vigorous campaign' to get 'government action on minimum wages'. In later years, without even the slightest nod to what so patently had been a trade union initiative, Blair claimed the introduction of a minimum wage was one of the defining achievements of his Premiership.

In the long lead-up to the 1997 general election Blair was in the fortunate position of finding that was pushing at an open door. After years of declining membership, and ever more restrictive employment laws, most union leaders were ready to lower their profile, anxious at all cost, as they had been in 1992, to do all they could to help bring about John Major's defeat. They seemed confident that a Labour victory would improve employment prospects and the welfare of their members. In the event they were guilty perhaps of wishful thinking because hopes of a revival in their fortunes under the Premiership of Blair and later Gordon Brown remained unfilled.

Eighteen years of Conservative government had exacted a terrible price on the union movement. Margaret Thatcher's dismantling of the nationalised industries had cost hundreds of thousands of jobs, and her government's step by step moves to curb strike action had produced the toughest employment legislation in Western Europe. Union membership halved during the Thatcher and Major years, necessitating a series of mergers that led to the winding-up of many craft-based groupings and the creation of two super unions, Unite and Unison.

My decade on the labour and industrial beat spanned the rise and fall of union influence. Mrs Thatcher's election victory in May 1979 coincided with a landmark moment, the year that the TUC's total affiliated membership reached an historic high of just over twelve million. One of my early post-election assignments was being sent to Scarborough in July to report the 28th biennial delegate conference of the Transport and General Workers' Union; its membership had just topped two million. On arriving at the Spa grand hall, I checked with the news desk and was told I would be the 'lead story' next morning: Britain's biggest union 'starts the fight back' against Mrs Thatcher.

For some days there had been speculation about the imminent publication of a consultative document outlining the new government's proposals for strengthening industrial law through the introduction of a limit on picketing; a right of appeal against the closed shop; and subsidised postal ballots. 'What's their plan', asked the news editor. 'What sort of strike action will it be?' He seemed convinced the union movement was on the brink of launching a 'summer of discontent'.

An emergency resolution on the agenda in the name of the T&G's executive council did call on the conference to urge the TUC to 'mobilise maximum trade union resistance' in defence of trade union rights. A rallying cry of sorts but a worthy dose of conference rhetoric rather than the promise of a repeat of the rolling stoppages and widespread secondary action of the winter of 1978-79.

I had no hesitation in asserting that the conference was providing the 'first major test of rank and file opinion' since Mrs Thatcher's election, but I was perhaps as guilty as the T&G's leadership in failing to take stock of the true impact of Labour's defeat. In my conversations that week in Scarborough with the union's general secretary Moss Evans and his two deputies, Harry Urwin and Alec Kitson, I formed the impression that although they were in a state of shock they believed the unions were somehow invincible, and that the movement could easily withstand any punishment which the Conservatives might attempt to inflict.

There was no plan B and with hindsight I sense a missed journalistic opportunity: there appeared to be no wish to devise a long-term strategy to counter a newly-elected government that had scores to settle. My regret is that I did not see the writing on the wall at Scarborough. I should have realised that the blind faith of the T&G and TUC leadership was based on an artificially high membership bequeathed by the Wilson and Callaghan governments.

Much of the growth had been in the nationalised industries and public services where payment of union subscriptions was usually compulsory due to the expansion of the closed shop and the employers' enforcement of automatic check-off of union contributions, an arrangement that would gradually be dismantled once the Thatcher government began selling off state-owned industries and privatising public services.

One longer lasting legacy of the rapid rise in membership during the 1970s was that the union movement could always be relied upon during general elections to deliver a powerful punch where it mattered most, out in the constituencies. For a time sponsorship by a union was a requirement for Labour's parliamentary candidates; on polling day staff at trades clubs and the local offices of the various affiliated unions helped to organise the knocking-up of the core vote; and an army of volunteers was on hand to drive electors to polling stations. Years of retrenchment in the wake of the mergers of the past has resulted in the closure of countless branch offices and a haemorrhaging of staff.

My first taste of election reporting was in the 1960s for local newspapers in Portsmouth and Oxford, two cities with strong trade union roots. Doing the rounds on polling day involved calling in at union offices, especially those of the T&G and Amalgamated Union of Engineering Workers; they were always a hive of activity; branch officials and shop stewards, mostly men, often smoking, organised a constant stream of cars going back and forth ferrying voters. There would be same buzz at the Conservatives' constituency office and the local Conservative clubs; more often than not the room would be packed with elderly volunteers, usually women, checking off the electoral roll, ticking off the names sent back by tellers, ready to remind committed supporters that they had yet to vote.

Going from one campaign office to the next one saw the full force of two-party politics in action, two different tribes helping to deliver their supporters to the ballot box, in an era when the overall turnout regularly exceeded 75 per cent and the combined vote of Labour and the Conservatives often approached almost 90 per cent of the total electorate. A tidal wave of votes delivered by the SNP in favour of independence in the 2014 referendum, and the tsunami seven months later on polling day, was a reminder if one was needed of Labour's failure to tackle decay at the heart of an election-winning machine that had been so effective for so long in what were once its impregnable Scottish heartlands.

UKIP

Family history has unexpected ways of repeating itself. My father discovered to his cost that he had unwittingly provided Enoch Powell with advice that helped him to promote his infamous 'rivers of blood' speech. Thirty years later I realised that I had inadvertently given a helping hand in boosting the political career of Nigel Farrage, leader of the *United Kingdom Independence Party* and an ardent Powell admirer. Our shared experience as newspaper man and broadcaster reflects a reciprocal but often hidden trade-off between journalist and politician. In return for inside information, and perhaps the possibility of an exclusive story line, we can offer guidance on the inner workings of the news media, invaluable assistance for a promising parliamentarian.

In 1968 my father Clement Jones was editor of the Wolverhampton *Express and Star*, the evening newspaper that circulated in Powell's constituency. The two men had become friends in the early 1950s and together they had been on a fast track for promotion, a local reporter heading for the editor's chair and an up-and-coming MP about to become a cabinet minister.

My minor but at the time perhaps influential role in Farrage's seemingly inexorable rise had many parallels: the two politicians had each taken a keen interest in the art of news management and both would go on to shake up the established political order of their day. After his death I realised the full extent of the heavy price that my father had paid for assisting in the presentation of a speech on immigration that was so contentious that it shattered a friendship and resulted in his becoming the local newspaper editor who faced a storm of protest for challenging Powell on the MP's home patch. By contrast, my advice, also freely given, and again without any real expectations on my part, engendered nothing but thanks and the unexpected offer of a job. On the strength of having put in a good word that assisted his breakthrough into political broadcasting, Farrage tried on two separate occasions to persuade me to become UKIP's press officer. The full extent of our inter-locking family connections was only brought home to me in December 2014 when the *Daily Telegraph* published details of private correspondence dating from the mid 1990s that revealed that Farrage had written several times asking Powell to endorse him as a parliamentary candidate for UKIP.

Our behind-the-scenes roles in promoting politicians might surprise some former colleagues given the subsequent notoriety of Powell and Farrage but there can be very few journalists who have not been asked at some stage in their careers to give a pointer, or at least encouragement, to those desperately seeking publicity. We can offer all kinds of advice: the most opportune timing for a speech or an event in order to meet newspaper deadlines or to catch the main radio and television news bulletins; guidance on how to present a potential story in a way most likely to secure the interest of a news room; or perhaps tips on the darker arts involved in trailing or leaking sensitive information.

The fall-out from the 'rivers of blood' speech is imprinted on family memory. Such was my father's subsequent misfortune that he had no alternative but to accept early retirement at the age of 55. As was the case years later with my acquaintance with Farrage, the starting point for our involvement was the fraternisation that often occurs between journalists and politicians. We lived only a short walk from Powell's constituency home in Wolverhampton, and he quite frequently dropped in to see my father. They would talk animatedly for hours; my father admired Powell's diligence as a constituency MP and Powell, who was fascinated by the processes involved in news management, was eager for tips on how to use the media to promote his career.

Three decades later I found myself having comparable conversations with former Conservative Euro-sceptics who had helped to establish UKIP and who were keen to discuss how best to promote their campaign to secure the UK's withdrawal from the European Union. I had met Farrage, one of the party's founder members, when he stood in the 1994 Eastleigh parliamentary by-election but it was not until after the 1997 general election that he began seeking advice. At the time my status as a BBC political correspondent was regarded by both the Conservative and Labour Party machines as being rather an irritant because of the books I had written on the news media's role in political campaigning. My third book, *Campaign 1997*, was considered even more 'unhelpful' than *Election '92* and *Soundbites and Spin Doctors* (1995). Its launch at Politicos book shop in the summer of 1997 was boycotted by New Labour's leading media apparatchiks, anxious not to be seen in the company of a journalist who had incurred the wrath of both Peter Mandelson and Alastair Campbell and had been deemed 'unreliable'. Farrage and a UKIP contingent had no such inhibitions, and afterwards they were determined to keep in touch. Subsequently, I found myself bombarded by their complaints about an alleged pro-European bias in the BBC's news coverage. At one point I remember suggesting that they should monitor the output and prepare some statistics because what programme editors feared most of all were complaints that were backed up by a precise chronology of the relevant output.

My advice had obviously been put to good use because I discovered to my embarrassment that editorial staff on the *Today* programme had been subjected to sustained and detailed criticism of what was perceived to be their failure to give a representative amount of air time to UKIP and other leading Euro-sceptic voices. After his election as an MEP for South East England in the 1999 European Parliament Election, Farrage became one of UKIP's most quoted politicians and I was well aware of how assiduous he had become in seeking publicity. My contacts with UKIP led to a chance inquiry: Lisa Jenkinson, a BBC producer, asked how I thought Farrage would acquit himself if he were invited on to the panel for the Radio 4 programme *Any Questions*. I assured her that Farrage would be an admirable panellist, more than capable of answering topical questions, holding his own and defending himself if need be. He subsequently made his debut in March 2001 and I thought he lived up to the advance billing I had given him.

Later in the following year, after I had left the BBC on reaching sixty, Farrage rang me at home to ask whether I would like to become UKIP's press officer; he assured me it would be worth my while as the party had strong financial backing and would offer a decent salary. Farrage was a smooth operator, keen to remind and thank me for having put in a good word for him with the BBC's *Any Questions* team: 'You know you were the one who helped get me launched into broadcasting'. I had no hesitation in turning down his offer, explaining that I valued my political independence as a journalist and broadcaster.

While I had no intention of ever working for a political party, I said that I was always happy to discuss tactics. Having written so much about the dark arts of political manipulation, I had no objection to talking to all and sundry about media related issues and where possible offering advice. Farrage did not a miss a trick: when did I think was the best time for UKIP to hold its annual party conference? Would it be wise to stick to the week immediately after the Conservative conference or should they go later in the autumn so as not to be overshadowed? I said UKIP's tactic should be to try to upstage the Conservatives by generating damaging headlines just as the Tory delegates were arriving for their own conference. Ideally the UKIP conference should be squeezed into the weekend before the Tory gathering and their aim should be to grab the headlines and become an irritant to the Conservatives.

Labour had deployed that trick in the past: I described how Alastair Campbell upstaged the Conservatives in 1995 by releasing on the eve of the Tory conference news of the defection to Labour of the former Conservative MP Alan Howarth. There is no doubt that UKIP's success in seizing the political agenda in the long haul to the 2015 general election was a testament to Farrage's news sense and his acute grasp of the importance of timing.

Not surprisingly I smiled with amusement when the defection to UKIP of the former Conservative MP Mark Reckless was announced by Farrage at his party conference in late

September 2014, on the eve of the Tory conference. In his column in the *Mail on Sunday*, James Forsyth, political editor of *The Spectator,* berated Farrage for 'an act of malice' that had 'rabbit-punched' David Cameron ahead of his set-piece speech. Boris Johnson, writing in his *Daily Telegraph* column in 1995, had paid the same back-handed compliment to New Labour's spin doctors for their 'vicious timing' of Alan Howarth's defection. Farrage telephoned me again at home and repeated his offer of a job with UKIP not long before the announcement in April 2014 that Patrick O'Flynn, political editor of the *Daily Express*, had been appointed UKIP's director of communications.

A fascination with the interplay between politicians and journalists dates back to my school days. My father's dedication to his work as news editor and then editor could not be faulted. I remember so well seeing him each evening go through the various editions of the *Express and Star*, marking up the pages with a blue pencil, perhaps with a comment or note to the effect that a story needed a follow-up, ready for the first newsroom meeting next morning.

As with my father and grandfather, local newspapers were the starting point of my career, first at the Portsmouth evening paper, *The News*, and then, by the year of the 'rivers of blood' speech, I was local government correspondent at the *Oxford Mail*. In the late 1960s Enoch Powell was at odds with the Conservative leadership, dissatisfied with the way his speeches were being handled by the party machine. My father had instructed him on how to short-circuit Central Office. His advice was that Saturday afternoon was perhaps the most opportune moment to deliver a hard-hitting political speech. The trick was to deliver an embargoed copy the previous Thursday or Friday to a hand-picked group of political editors and leader writers on the Sunday newspapers; they would be only too keen to preserve the embargo, and if all went as planned Powell, would end up getting sustained coverage throughout the weekend.

The aim of my father's strategy was to stretch coverage over three days: first it would be reported on Saturday evening news bulletins; then in the Sunday newspapers and their coverage would be picked up again in Monday's papers. Powell's first public references to anxieties in Wolverhampton about the influx of immigrants, mainly West Indians and Kenyan Asians, was in a speech in Walsall in March 1968 in which he described the concerns of a constituent who claimed that his daughter was the only white child in her class at primary school.

After journalists from the *Express and Star* failed to track down either the child or the class, my father challenged Powell. He explained that as editor he had been receiving similar anonymous complaints but they had all proved to be false and could be tracked back to members of the National Front. Powell would not accept it and three weeks later in April 1968 he told my father he was planning another speech at three o'clock that Saturday afternoon. He would not say what it was about but made the tantalising comment: 'Look, Clem, you know how a rocket goes up into the air, explodes into lots of stars and then falls down to the ground. Well, this speech is going to go up like a rocket, and when it gets up to the top, the stars are going to stay up.' Powell had followed my father's instructions on distributing advance copies and his prediction proved correct. The repercussions from the 'rivers of blood' speech reverberated for months, and its meaning and impact are argued about to this day.

My parents had been looking after the Powells' two daughters that Saturday afternoon and when Powell returned to collect them my mother told him they would not be 'seeing each other again for a very long time'. The following weeks were a searing experience for my father who was appalled by Powell's racist tone. Few provincial editors have had to face a stiffer test of their duty to provide balanced coverage when, as far as the *Express and Star's* circulation district was concerned, 'virtually the whole area was determined to make a saint out of Powell'. My father's principled stand came at price. He announced his early retirement within three months of the conclusion of a protracted libel case after the *Sunday Times* and the *Express and Star* agreed to publish an apology and retraction for having repeated an allegation that Powell had indulged in Nazi-style propaganda.

V

votes

Wider cross-party support for electoral reform was one of the few unifying themes that emerged from the political wreckage left in the wake of the 2015 general election. Massive anomalies in the way 650 MPs were elected to the House of Commons gave further impetus to a campaign to change a first-past-the-post **voting** system that critics believed could hardly stagger on much longer. David Cameron returned to Westminster with 331 MPs after the Conservatives gained 11.3 million votes. A re-elected Prime Minister was able to claim that achieving an outright majority of 12 MPs was the 'sweetest victory of all'. His celebrations contrasted with the anger and despair of smaller parties whose hopes were dashed yet again by a winner-takes-all lottery that they argued deprived them of a fair proportion of the seats at Westminster.

Candidates standing for the Liberal Democrats, United Kingdom Independence party and Greens secured 7.4 million votes, but the three parties ended up with only 10 MPs between them. Their combined share of votes cast was 24.3 per cent whereas the Conservatives, although they topped the poll in just over half of all constituencies, did so with the backing of only 36.9 per cent of the electorate.

Campaigners for electoral reform pointed to even greater disparities in Scotland where the Scottish National party won 56 out of 59 constituencies after securing 1.5 million votes; a 50 per cent share of votes cast had delivered 95 per cent of Scotland's seats at Westminster. Nigel Farrage blamed a bankrupt electoral system for failing to respond to the significance of UKIP's achievement in having gained a 12.6 per share of the total vote. Although his party had picked up 3.9 million votes, and finished second in 118 constituencies across the country, UKIP had only one MP to show for their efforts, whereas the SNP leader Nicola Sturgeon, could boast of having 56 MPs on what in UK-wide terms was only 4.7 per cent of the total vote.

Caroline Lucas, re-elected in her constituency of Brighton Pavilion, was equally disillusioned: the Greens had gained 1.2 million votes, a 3.8 per cent share, but she remained the party's only MP. Unlike UKIP and the Greens, whose share of the vote had increased significantly, the Liberal Democrats were hit by a catastrophic fall in support, down by 15 per on the 2010 election. The loss of 49 MPs was a momentous setback for Nick Clegg whose only consolation was that his party still managed to retain eight seats on what proportionally was a far worse performance than that of UKIP. Clegg could also take some comfort from the strength of the post-election recriminations over the unfairness of the voting system, and the hope that the mounting resentment would re-awaken demands for some form of proportional representation, a cause that the Liberal Democrats had championed for so long.

Scars have been left on the back of many of Clegg's predecessors by the contrariness of a first-past-the-post voting system steadfastly defended by both Labour and the

Conservatives, its two principal beneficiaries. While she was only too happy to commiserate with the disenchantment of rival parties, the Liberal Democrat life peer Baroness Shirley Williams was keen to remind them that their grievances in 2015 paled into insignificance when compared with the injustices of the 1983 election. Candidates for the SDP-Liberal Alliance gained 7.8 million votes, a 25.4 per cent share of the electorate, but won only 23 seats, whereas Labour on 8.5 million votes (27.6 per cent) returned to Westminster with a grand total of 209 MPs. There had been a similarly devastating outcome in 1964 when the Liberals managed to double their support, gaining 3.1 million votes (11.2 per cent), but secured only nine MPs.

Renewed pressure for change from the Liberal Democrats, strengthened by the exasperation of UKIP and Greens, had to be set against the satisfaction of those voters who had backed the election of a majority Conservative government, fearing the possibility of another hung parliament and an unstable coalition. However brutal the system might be, those who have always backed the retention of first-past-the-post insist that it did deliver another single-party government, and with few exceptions that had been experience of post-war politics. Long-standing advocates of a winner-takes-all result were accused of having overlooked the consequences of fragmenting support for two-party politics, and the emergence of strong political movements that had succeeded in attracting votes from both Labour and the Conservatives.

A Liberal Democrat-inspired proposal for a system of proportional representation was put to a referendum in 2011, one of the conditions of the 2010 coalition agreement with the Conservatives. Although defeated by a majority of more than two to one, the Electoral Reform Society believed the unfairness of the 2015 election result would breathe fresh life into the campaign to replace first-past-the-post. Katie Ghose, the ERS chief executive, considered the scale of the setback suffered by UKIP and the Greens was 'a game changer' because millions more voters from across the political spectrum had failed to get their views represented in parliament.

Data compiled by the ERS for the *Observer* suggested the 2015 election was the 'most disproportionate' in UK political history. Electing one MP had required 3.86 million UKIP votes; 299,000 Liberal Democrat votes; 40,000 Labour votes; 34,000 Conservative votes; and 26,000 SNP votes. If a proportional voting system had been in place nearly a quarter of MPs elected to Westminster would not have won a seat. Ms Ghose believed a fairer system was needed to reflect fundamental shifts in political support. 'People are shopping around, yet our voting system, designed for a long-gone era, is failing to cope with the choices modern voters want to express. That Labour and the Conservatives managed to get 87 per cent of seats on just over two thirds of the vote is a damming indictment. Why should 5 million voters be marginalised for voting UKIP or Green? At a time when more and more people are turning away from politics, our broken voting system accentuates divides and is making it worse.'

The ERS believed the case for proportional representation would gain support once voters understood that so many of them played no effective role in the election: 74 per cent of votes were wasted because they did not contribute towards electing an MP. Shortly before the election the ERS identified 368 safe seats which would not change hands, of which 363 were called correctly. There were 26 million voters in constituencies where the result was a foregone conclusion, 'another blight' that could be eradicated by changing the system.

Campaigners for electoral reformers have failed to

reach agreement on the most effective form of proportional representation. The option put forward in the 2011 referendum was the alternative vote system, allowing voters to number candidates in order of preference. An additional member system is used to elect the 129 members of the Scottish Parliament. The single transferable vote, used for local elections in Scotland and Northern Ireland, is the method favoured by the ERS because candidates are ranked in order of preference, and the system keeps the constituency link with local electors. Larger constituencies would be required, and each would have a team of MPs, but the ERS says there is likely to be at least one MP backed by most voters.

If the single transferable vote had been applied to the outcome of the 2015 general election the outcome would have given no party an outright majority. The Conservatives would have been the largest party, and would have needed to find coalition partners to form a government. The result would have been: 276 Conservative MPs; 236 Labour; 54 UKIP; 34 SNP; 26 Liberal Democrats; 3 Greens; and 3 Plaid Cymru.

Within a few days of the election there was a public demonstration of the cross-party unity behind the demand for an overhaul of the electoral system. A petition backed by 478,000 signatures was delivered to Downing Street by a delegation that brought together representatives of the Greens, Liberal Democrats, UKIP, SNP and Plaid Cymru. Nigel Farrage and the Greens' leader Natalie Bennett joined the group for a photo-call on the steps of No.10. Ms Bennett said she was ready to work with Farrage to build up a grassroots campaign to urge a total rethink in the way the country voted. 'We haven't seen a significant reform at Westminster since women got the vote in 1918, and we shouldn't get to that centenary without achieving a fair voting system.'

political wives

Having made a career in what for most of my time were the male-dominated worlds of industrial and political reporting, I readily acknowledge that collectively we should have responded far earlier and done much more to welcome women journalists. Our failure to be more understanding and accommodating mirrored the attitude of trade union leaders and politicians of that era. In truth we correspondents quite enjoyed our erratic hours, late nights and socialising after work, hardly an enticing prospect for women anxious to combine a career with a demanding family life. But great strides have been made in the news media, especially in broadcasting, where every effort has been made to achieve a balance on air and on screen between male and female reporters and presenters.

By comparison progress at Westminster has been painfully slow: Labour made a breakthrough in the 1997 general election when all-women constituency short lists pushed the party's count to a record 101 of the 120 women MPs elected that year. A comparable push in 2010 took the Conservatives' tally to an unprecedented 49, but the overall total of 143 left women holding around only a fifth of the 650 seats in the House of Commons. Another significant advance in 2015 took the total to 191, almost one in three, with Labour remaining well ahead with women holding 43 per cent of the party's seats and a third of the SNP's record intake.

Despite remaining woefully under represented at Westminster, women politicians have secured a far more effective voice than their numbers might suggest. Three women in a line-up of seven party leaders for the only head-to-head televised debate of the 2015 election indicated the extent of the step change that has taken place. Limited though their success has been in shaking up the political establishment and in achieving full equality at Westminster, their higher profile has had an incremental impact on the **wives** of party leaders, and imposed fresh demands on the campaigning duties that are required of them. Instead of maintaining a discreet presence in the background, perhaps sitting or standing on the side lines holding a hand bag or a party programme, they are now expected to enter a conference hall hand in hand with their husbands so as to provide compelling images for live television coverage and photographs for the press. Rather than having the option of restricting themselves to a few pleasantries when seen in public with party workers or greeting potential voters, today's wives are definitely on parade and on camera, well advised to take a spin doctor's advice on the supportive soundbites they will be expected to deliver when their husbands arrange family-friendly photo-opportunities or have to give interviews for celebrity-style profiles.

Unlike Westminster and the national media, local politics and provincial journalism were always in my experience far more welcoming to women. As local government correspondent for the *Oxford Mail* in the mid-1960s, I had to contend with two formidable group leaders on Oxford City Council, Janet Young (Conservative) and Olive Gibbs (Labour). On joining *The Times* at Westminster in 1968, there were several women in the Parliamentary Press Gallery, mainly reporting debates for the Press Association news agency and Hansard on the strength of having a fast shorthand note, but only one political correspondent, Nora Beloff of *The Observer*. By the mid-70s, on becoming a political reporter for the BBC, I recall the buzz there was in the lobby when Christine Eade was the first woman to be appointed a BBC political correspondent. Similarly in the late 1970s, having switched by then to industrial reporting, the only woman in the Labour and Industrial Correspondents' Group was Isolda McNeil of the *Morning Star*, and she had only recently been granted full access following a rule change to admit women members. In the early 1980s we were joined on the industrial beat by Julia Somerville, the first woman to become a BBC labour correspondent.

Looking back on those years perhaps the criticism that hurts most of all is that we were patronising to women, safe in the belief our all-male cliques were somehow superior, and that when it came to dealing with union leaders and employers, ministers and MPs, only we were capable of withstanding the hard graft of late-night reporting and impossibly tight deadlines for filing news copy and voice reports. Plucky pioneers were starting to break down those barriers, and while equality campaigners have every right to be critical about the tardiness of our response, industrial and political journalists had been left in no doubt by our editors and producers that we should not be caught indulging in the kind of sexist abuse and banter that was so commonplace at Westminster.

Women who had succeeded against the odds in getting elected to parliament were admired for having done so on their merit. A Labour high flyer in the early 1970s was Shirley Williams, then the shadow Home Secretary and one of only 26 women in the House of Commons. Labour were fighting back after Edward Heath's defeat of Harold Wilson and she often spoke at news conferences held in Transport House. On the platform would be other shadow ministers, and perhaps also trade union leaders, but on several occasions we had to wait for her arrival. I recall top-table muttering, plus a few guffaws, to the effect that we journalists would have to patient; we should understand women were allowed to be a little late.

Leaders' wives were invariably seen but not heard at party and constituency events. Their presence during speeches, and on other high-profile occasions, was of great importance to their husbands. At campaign meetings in Scotland throughout the 1970 election, the shadow Foreign Secretary and former Prime Minister Sir Alec Douglas-Home was almost always accompanied by his wife Elizabeth. She would join her husband in shaking hands with their hosts, perhaps exchanging a few words with a local laird. As Sir Alec usually repeated the same speech there was rarely anything fresh to report for *The Times* and I would often chat with her as we waited while her husband did the rounds before leaving for yet another village meeting. She confined herself to small talk when I was in the vicinity, but there was no doubting that the Conservative faithful expected an MP's wife to put in appearance, and I admired her enthusiasm in supporting her husband night after night.

Such was her diligence I was sure that if Elizabeth had been younger, and Sir Alec's schedule less hectic, she might have emulated Clement Attlee's wife Violet who regularly drove her husband to political events in the post-war years. In the 1945 election she was regularly seen at the wheel of their Hillman, the map on her husband's knees. When Attlee fought the 1950 election there was a detective on the back seat so as to provide protection for the Prime Minister. If the couple stopped at the roadside ahead of schedule, Vi caught up on her knitting, her husband did the crossword and they would eat their sandwiches.

In my early years on *The Times* and later with the BBC an opportunity for a journalist to fraternise with the wife of a party leader or Prime Minister was an exception. Their arrival at party conferences or campaign engagements was invariably low profile; there was little if any stage management and there were certainly none of the media scrums or shouted questions of today. I remember seeing Mary Wilson and Audrey Callaghan at significant events; they might have been filmed or photographed from a distance, but they were strictly off limits for reporters and broadcasters.

Glenys Kinnock was the first spouse to emerge from the side lines, embrace the demand for photo-opportunities and take the knocks that would follow once she allowed her presence to be exploited on her husband's behalf. At the 1983 Labour conference in Brighton she had a starring role in an ill-fated publicity stunt intended to promote the newly-installed party leader. Neil Kinnock was being filmed walking along the beach hand in hand with his wife: he tripped and, at the very moment he fell on to the shingle, he was hit by an incoming wave. Television footage of his slip-up was immortalised by being replayed time and time again in the opening titles of *Spitting Image*.

A highlight of Labour's campaign in 1987 was an election broadcast directed by Hugh Hudson which was dubbed 'Kinnock: The Movie', depicting Neil and Glenys walking along a cliff top to the strains of Brahms. She was at her husband's side for the main events of the 1992 election, and in conceding defeat he paid tribute to her fortitude in withstanding the vilification they had both been subjected to in the tabloid press. 'She has been the target of such spite that it disgraces those who offer it...and she bears it with a dignity that makes me proud.'

Norma Major, unlike Glenys Kinnock, disliked election razzmatazz and she made only fleeting appearances during the 1992 campaign. On the day her husband stood outside 10 Downing Street to declare the election, she was at their constituency home in Huntingdon. A Conservative press officer, Vanessa Ford, was with her when the announcement was made, and sat close by at the launch of the party's manifesto. Norma was placed near the front in one of the press seats but I had overheard party workers anxiously saying they must make sure journalists did not get too close because we might ask awkward questions and she could find that unsettling.

Again in the 1997 election she kept the lowest possible profile. On the final Saturday of the campaign Major was filmed with Norma chatting to some of his constituents in the Market Inn at Huntingdon. But she appeared to have no illusions about the likelihood of her husband being defeated by Tony Blair. On the return flight to London after Major's last regional campaign tour, she joined in the party atmosphere on board. Champagne and cakes had been laid on by the cabin crew. Clarence Mitchell, a BBC correspondent on the flight, told me he noticed her taking her own snaps of the party, as though she knew it was his final flight as Prime Minister and she wanted some pictures for the family album.

Her insistence on keeping herself at arm's length from the media, already justified in her judgement by the treatment meted out to Glenys Kinnock, had been reinforced during the long haul to the 1997 election as Cherie Blair found that she too was increasingly becoming a target for the tabloids. Peter Mandelson singled out the *Daily Mail* and *Daily Express* for their 'vicious' pursuit of the Labour leader's wife. A constant theme of the coverage was that she was the power behind the throne, influencing party policy. After she had been dubbed 'Britain's would-be Hilary Clinton' by the *Daily Express* correspondent Peter Hitchens, he argued that she was a leading barrister and QC who had made frequent speeches on legal reform. She was also a 'highly political' figure in her own right, having stood as a Labour candidate in Thanet North in 1983 under her maiden name of Cherie Booth.

During their decade in 10 Downing Street, the Blairs were generous hosts. Instead of holding largely private and informal gatherings they staged more events that offered access to the news media, and hence the accusation that they exploited government hospitality for political advantage. Cherie continued her legal career, being appointed a crown court recorder in 1999, and she held firm to her political convictions by supporting the sometimes controversial causes in which she had an interest. Whenever she expressed her opinion she was roundly condemned by newspaper columnists, especially if they managed to find a way to suggest she was interfering in government affairs

Extra care had to be taken managing her appearances at political events but she was at her husband's side for the all-important family photo-calls. On polling day in the 2001 election Blair, holding hands with his wife and daughter Kathryn, together with the couple's two eldest sons, Euan and Nicky, strolled across a playing field covered with buttercups and daisies on the way to the polling station in the Trimdon Colliery community centre, near their constituency home. Together as a family, on a sunny morning in June, with all but baby Leo who was asleep at the house, they provided a lingering sequence of pictures which mirrored the same walk on polling day in 1997 – and once again it would not have looked out of place in *The Sound of Music.*

Next door in 11 Downing Street, home of Chancellor of the Exchequer Gordon Brown, Cherie's mauling by the popular press had not gone unnoticed by his wife Sarah. When her husband finally became Prime Minister in June 2007 she unashamedly started to present herself as the First Lady of British politics. Instead of continuing to pursue her earlier career as a public relations consultant, or opting to become a demure and often silent companion, she began to refashion the public's expectation of the role to be performed by the premier's spouse. From her courtship through to their marriage in 2000 and the loss the following year of their baby daughter Jennifer, she had never wavered in her dedication to the dual cause of humanising her husband's dour image and becoming an informal ambassador for the Labour government. At summits of world leaders she took her place alongside the other wives during social gatherings, striking a pose that won an affectionate response from women journalists.

Using Twitter and other social media sites she managed to by-pass official channels and develop an engaging dialogue with the public. Within a matter of months she was writing regularly under her own by-line as a celebrity commentator and columnist. Editors and Downing Street press officers admired her news judgement; her ability to censor herself by steering clear of blatant political propaganda; and knowing how to avoid embarrassing the government.

She used her new-found celebrity status to support her embattled husband's fightback with a novel intervention at the 2008 party conference. Setting aside procedure, she stepped on to the stage to introduce 'my husband, the leader of the Labour Party, your Prime Minister'. She could not be faulted on her timing as her emotional gesture seemed to chime with the mesmerising campaign being waged by Barack and Michelle Obama in the lead-up to the US Presidential election that November. Next day's newspapers were filled with photographs of the Browns' platform embrace.

Her empathy with the press pack was so intuitive that I have always thought that her husband's disastrous confrontation in the 2010 election campaign with a Rochdale grandmother whom he later referred to as 'just a sort of bigoted woman' might never happened if she had been at his side. Her very presence would have so charmed Gillian Duffy that they would probably have engaged in nothing more than simple pleasantries, and even if the conversation had gone awry, I am sure she would have noticed immediately, once her husband returned to a waiting car, that a Sky News radio microphone was still attached to his lapel.

Sarah and Cherie shared a common desire to limit media intrusion into their family life and keep their children out of the public eye. So anxious was he to protect his sons John and Fraser from the 'glare of publicity' that Brown purposely avoided sitting next to them at the Olympic Games in Beijing so that they could not be photographed with him. He justified his refusal to serve his two boys up 'for spreads in the papers' in a speech at the 2008 party conference: 'My children aren't props; they're people.' Finally he relented on the day he resigned in May 2010 after Labour's defeat, and the agreement by the Conservatives and Liberal Democrats to form a coalition government. Brown and his wife walked the length of Downing Street holding hands with John and Fraser, an abiding image of his final, tortured days in office that begged the question, 'Why hadn't he shown the country before that he was a caring family man as well as Prime Minister, the proud father of two small boys?'

David and Samantha Cameron held the key to that puzzle, an explanation of sorts for Brown's irritation. Well before he was elected Conservative leader, Cameron had accepted that an MP's family was part of a politician's public persona. He had made frequent reference to his commitment as a father to the task of looking after his two-year-old disabled son Ivan, and after his promotion to the shadow cabinet in September 2004, he and Samantha were photographed for a profile in *The Times* with Ivan and their nine-month-old daughter Nancy. During the lengthy leadership contest in the summer and autumn of 2005, the couple were often photographed in their kitchen or out walking with Ivan and Nancy, sometimes held in their arms or in push chairs. Brown's defence of family privacy in 2008 had been preceded by a television profile of Cameron in which a BBC correspondent Carole Walker contrasted the access offered by the Conservative leader with the Prime Minister's refusal to allow his sons to be photographed. Cameron had no hesitation in explaining why as party leader he invited camera crews and photographers into his home: 'The public have a right to know quite a bit about you, your life and your family…so this is a natural thing to do.'

Ivan's death in February 2009 prompted Brown to cancel Prime Minister's questions and the Camerons' grief was front-page news next day. Six weeks before polling day in the 2010 election, Cameron revealed that his wife was pregnant, a lucky break for Conservative spin doctors. To coincide with the news they were filmed for WebCameron, a Conservative online video site. Samantha was seen boiling a kettle at their London home and then sipping her drink as her husband sat at a computer. She had always refused to be interviewed at length, restricting herself to a few casual remarks. When asked if she needed any tips on campaigning, he replied: 'She's a natural…she's eclipsing me completely.' Samantha chipped in: 'I think the bump is.'

Once the go-ahead was given for the first ever televised debates between the three party leaders, campaign strategists had to prepare for another inexorable shift towards a US-style 'presidential' election. Sarah Brown's high profile had created a dilemma for Samantha and Miriam Gonzalez, wife of the Liberal Democrat leader Nick Clegg: were they too prepared to present themselves as political activists and join the 2010 campaign trail? Unlike Sarah, who had already been devoting her energies to supporting the Prime Minister, they were working mothers determined to continue their own successful careers. Each of the parties knew they would have to contend with highly personalised campaigns, but to the delight of their respective spin doctors the three leaders had attractive wives, young children and were devoted fathers.

Conservative-supporting newspapers were captivated by images of the pregnant Samantha but the more she was paraded as Cameron's 'secret weapon' the greater the admiration for Miriam, an international trade lawyer. She was applauded by some women commentators for her feisty declaration that she could be 'supportive without being submissive'. Nonetheless the tabloid fashionistas were soon assembling photographs of the wives' ever-changing outfits ready to determine which of the 'Westminster WAGs' was the most stylish.

Miriam stuck resolutely to her own election pledge to put career and family first rather than spend her five weeks' holiday on the campaign trail. After she had been photographed helping Clegg build a dry stone wall in his Sheffield Hallam constituency, the columnists promoting the 'war of the wives' finally had a real contest and offered their assessment of her blue jeans and grey cardigan. Next day Miriam told ITV News that voters deserved better than patronising remarks about her clothes. However much she disliked the focus on her appearance, the wives were the subject of a *Mail on Sunday* opinion poll to determine which of them was having the best campaign. Samantha was way out in front on 22 per cent; Sarah on 13 per cent; and a puny 4 per cent for Miriam. A YouGov survey provided an antidote: 89 per cent thought the wives would have little or no influence on how they voted.

In the five years that elapsed before the 2015 election Samantha and Miriam had both been photographed on countless occasions, as had Justine Thornton, wife of the Labour leader Ed Miliband. Unlike the Cleggs who resolutely refused to allow any media access to their children, the Milibands had been pictured occasionally with their two sons, Daniel and Samuel, and as polling day approached they readily agreed to family photo-opportunities. Although there was nothing like the 2010 feeding frenzy surrounding the 'Westminster WAGs', their appearance at campaign events did command widespread coverage and was far more partisan with Conservative-supporting newspapers printing many more flattering photographs of Samantha than either Justine and Miriam. Opinion polls again put the Prime Minister's wife well ahead. When YouGov asked which wife was the best election asset, 54 per cent went for Samantha, double the proportion for either Justine (26 per cent) or Miriam (20 per cent). A survey of mothers by the parenting website Netmums suggested 14 per cent identified with Samantha, 8 per cent with Justine and 5 per cent with Miriam.

Again the *Daily Mail* led the press pack in its scrutiny of the wives. A page of photographs of Justine cycling to and from work showed her jumping red lights, travelling the wrong way down a one-way street and riding on the pavement. When asked why as a top barrister she did not know the Highway Code, a party spokesman said she had promised to be more careful in future. Samantha was mortally offended when the *Mail* published a two-page feature asking an acutely embarrassing question: 'Have you got tootsie trouble?' On a visit to Hounslow the Prime Minister had removed her loafers when taking a rest and photographs of her bare feet showed that she had 'paid the price for lifelong devotion to fashionable footwear in the form of bunions, yellowing toenails, corns and red and flaky skin'. Cookery writers praised Miriam's taste for practical photo-opportunities helping to prepare food for hungry constituency activists once they discovered her recipes for the meals she cooked her three boys were published on her own blog mumandsons.com. At the end of a marathon election the wives' final campaign photo-opportunity ran true to form: they were each filmed in good time for the lunchtime news bulletins walking hand in hand with their husbands towards the polling stations in their constituencies.

Xavier (Michael Portillo)

"**I**f this had happened, that could have happened"… journalists love nothing more than to speculate about how an outcome might have been entirely different if only events had gone the other way. Armed with information gleaned from the Westminster village, political correspondents are particularly prone to second guessing any eventuality, always ready to offer a variety of tantalising alternative scenarios. Such is the lottery of a first-past-the-post voting system, and so captivating can be the live coverage from counts and declarations, that sometimes a general election is remembered for a totally unexpected result, an event that encapsulates the drama of the night. As the election map was turning from blue to red in the early hours of Tony Blair's landslide victory in May 1997, Michael Denzil **Xavier** Portillo earned his place in the hit parade of election night highlights.

For political aficionados the 'Portillo moment' remains a visual reminder of an historic shift in political power. 'Were you up for Portillo?' became a constant refrain of Blairites, a mantra for expressing their jubilation at New Labour's resounding success in persuading so many electors to reject all that

Margaret Thatcher and John Major had stood for. By contrast the haunted look on Portillo's face marked the end of an era: Major's comprehensive defeat finally drew to a close 18 years of Conservative government.

The devastation Thatcherites were witnessing live on television was compounded by the loss of their favourite contender for the future, the Tory MP whom they were convinced was her anointed successor. A setback that seemed unthinkable had put paid to a secret, carefully prepared plan for Portillo to declare his hand that weekend as a candidate for the leadership of the Conservative Party, given the widespread expectation that Major would lose the election and then resign. I had been on the inside track of what Portillo's supporters were planning, and I realised how deeply the shock of his defeat would have been felt among those who regarded him as the true heir to the Thatcherite inheritance.

Portillo looked mortified as the count was declared. His 1992 majority of 15,545 in his hitherto impregnable constituency of Enfield Southgate had been obliterated on a 17.4 per cent swing to Labour. Stephen Twigg, a former president of the National Union of Students, had won by the narrow margin of 1,433 votes. Enfield Southgate was by far the safest of the seven seats lost by Cabinet ministers that night, and Portillo had fallen victim to an army of young Labour campaign workers drawn from all over London. His seat was one of the constituencies identified in *The Observer* as a target for tactical voting by Liberal Democrat supporters.

Politicians and their families are of course the real casualties of the often cruel swings and roundabouts of polling day but political correspondents do sometimes have a small, personal stake in the outcome. Building up good contacts, and keeping an eye out for potential future stories, are all part and parcel of a journalist's daily life. I had gained my inside knowledge of preparations for the launch of Portillo's leadership bid from one of his closest confidants, the late David Hart, a former adviser to Mrs Thatcher, whom I had known since the aftermath of the 1984-85 pit dispute.

During the year-long strike, Hart helped to establish the National Working Miners' Committee and he had been an adviser to both the Prime Minister and Ian MacGregor, the chairman of the National Coal Board. In the years after Arthur Scargill's defeat, I had gained valuable insight from Hart into Mrs Thatcher's tactics, and on my return to political reporting, he had impressed me by the extent of his knowledge about the activities of the Tory right and the accuracy of his predictions.

Portillo's humiliation at the count had triggered another very personal flashback, one that dated from the year before the general election. Unknown to Hart, in February 1996, when he was then Secretary of State for Defence, Portillo had asked me to call in at the Ministry of Defence to discuss the way he was being presented in the news media. He was aware of my regular contact with Hart, and I was naturally curious to discover what was troubling him. He had featured in my most recent book *Soundbites and Spin Doctors* (1995), and I presumed he thought I might conceivably be able to give him some tips from a broadcaster's perspective.

I found the Secretary of State was decidedly queasy about the way he was coming across to the public; indeed he seemed almost repelled by the super-macho image that he had acquired as a standard bearer for the Thatcherite Euro-sceptics who were proving so troublesome to John Major. Hart's name was not mentioned but my gut reaction was that all was not well in their relationship. I made some suggestions as to how Portillo might seek to present himself differently in television interviews, in a more engaging manner, but our conversation was relatively short and inconclusive. I left feeling extremely puzzled by Portillo's self-doubt, and also somewhat uncertain about my own position: was I in danger of comprising the prized political neutrality of a BBC correspondent?

As it happened life had become so hectic for political journalists that I did not have time to dwell on my misgivings. New Labour was on the march in Westminster; the Major government was in dire straits; and the ideas and initiatives of Tony Blair and his colleagues were commanding the news agenda. Nonetheless I sensed that I might have crossed the line. Had I been a little too friendly with both Hart and Portillo, the danger being that such familiarity might adversely be influencing my independence as a journalist?

After the 1992 general election, once I began using my free time to write on the way politicians tried to manipulate the news media, I had decided to shun the regular practice of many lobby correspondents of taking politicians out for a drink, lunch or dinner in the hope of obtaining useful off-the-record information in return for hospitality. Instead I tried to make it clear that I believed conversations between journalists and politicians should, whenever possible, be on the record. If I was seeking to expose how party leaders and their spin doctors exploited the media, I wanted to avoid the charge of double standards, of being accused of seeking information on an off-the-record basis and of then breaking that confidence.

On starting my research for *The Election A-Z* I realised this was an opportune moment to revisit my insight into Portillo's tormented look on the night of his defeat, a way also perhaps of describing the role of influential but often shadowy fixers whose hidden hand can be so decisive in shaping the fortunes of political high flyers. Such has been my reluctance to take advantage of notes of private conversations relating to Portillo that my file on the part played by Hart has remained unopened for a decade or more. There was a nagging question I struggled to resolve: does there come a time when a journalist should no longer feel constrained by the confidences of a private conversation or guidance given off the record?

First I have declare another interest: to use criminal parlance, I have to admit that I have 'form' when it comes to leaking secret or confidential information. I was the BBC journalist who had surreptitiously taken a shorthand note of John Major's 1993 indiscretion about there being 'three more of the bastards out there' – one whom was said to be Portillo – and had then leaked the quote to *The Observer* after being told by my editor that I had overhead a private conversation and that what had been said could not be reported by the BBC. In the event 'Bastardgate' became one of the many media feeding frenzies that dogged a beleaguered Prime Minister who was so often at the mercy of the Conservatives' Euro-sceptic tendency. Not surprisingly I was carpeted by the BBC for my mischief. I was lucky to keep my job, and I owned up only publicly to being the source of the 'Bastardgate' quote in my book *Trading Information: Leaks, Lies and Tip-offs* (2006).

David Hart, a banking heir and Old Etonian, died in 2011. He was a latter-day Machiavelli, a throwback to the days of wealthy political adventurers who could indulge their interests and who believed they had a right, almost a duty, to help influence the politics of their day. He revelled in his role as a Thatcher adviser, and delighted in the recognition he gained after the pit strike for having become the scourge of Arthur Scargill. When visiting the working miners of the Nottinghamshire coalfield, he used to pass himself off as correspondent for *The Times*, an example of the subterfuge he regularly deployed, and perhaps a justification in itself for my journalistic licence in revealing how he devoted his energies behind the scenes trying to groom a potential party leader.

My interest in Hart's political activities intensified on my return to Westminster in 1988, once I began to investigate the work of the Committee for a Free Britain, which he had established in the run-up to the 1987 general election, and which had paid for controversial newspaper advertisements 'warning the country of the consequences of a Labour victory'. The committee was a firm advocate of the ill-fated community charge, or poll tax, and at the time I found his guidance of value. He must have thought that I was a useful sounding board because he started to ring me quite regularly, initially to offer guidance on running news stories and later to get my opinion on how the news media was reacting to the dramatic sequence of events in November 1990 that began with Michael Heseltine's challenge for the Conservative Party leadership, the resignation of Margaret Thatcher and John Major's appointment as the new Prime Minister.

After her downfall, Thatcher loyalists wasted little time in preparing for what they were expecting would be Major's defeat in the 1992 general election. Ahead of the 1991 party conference, Hart's briefing concentrated on his efforts to promote Portillo for the leadership in the event of Major's resignation. He had written a speech that Portillo would give to a lunchtime fringe meeting of the No Turning Back group. 'This is a very honest attempt by a genuine Thatcherite to make sense of being in a Major government...Michael is not a trimmer...only the Thatcherites have a coherent set of principles…and if the Tories lose, Michael is the soundest in this crucial area, and very clever tactically.'

Major's victory against the odds ruled out an immediate contest but it gave Hart the time he needed to promote his protégé as a long-term favourite for the leadership. After the election Portillo was promoted to Cabinet as the new Chief Secretary to the Treasury where he worked with another of Hart's close friends, the Chancellor of the Exchequer Norman Lamont. Within a matter of weeks I was told that Portillo was preparing a 'very tough' spending round and that the cuts would be 'much more ferocious' than the media expected. Two days later Hart rang again, this time to ask a favour: the *Mail on Sunday* had been digging into Portillo's past and they both wanted to know if there had been talk of the story among lobby correspondents. His request was a typical example of the two-way trade between contact and journalist, but I had no insight to offer. However, Hart expanded on the advice he was giving: 'All along I have told Michael never to give profile interviews, never to answer questions about his private life because you never know when the information can be used against you.'

My respect for the accuracy of Hart's guidance was assured a year later, during the 1993 cabinet reshuffle when Major sacked Lamont. Initially Hart was convinced Lamont would remain Chancellor and deliver the Budget in the autumn. 'Norman is the only bloke with the bottle to back Michael and stick by him on public spending, so it's vital Lamont stays.' The previous week Portillo had hit the headlines over a warning on prescription charges. 'A lot of that speech was my handiwork… it shows Michael's readiness to court unpopularity…it gives the impression he wouldn't mind if he was in the government or not.' In the event, Hart's confidence in Lamont's position was misplaced; and on the evening of the reshuffle he predicted that the now sacked Chancellor would not go quietly. 'Major is crazy to have got rid of Norman on such terms…he is boiling over with rage…he will cause a lot of trouble.' Several days later Hart tipped me off that Lamont's resignation statement would be a 'bombshell'; the ex-Chancellor accused Major's government of giving 'the impression of being in office but not in power'.

The constant threat of a possible leadership challenge to Major encouraged Hart to do all he could to strengthen Portillo's position as the right's leading contender. After writing a speech for a fringe meeting at the 1993 party conference, designed to show that Portillo was 'tough and statesmanlike', Hart outlined his strategy. 'I wanted people to think Portillo should be Prime Minister…it's a warning to Major to stick to his principles…We have professors and the like coming in every month to brief Portillo on defence, foreign affairs, social services and law and order…we've got to get him up to speed'.

Four months later Hart opened up again on the tactical planning being done by what he called the 'Portillo team': if the forthcoming elections to the European Parliament were a disaster for the Conservatives, one option would be for him to resign from the cabinet and build a platform for a leadership challenge. Portillo's third 'provocative' speech of the year would be a 'redefinition of Conservativism', the party had to 'listen to the small voice of Britain's quiet majority'. His opening remarks included a strong defence of 'a free press in Britain', a pledge that Hart said had been included because Portillo had been promised the support of two leading newspaper proprietors, Rupert Murdoch and Conrad Black (*Daily Telegraph*).

But the following year, when Major resigned in June 1995 and staged a mid-term leadership election order to flush out his opponents, Portillo hesitated. His ignominious retreat from the fray damaged both his future prospects and his campaign team. Hart was revealed as having been responsible for installing telephones and fax machines in a house in Lord North Street, a short walk from the Palace of Westminster. Portillo, who by then was Secretary of State for Employment, held back out of loyalty to Major, telling his supporters that he would stand only if the Prime Minister was defeated by John Redwood and the contest went to a second round.

Undaunted by the overwhelming vote in favour of Major's re-election, Hart and the rest of the team re-grouped, intent on re-launching Portillo as the heir apparent at the October party conference. In the summer reshuffle Portillo had been promoted to Secretary of State for Defence and Hart was appointed his unpaid special adviser, a role that he had undertaken for the previous Secretary of State Malcolm Rifkind. Hart prided himself on his military expertise; he had advised Mrs Thatcher; and he wanted the conference speech, which he had written with Portillo, to restate Conservative values on defence.

'I want Michael to be the darling of the conference again this year…he won't allow Blair to wrap the Union Jack round the Labour Party…Labour's defence policy is surrender and withdrawal…a retreat that would end up with Britain joining a single European army.' Hart had not warned me that Portillo had an electrifying punch line: 'The SAS have a motto: "Who Dares Wins." We dare. We will win.' Major joined in the applause and there was little doubt among party representatives that Portillo had reclaimed the leadership of the Tory right.

Portillo might have succeeded in rallying the party faithful at the Winter Gardens in Blackpool but his jingoism was widely condemned, and he was stunned by the criticism. The word among civil servants at the Ministry of Defence at parties that Christmas was that Portillo was 'definitely not hungry any more'; the joke against him, 'Who dares puts in phones', harked back to his failure to rise to Major's 'back me or sack me' challenge the previous summer. Hart agreed that Portillo was 'very depressed', determined to keep his head down so that he could not be blamed if Major was defeated by Blair.

Two months later, when we met at Portillo's office in Whitehall, he appeared devastated, unsure how to project himself. His refusal to be interviewed for newspaper profiles, as Hart had advised, meant that he continually came across in 'a stereotyped, one dimensional way'. To break the run of negative publicity, I suggested he might try doing more photo-opportunities with young service men and women to soften the hard-line, macho image that he had acquired.

In the lead-up to the May 1997 general election, I heard no more talk from Hart of leadership ambitions, but early on polling day he revealed that if Major lost to Blair, Portillo would stand. 'I don't want Michael coming out too early but we're thinking of doing it in an article I've already written for the *Sunday Telegraph* in which he sets out his vision…We are the front runner…Michael has earned lots of points recently by being so loyal and it'll be so much easier now 99 per cent of the party is Euro-sceptic.' In our conversation next day discussing the reasons for the Conservatives' defeat, Hart conceded that Labour's 'brilliant operation' in targeting constituencies such as Enfield Southgate had cost Portillo his seat.

After a much chastened Portillo spent some months coming to terms with his defeat, and with what he acknowledged was the mistake of getting pigeon holed by an image of himself that even he did not recognise, he told *Breakfast with Frost* in March 1998 that he wanted to return to Parliament. To prepare for the possibility of finding another constituency, he agreed to be interviewed in July 1999 for a profile in *The Times*; he was asked about his time as a student at Cambridge and told his interviewer Ginny Dougary that he had 'some homosexual experiences as a young person', an admission that finally explained Hart's advice to avoid the personal questions that are asked for newspaper and magazine profiles.

The death that September of Sir Alan Clark, MP for Kensington and Chelsea, meant that one of the Conservatives' safest seats was suddenly up for grabs, a vacancy ready-made for a re-emerging Portillo. Once he confirmed his interest, *The Times* published its highly-revealing profile. Next day he told journalists that he had been keen to put to rest some vile rumours that had been circulating. 'I thought the best thing to do was say what was true and what was untrue.'

Despite being the most prominent senior Conservative to admit to past homosexual experiences, the fact that he had supported the ban on homosexuality in the armed forces, and opposed changes in the age of consent, led to demonstrations during the by-election by the gay rights group OutRage. On being returned again as the Kensington and Chelsea MP in the 2001 election, he entered the leadership contest to choose William Hague's successor. Portillo was a regarded as the favourite by many of his fellow MPs, having promised a 'moderate and understanding' agenda, but he failed by one vote to secure a place in the Conservatives' first-ever leadership ballot by one member one vote, a contest that was eventually won by Iain Duncan Smith. Portillo did not seek re-election in 2005 and went on to achieve success as a broadcaster and journalist.

As the years rolled by, and Portillo became ever more tolerant and open in his approach to public life, there was often mention in interviews and articles of his personal turmoil. Reminders of his misgivings made realise how the inner Portillo had conflicted with the image that Hart had presented to me:

'I have always been someone with many self-doubts…I have been nervous about what I have had to do.' (*Desert Island Discs*, 21.7.2000)

'The most disastrous day of my political career…I praised the heroism of the SAS…I strayed into absurd chauvinism because I knew what the Tory activists wanted to hear and I was fixated with getting a standing ovation' (*Sunday Times*, 4.1.2004)

'I made two hideous errors in 1995. John Major told me personally of his decision to seek re-election…I could not stand against him…But most people thought he would be mortally wounded…I authorised preparations for that eventuality, including installing phone lines…I felt that if I could wow the party conference with a rabble-rousing speech I could climb back.' (*Sunday Times*, 22.2.2004)

Hart's protégé had accepted responsibility for the past. His lesson in contrition made me realise how mistaken I had been all along in contemplating an 'If only…' scenario.

youth vote

C ountless encounters with sixth formers and students have convinced me that most of them do take a keen interest in issues that affect their lives. With a little encouragement their sense of awareness about every day concerns can provoke an engaging a debate, and potentially lead to their active participation in the political process. If I succeed at a school or college in prompting plenty of questions, I leave buoyed up by the enthusiasm that a lively discussion has generated. **Young** voters get criticised for not turning out on polling day, but they can hardly be blamed for opting out of politics when so many policies are skewed towards the needs of their grandparents rather than those choosing a career and starting out in life.

I have long been a supporter of the campaign to lower the voting age from 18 to 16 for all UK elections, as happened for the first time in the 2014 referendum on Scottish independence. A way has to be found to reverse rising levels of disengagement: voting at 16 would help to foster a lifetime's involvement in politics, and perhaps start to redress both a reluctance to register and the recent sharp falls in turn out on polling day.

Having a say in deciding whether to leave the UK and become an independent country was a question that clearly excited and engaged teenagers in Scotland. Around 100,000 under-18s signed up to vote – 80 per cent of the total that were eligible – and an opinion poll taken on the day of the referendum suggested that 71 per cent of those aged 16 and 17 had voted Yes.

There could hardly have been a clearer illustration of the justification for lowering the voting age. Schools and colleges across Scotland did all they could to encourage their pupils to engage in the argument. Thousands of first-time voters attended 'The Big, Big Debate' at Glasgow Hydro and had chance to quiz politicians from the Yes and No campaigns. In my own discussions around the country in the months before the referendum I found that many youngsters south of the border were rather envious, wishing they too were being consulted on whether Scotland should become an independent country.

While many teenagers have turned away from the political loyalties of their parents, and express little or no interest in the process of government, when challenged they are quick to voice an opinion on day-to-day affairs. Three topics that have cropped up regularly in recent years have been the rate of the national minimum wage paid to young people, the lack of affordable housing to rent or buy, and a range of concerns about climate change.

My support for lowering the voting age grew out of the unprecedented involvement of young people in the long lead-up to the 1997 general election. Tony Blair widened his electoral base by pulling together support for a rainbow alliance of causes that had a strong appeal to first-time voters, ranging from the gay rights campaign against Section 28 to the demand for a ban on fox hunting.

Blair's victory celebrations turned into a party to end all parties at the Royal Festival Hall. Spilling out on the South Bank was a political gathering of a kind I had never witnessed before. Hundreds of young people, many in their late teens and early twenties, who like me had been unable to gain access, were milling about in front of an enormous stage where Blair was due to speak at 4 a.m. on return from his count in Sedgefield. I had been at youth rallies in support of Margaret Thatcher during the early years of her premiership, and I had marvelled at the enthusiasm with which she was greeted by members of Young Conservatives and Conservative Students. But, as I began talking to Labour's young activists while their election theme song, 'Things Can Only Get Better', blared out from loudspeakers, I discovered not just admiration but adoration for Blair, and I had to force myself to remember that they were talking not about a pop star but a politician.

Among the great throng who cheered Blair so enthusiastically I found three young women eager to explain why they had been so deeply moved by New Labour's crusade to sweep away Thatcherism. 'This is the best moment in my life. I think Tony Blair is the only person who can lead us into the future.' His speech had captivated another: 'I've got the greatest hope in the world for the future with Tony Blair.' The third was equally optimistic: 'He's the best thing that's happened to this country. I'm so looking forward to the next five years when he can put all that he said into action.' Over the years I had recorded plenty of gushing political soundbites but these three first-time voters seemed refreshingly honest and gave me the impression that they felt they had participated in what they regarded as an historic moment for the country.

Despite New Labour's success in engaging with young people, and in uniting many of them around a shared political goal of ending 18 years of Conservative government, Blair's appeal was still not enough to halt rising levels of apathy among first time voters. A turnout of 51 per cent among those aged 18 to 24 was well down on the 63 per cent recorded in 1992, and it fell to 39 per cent in 2001, 37 per cent in 2005, and recovered slightly to 44 per cent in 2010, perhaps partly in response to an ill-fated pre-election pledge by the Liberal Democrat leader Nick Clegg to oppose any increase in student tuition fees.

Given the extent of political disillusionment among young adults across the UK, Scotland's record levels of registration and turnout for the vote on independence proved beyond doubt that if an issue has sufficient appeal voters aged between 16 and 24 are as keen to participate as their parents or grandparents. The closer the result appeared, and the more the SNP stepped up its efforts to recruit teenagers voting for the first time, the more I was reminded of New Labour's pitch in 1997 to the effect that Blair was offering the country a fresh start. That same sense of a playing a part in what could be history in the making had galvanised many of the 16- and 17-year-olds who supported the SNP. Young people had a single issue to consider, a straight choice of Yes or No to the question, 'Should Scotland be an independent country?'

Alex Salmond, First Minister of Scotland, had secured a tactical advantage in his negotiations with David Cameron. Campaigning for a Yes vote meant the SNP could be positive rather than negative. Sixth formers and students interviewed on radio and television sounded engaged and enthused, well aware of a shared responsibility to think about Scotland's future and then cast their vote in what the SNP said was a 'once in a lifetime' decision. I was struck by the clarity of their answers and their enthusiasm to take a step into the unknown, a readiness to embark on a journey to establish and belong to an independent country, whatever the difficulties that lay ahead.

So great was the resolve of so many teenagers to get involved that they made sure through the strength of their commitment that Scotland would remain out in front when it came to electioneering. The No campaign might have won the day with the 55 to 45 per cent vote to reject independence, but the Scottish political process had once again leapt ahead of the rest of the UK. The go-ahead to allow votes at 16 in all future Scottish elections was one of the lasting changes secured by the SNP in the post-referendum agreement for Scotland, and would be the law in time for the 2016 elections to the Scottish Parliament.

The SNP's success in mobilising first-time voters re-invigorated the campaign to lower the voting age across the UK. In the months leading up to the 2015 general election, the Liberal Democrats repeated their 2010 pledge to support votes at 16. Labour renewed their undertaking, first given in 2013, to legislate in the first session of a new parliament. Spurred on by Scotland's example, Ed Miliband promised that a Labour government would change the law in time to allow 190,000 16- and 17-year olds to vote in the 2016 election for Mayor of London. For their part, the Liberal Democrats insisted that voting at 16 should be in place before the in-out referendum on UK membership of the European Union that the Conservatives had promised to hold by the end of 2017. Only the United Kingdom Independence party expressed outright opposition to lowering the voting age, arguing that schoolchildren were being unduly influenced by pro-European propaganda paid for by the European Commission.

Ahead of the election of far greater immediacy than a future extension of the franchise to a further 1.5 million teenagers was a pre-election drive to ensure that the electoral roll included as many as possible of the 3.3 million 17- to 22-year-olds who would be eligible to vote by May 2015. At the start of the year there were dire predictions that up to a million first-time voters had not bothered to register, many were said to be students caught out by the introduction of a new individual electoral registration system. Bite the Ballot and No Vote No Voice were at the forefront of a non-partisan coalition to encourage people to check whether their names were on the electoral roll, and to remind them that they could register on line.

Students disenchanted by the Liberal Democrats' broken pledge on tuition fees were regarded as one of the hardest groups to reach, and as with other disillusioned teenagers and young adults there were fears they might have been influenced by the anti-voting, anti-capitalist agenda promoted by the comedian and activist Russell Brand. In a much-publicised interview on *Newsnight* in 2013, he told the presenter Jeremy Paxman that he had never voted because of 'absolute indifference and weariness and exhaustion from the lies, treachery and deceit of the political class'.

Brand justified his argument that young people had every reason to abandon the political process in his book *Revolution*, but his mantra that 'politics is dead' provoked a radical response. One proposal was that young people should be forced to vote in the first election after they turned 18. Research quoted by the centre-left Institute for Public Policy Research showed that taking part in elections was a habit formed early in life. Mathew Lawrence, the report's author, thought compulsory voting for first timers would be a way to 'reboot democracy'. If a duty to vote was introduced, ballot papers would offer electors the option of being able to vote for 'none of the above' candidates. Lawrence was convinced that if more young people voted, politicians would have to address their concerns. 'President Obama has come out in favour of compulsory voting. Achieving a higher turnout is a way of forcing the political system to respond to marginalised groups in society.'

Ten days before polling day Ed Miliband was ridiculed by David Cameron and mocked by the tabloid press for going to Brand's £2 million home in Shoreditch, east London, to be interviewed for the comedian-turned-activist's YouTube channel *The Trews*. Extracts from their conversation, recorded in his kitchen, were greeted with derision when the Labour leader was seen to have adopted an estuary accent and the streetwise hand gestures of the self-styled revolutionary. Miliband was forthright about the need to vote: politicians could not transform the world. 'It ain't going to be like that.' The creation of the National Health Service and equal pay were two of the changes the political process had achieved.

When derided by Cameron for hanging out with 'a joke' who had not registered and did not vote, Miliband argued that Brand could reach out to young people disengaged from politics, and the opportunity had to be taken. Brand had 9.5 million followers on Twitter and more than a million watched *The Trews*. Three days before polling day Brand updated his YouTube channel and urged his supporters to end 'the danger of the Conservative party'. He said they should vote Labour except in Scotland and Brighton Pavilion where the Green MP Caroline Lucas was standing for re-election. Miliband was given a personal endorsement: 'This bloke will be in parliament and I think this bloke will listen to us'.

Groups urging young people to vote welcomed the Miliband-Brand initiative to encourage a higher turnout. There was some disappointment they had not intervened earlier, before the final date for registering on the electoral roll. A total of 6.8 million 18- to 24-year-olds had registered by the deadline, 70 per cent of those eligible, and 14 per cent higher than in 2010. Pre-election surveys forecast that turnout would also be up. A poll by YouGov indicated 69 per cent were 'absolutely certain' to vote, although other surveys had lower figures suggesting, for example, that only 41 per cent of the 3.3 million first-time voters would get to a polling station.

Post-election analysis appeared to vindicate all the extra effort there had been. Ipsos Mori suggested the turnout among 18- to 24-year-olds reached 43 per cent, only one point below 2010. But another survey carried out for Sky News by the British Election Study suggested a figure of 58 per cent, which if confirmed by other surveys would be higher than Blair's landslide in 1997, and the highest since 1992. Success in stemming the long-term decline was seen as a spur to redouble efforts to increase registration in the lead-up to the promised referendum on UK membership of the European Union, an issue which campaigners were convinced would engage the attention of many young voters.

Shortly before the election David Cameron told MPs that although the Conservatives believed 18 was the right age, if re-elected Prime Minister he would allow a free vote at Westminster to decide whether the voting age should be reduced. On returning to office with an outright majority, one of the first decisions of the new Conservative government was to rule out a reduction in time for the EU vote. On one issue at least Labour and the SNP were united. They both said that once the EU Referendum Bill was published they intended to table amendments demanding votes at 16. Opposition parties believed they could win support for the change in the House of Lords, and that Cameron would find stand was untenable having accepted that 16- and 17-year-olds could vote in the 2016 elections to the Scottish Parliament.

Z

Zelig

By the very nature of their trade political correspondents have to be chameleon-like in the way gather information, able to win the confidence of contacts from left or right, from those in authority or perhaps on the extremes of society. However difficult they might find the prospect of accepting let alone endorsing some of the views that are being expressed, journalists have to sound interested, even enthusiastic, and are ill advised to reveal their true feelings, as this might lead to misunderstandings or create an unnecessary barrier. MPs require the same self-discipline when dealing with the concerns of their constituents. But by sheer necessity most politicians, unlike many reporters, tend to have a clearly defined set of opinions and values; their party allegiances usually last a life time. Defections across the floor of the House of Commons are not uncommon though few can reinvent themselves and their thinking with the consummate ease of Leonard **Zelig**, the Woody Allen character able to look and act like whoever he was around.

Newspaper columnists often complain of being required by their editors to write opinion pieces that conflict with their own beliefs, and the same goes for MPs who feel duty-bound to support the party line whatever they might think privately. But politicians who switch sides tread a dangerous path because their erstwhile colleagues seize on contradictions and U-turns that become part and parcel of their defection to accuse them of having lived a lie and of doubling crossing their constituents.

The Westminster press corps like to think they are a good judge of the strengths and weaknesses of the politicians they write about. During my first years at the House of Commons I spent hour upon hour in the reporters' gallery, looking down on the chamber below, and I became quite familiar with the characteristics and temperament of leading MPs and ministers. Occasionally I did wonder whether whoever was speaking really believed in some of the points they were making. Sometimes we gallery reporters did joke about this among ourselves and cooked up far-fetched imaginary quotes, rather like the Woody Allen thought-bubbles above the characters' heads that bore no relation to what they were actually saying.

Nonetheless this was the heyday of parliamentary reporting, when broadsheet newspapers provided verbatim reports of the main debates, a service to readers that became redundant once proceedings in the two Houses of Parliament started being broadcast on radio and then television. I was one of a team of 12 reporters on *The Times* and we often filled up two pages a day with column after column of who had said what. We took it in turns, sitting in the gallery for 10 to 20 minutes taking a shorthand note, and then typed out our copy. Accuracy and immediacy were the by-words of *The Times'* parliamentary pages; we liked to think our reporting was as reliable as that of Hansard.

The late 1960s were a testing time for Harold Wilson's government. There were frequent late night sessions and plenty of drama in the chamber. Sitting up in the gallery we enjoyed the jousting below, especially the wind-up speeches when Labour ministers and their opposite numbers on the Conservative benches went to head to head. Wilson's defeat by Edward Heath in the 1970 general election had shocked and surprised the Labour cabinet; former ministers were having to go through the uncomfortable transition from government to opposition and their misfortune heightened the cut and thrust of debates.

We reporters all had our favourites: MPs and front benchers who had the knack of bringing a debate to life, as well as providing good copy. One who had impressed me was the Labour minister Reg Prentice who took the loss of office in his stride and bounced back on the strength of his popularity in the annual elections for a place in the shadow cabinet. Prentice, red-faced and pugnacious, thrived on adversity, always ready for a fresh challenge, attributes that would serve him well during other Zelig-like transformations in his subsequent career.

After Heath's defeat in the 1974 general election and Labour's return to office, Wilson appointed Prentice Secretary of State at the Department for Education and Science where he worked on regulations to abolish direct grant status for grammar schools, so as to strengthen still further the comprehensive system. But he was demoted to Minister of State for Overseas Development the following year after having angered Wilson by his criticism of trade unions for failing to keep to their side of social contract. Despite having been an official of the Transport and General Workers' Union before entering parliament, Prentice did not hold back in deploring industrial militancy and in attacking Marxists in the labour movement. His uncompromising attitude made him a target of left-wing activists who had infiltrated his London constituency of Newham North-East. He was about to become the first prominent casualty of what became known as entryism, a concerted attempt to take control of Labour constituencies and impose candidates from the left. A cabinet minister battling against what he dubbed bedsit Trotskyists was a storyline that excited the news media, and on my visits to his constituency, having joined the BBC, I found he was a forthright interviewee, only too ready to denounce what he claimed were the gang that were conspiring against him. His fight-back was in vain as he was ousted in 1976, and failed to get his de-selection overturned at that year's party conference.

Prentice resigned from the cabinet that December and the following year became the highest-ranking Labour politician of the post-war era to cross the floor of the house. He defected to the Conservatives on the eve of the party's 1977 annual conference and within a month had made his first speech from the Tory benches. He refused to give up his seat to fight a by-election, arguing that it was the Labour Party that had deserted him. At his fourth attempt he was fortunate to be selected Conservative candidate for Daventry in the 1979 general election; returned to Westminster with a majority of 21,483; and was appointed Minister of State for Social Security in the newly-elected government of a victorious Margaret Thatcher.

I was intrigued by Prentice's career progression straight to Mrs Thatcher's front bench after his earlier roles as a union official, Labour councillor, MP and cabinet minister. When I first reported his speeches in the late 1960s I had been struck by strength of his conviction and commitment to the labour and trade union movement; I could not have imagined him switching sides. I was to prove equally mistaken about another Zelig-like transformation, this time by Shaun

Woodward, a former BBC television producer who helped secure John Major's 1992 general election victory and became a Conservative MP. After two and half years on the Tory benches he defected to Labour and was appointed a minister in Tony Blair's government, later being promoted to Secretary of State for Northern Ireland under Gordon Brown. Unlike Prentice's metamorphosis, I was able to observe at first hand Woodward's ability to reinvent himself, and the fact that we were BBC contemporaries only added to my fascination.

Because of his experience as a television producer, Woodward's recruitment in 1991 as the Conservatives' director of communications was regarded by the party chairman Chris Patten as a trump card in his plan to present the Prime Minister as 'Citizen John Major' in the 1992 general election. Woodward had spent eight years with the BBC, at *Newsnight* and *Panorama* before editing *That's Life*, where he worked with its star presenter Esther Rantzen. He seemed to have had no difficulty making the transition from the political neutrality of BBC programme making to the partisan world of Tory Central Office and was soon putting his production experience to use.

Sitting the Prime Minister on a bar stool in the middle of village halls for intimate 'Meet John Major' sessions was Woodward's first attempt to give the Conservative campaign a televisual makeover. I remember him telling me how peeved he was when they were mocked for being 'desperately tame'. Eventually Major broke free from the concept of friendly fireside chats, pulled out a soapbox when his battle bus drew into shopping centres and, armed with a loud-hailer, enjoyed taking on the crowd in forthright street-corner oratory.

A stunt that had all the hallmarks of a That's Life running order, although it lacked Rantzen's singing dogs and comic characters, was Woodward's offering in the second week of the campaign. Laid out in Smith Square was the model of a factory with the words 'investment', 'jobs' and 'recovery' written on the chimneys. No sooner were the television cameras in place than a steamroller trundled into view and proceeded to smash the wooden model to smithereens. A red L-plate of the kind used by learner drivers had been attached to the rear of the steamroller, a reminder of the superimposed red L used in a Saatchi and Saatchi poster with the slogan 'You can't trust Labour'. Tory press and broadcasting officers thought the stunt was hilarious, the kind of jape *That's Life* would have been proud of.

On leaving Central Office three months after the Conservatives' unexpected victory, Woodward was thanked by Major for his loyalty and commitment and praised by Patten for his invaluable experience in media communications, plaudits that stood him in good stead when he won the nomination to stand as parliamentary candidate at the 1997 election in the safe Oxfordshire seat of Witney, in succession to Douglas Hurd. He went straight to the front bench as the Conservatives' spokesman for London but found himself increasingly at odds with party policy as the Conservatives adjusted to life at Westminster under Tony Blair by moving further to the right. After his refusal in 1999 to vote in support of a provision known as section 28 (of the Local Government Act 1986), which prohibited the promotion of gay sex in local authority schools, Woodward was sacked by William Hague and defected almost immediately. His defection had been timed to cause Hague the maximum damage and was regarded by New Labour as a considerable coup. His refusal to resign and stand in a by-election prompted the same vicious backlash that Prentice had to endure in the late 1970s when his enemies in Newham claimed his self-fulfilling betrayal had warranted their deselection of 'a nauseating traitor'.

Woodward's Zelig-style contortions in seeking to justify imposing himself as a Labour MP in one of the Conservatives' safest seats appalled the Tory hierarchy. Michael Ancram, the party chairman, said 'no amount of sincerity or fake sincerity' could hide the fact that he had defected for his own careerist reasons. 'Shaun is a man of great ability and he is also a man of great plausibility...but I have never felt able to take him at face value. I am confirmed in this view by the speed and ease with which he has moved from protestations of firm loyalty to the Conservatives last week to this self-promoting defection.'

As luck would have it I had a ringside seat for next act in a drama in which Woodward tried again to pull off a performance that did justice to Leonard Zelig's chameleon disorder of being able to resemble anyone in whose company he found himself. Finding a safe seat for a defecting MP is often a tall order. Witney's soon to be ex-MP presented Labour with a particularly acute problem in the run-up to the 2001 general election. Woodward's wife Camilla was an heiress to the Sainsbury supermarket fortune; the couple lived in a country mansion and kept a butler, hardly the profile that would appeal to working-class constituencies in Labour's heartlands. Two days after Blair called the election two senior Labour MPs announced unexpectedly that they would be standing down, and St Helens South on Merseyside was one the constituencies that was suddenly up for grabs. At this stage party managers were in control. A shortlist was agreed that included Woodward but excluded candidates who lived or worked in the constituency, and who might have appealed to local activists.

I had to make an early start that Sunday morning for the long drive north to report the selection meeting at the West Sutton Labour Club. St Helens had been hard hit by redundancies in coal-mining and glass-making and the club was opposite the site of the former Sutton Manor colliery, which had been one of the last remaining pits in the Lancashire coalfield. Tattered plastic bags had attached themselves to the barbed wire that ran along the club's outer walls; some of the doors and windows were protected by steel shutters. There were posters up for the next big event, a concert by the Cockney duo Chas'n'Dave.

Woodward was one of the last to arrive. Television crews and photographers had been looking out for a chauffeur-driven car, but he had planned his entrance with the care one might have expected of a former television producer. He was first seen some distance away along the main road, walking with his wife, almost opposite the pit gates. On reaching the club he told the assembled journalists that if he became the MP he would become 'a champion for St Helens and the north-west of England'. He won the selection by only four votes and as party members left the meeting it was obvious the constituency had been split down the middle. After a short wait we were ushered into the main room next to the bar. Woodward, who was sitting with the three other candidates amid tables strewn with glasses, promised to represent 'all the people' of St Helens. 'This is a fabulous constituency and I'm in a party that recognises we are one nation whatever people's background or race.'

Outside the club there were quite a few local youngsters who had been attracted by the television cameras. Some were sitting on the wall drinking lager and enjoying the sunshine. When my producer started attracting wolf-whistles from some of the drinkers she ordered us inside to find another location. As I finally left the club Camilla Woodward was ahead of me and she walked out straight into the crowd of youngsters drinking in the forecourt. She looked lost for a moment and was quickly ushered towards a waiting car. A sunny Sunday afternoon outside a Labour club in St Helens was hardly the place to loiter, and quite a contrast from the calm and ordered existence of their family home in the Oxfordshire countryside.

Labour held St Helens South with its 1997 majority of 23,739 slashed to 8,985. The swing of 14.3 per cent against Labour was the largest of the election. Woodward was shown on the BBC's election night programme *Vote 2001* waiting for his count to be declared; sitting with him was Esther Rantzen. After the result was announced, Jeremy Paxman asked if the new MP's butler had voted Labour as well. Woodward insisted he had a loftier agenda: 'We won by talking about the real issues, jobs and schools...Yes, I spent some time in the Conservative Party and inevitably you must go along with the things they say but, as Winston Churchill said, I left the Conservatives to stop saying stupid things...I ended up with right-wing extremists and a bunch of people propelled by William Hague to say outrageous things against asylum seekers and a ludicrous policy against Europe.'

Initially I had not shared Michael Ancram's doubts about Woodward's plausibility. Having heard him in the chamber and in interviews during his brief stint as a Conservative MP, it had never occurred to me that above his head I should have put a Woody Allen speech bubble indicating that he believed the complete opposite of what he had just said. Calling in aid Churchill's edict that parliamentarians sometimes end up 'saying stupid things' was astute footwork on Woodward's part, even if it did confirm that he saw no need to apologise for having adopted a Zelig-like persona during a political career that peaked with a seat at the cabinet table and ended when he stepped down ahead of the 2015 general election.

index

A

Adams, Gerry 21

Advertising: 11–22l; direct mail 11, 13; online 11–4; posters 11–3, 20–2, 148; press 11-13; television 11

Advertising Standards Authority 12, 20,

Alexander, Douglas 198–9

Allen, Woody 257–8, 265

Amalgamated Union of Engineering Workers 208

Amess, David 188

Ancram, Michael 263, 265

Ashdown, Paddy: 120–1, 124–7; 1992 election 76; 2015 election 124–7; battle bus 28

Attlee, Clement 194, 226–7

Attlee, Violet 226–7

Axelrod, David 5

B

Baldwin, Tom 151

Balls, Ed 4, 135, 192

battle buses: 23–31;pink 30–1; security 26, 28, 88

BBC: 2, 23–5, 103, 109–110, 114, 137, 144, 151, 167, 187, 188, 191, 195, 211– 3, 225, 241, 260; political reporting 60, 64, 93–6, 157–9, 162–3

Beloff, Nora 225

Bell, Lord Tim 21, 170

Bell, Steve 171

Bennett, Natalie 30, 41, 61–6, 79, 221

Berry, Bez 43

Bickerstaffe, Rodney 205

Birt, Lord John 157

Black, Conrad 244

Black, Mhairi 199

Blair, Cherie 97, 228–30

Blair, Tony: 123, 141, 151, 204–5, 261; 1997 election 3, 16–9, 38, 189–90, 198, 205, 228, 250–1; 2001 53–6, 85; 2005 election 29; battle bus 29; election strategy 104, 107, 250–1; media access 112, 181, 229–30; media relations 16–9, 86, 95–7, 130, 139

Bloomberg, Michael 180–1

Boaks, Bill 42-3

Bradby, Tom 117

Braithwaite, Nicola 172
Brand, Russell 254–5
British Coal 53
British Polling Council 8, 155, 160, 164
British Rail 53
Brookes, Peter 135, 170
Brooks, Rebekah 132
Brown, Gordon: 48, 55–7, 84, 106, 199, 205, 261; and Gillian Duffy 71, 85, 87, 92, 231; media relations 112, 129, 131, 181–2, 230–33; televised debates 121– 2
Brown, Sarah 181–2, 230–3
BskyB 132–3
Bush, George 16
BuzzFeed 100
Byrne, Liam 72–4

C

Cable, Vince 192
Callaghan, James 2, 17–8, 25, 27, 48-56, 73, 82
Callaghan, Audrey 227
Cambridge, Duke and Duchess 74–5, 182
Cameron, David: 135, 214; 2010 election 47, 57, 121–2; 2014 Scottish referendum 142, 146, 147, 180–1; 2015 election 3–6, 57, 59, 125–6, 142, 147–8, 153–4, 160, 168, 175–8, 191, 217; advertising 20-1; battle bus 30; election strategy 71, 74, 81, 84, 88, 125–6, 168–70; gaffes 72, 79, 91–2, 116, 169, 180–1; media access 113–5, 232–4; media relations 131, 132-3; selfies 172; televised debates 60–6, 77–8, 84–5, 91–2, 121–2, 148; votes at 16 172, 252, 255–6
Cameron, Ivan 113, 232
Cameron, Samantha 113–4, 116, 168, 176, 181, 232–5

Campbell, Alastair 19, 54–5, 95–7, 107, 139, 151, 160, 204, 212–3
Campbell, Sir Menzies 121
Carswell, Douglas 65
Castle, Barbara 112
Channel 4 News 88, 106
Chapman, Sir Sydney 36–8
Churchill, Sir Winston 73, 112, 194, 265
Clark, Sir Alan 247
Clarkson, Jeremy 42
Clegg, Miriam – see Gonzalez
Clegg, Nick: 135, 146, 252; 2010 election 47, 57, 121–3; 2015 election 6–7, 35, 40, 85, 125-8, 171, 177, 218; battle bus 30; Deputy Prime Minister 6, 122–3, 127–8; election strategy 71, 125–8, 171; electoral reform 128, 218; media access 117, 233–4; resignation 127, 177; televised debates 61, 63, 77, 84, 121-2, 148
Collett, Jonathan 28
coalition government 3, 6, 8, 35, 47, 57, 59, 73, 84, 125–8, 154, 176–9, 219
Committee for a Free Britain 242
Conservative party: 2015 election 2-9, 48, 125–6, 159, 154, 217, 220–1; advertising 11–8; election strategy 106–7, 166–8, 187–8, 196–7
constituents 33-8
Cooper, Andrew 158
Coulson, Andy 132–3
Crosby, Lynton 5, 13, 61, 150–1, 162–3
Crow, Bob 44
Currie, Edwina 116
Curtice, Professor John 159

D

Dacre, Paul 135
Daily Express 214, 229
Daily Mail 5, 31, 63, 115, 117, 130, 134, 135, 142, 146, 148, 149, 151, 173, 177, 178, 229, 235
Daily Mirror 133, 151, 161, 180
Daily Telegraph 5, 130, 134, 142, 149, 151, 161, 180, 210, 244
Darling, Alistair 106–7
Democratic Audit UK 45
Democratic Unionist party 61
deposits 39–45
Dewar, Donald 193–4
Dinsmore, David 137
Dougary, Ginny 247
Douglas-Home, Sir Alec 73, 112, 195–8, 226
Douglas-Home, Lady Elizabeth 226
Dowler, Milly 132
Duffy, Gillian 71, 77, 85, 87, 92, 231
Dzon, Jonathan 43

E

Eade, Christine 225
Eden, Sir Anthony 112
Elections
   1999 European Parliament 212
   2014 European Parliament 3, 124
   by-elections Clacton 65; Eastleigh 211; Glasgow Garscadden 193–5; Glasgow Govan 194; Kensington and Chelsea 247; Paisley South 198; Rochester and Strood 65; general elections
   1945 175, 190, 226
   1950 227
   1951 194, 196
   1959 112
   1964 2, 73, 112, 196, 219
   1966 2
   1970 195–6
   1974 February 2, 26, 185–7, 259
   1947 October 2, 26, 185, 195
   1979 2, 17, 24–9, 40, 49, 94, 120, 167, 170, 206, 260
   1983 71, 75, 167, 219
   1987 242
   1992 3, 50–2, 71, 82, 154, 157, 161, 181, 188–9, 227–8, 261
   1997 3, 16, 38, 42, 120, 158, 161, 189, 198, 205, 211, 237–9, 250–1, 262
   2001 44, 53, 85–6, 106, 229
   2005 12, 29, 120, 252
   2010 11–2, 29–30, 40, 71–2, 85, 87, 100, 121, 155, 159, 176, 231, 255
   2015 2–9, 12, 30–1, 34-5, 40–1, 48, 59, 81, 84–5, 87–90, 91–2, 100, 113–8, 119–21, 125–8, 130, 134–7, 142, 146–52, 153–5, 158, 165–6, 168, 175–8, 182, 191–2, 199, 217–21, 274–5
election broadcasts 15, 67
election news conferences 104–7, 166–7
election results 183–92
election timing 47–57
Electoral Commission 45
electoral reform: 8, 66, 66, 218–21; first-past-the-post 8, 60, 66, 128, 183, 218, 237; proportional representation 128, 219–21; single transferable vote 221; winner-takes-all 66
Electoral Reform Society 8, 219–21
Evans, Moss 207
Evening Standard 90, 136, 156, 172
Everett, Kenny 71
Ewing, Winnie 194
Express and Star, Wolverhampton 194, 209, 214–6

F

Facebook 12–3, 23, 100
Farrage, Nigel: 1999 European
    Parliament election 212; 2014
    European Parliament election
    60, 124,143; 2015 election 21,
    41–2, 65–6, 218; advertising
    21; elected MEP 212; electoral
    reform 218, 221; gaffes 79–80;
    media attacks on 143; media
    relations 79–80, 209–11; selfies
    90 televised debates 60–1,
    63–4, 148
fixed-term parliaments 35–6, 47,
    57, 84, 181
Flanagan, Mark 43
Flint, Caroline 31
Foot, Michael 4, 71, 75, 129,
    138, 168
Ford, Vanessa 228
Forsyth, James 214
Foulkes, Lord 164
fragmenting political support 41,
    47, 59-66, 187, 217

G

gaffes 67–80, 116–8, 135–6,
    169, 171
George, Lloyd 7,
Ghose, Katie 220
Gibbs, Olive 225
Goldsmith, Beryl 111
Gonzalez, Miriam 117, 233–5
Gove, Michael 115
Grace, John 75
Green, Miranda 127
Green party 8–9, 30, 40–1, 48, 59,
    66, 217–21
Guardian 21, 75, 78, 79, 127,
    131–3, 151, 163, 171,173

H

Hague, William 107, 262
Hammond, Philip 73
Handley, Nathan 41
Harman, Harriett 30–1
Harries, Right Rev Richard 19–20
Hart, David: 239–48; 1984-5
    miners' strike 239, 241–2; and
    Michael Portillo 239–48
Hayward, Rob 161
Hayward, Ron 187
Healey, Denis 18–9, 82
Heath, Edward 2, 93, 186–7,
    197–8, 226, 259
heckling 81–90
Heseltine, Michael 162
Heywood, Sir Jeremy 178
Hill, David 190
Hitchens, Peter 229
Howard, Michael 29
Howarth, Alan 213
Hudson, Hugh 227
Hurd, Douglas 262

I

Independent Press Standards
    Organisation 133
Independent 127, 133, 137
Independent on Sunday 163
Instagram 100
Institute of Public Policy Research
    254
Interviews 91–7
ITV (ITN) 23, 96, 158, 167, 188–9,
    191
Izzard, Eddie 89

J

Jackson, James 41
Jenkinson, Lisa 212
Jenkyns, Andrea 192

Johnson, Alan 78
Johnson, Boris 90, 171, 214
Jones, Clement 194, 209–11, 214–6
Jones, Marcus 191
Jones, Sion 86
journalists: 2, 19, 25, 28, 40, 47-9, 69–71, 99–108, 183–5, 204–5, 209, 223–5, 237–40, 257–9; broadcasting 92, 102–4, 109, 184–7; online 100–4

K

Kaufman, Gerald 75, 124
Kavanagh, Trevor 189
Kellner, Peter 156, 159–61
Kennedy, Charles 7, 106, 120–1
Kinnock, Glenys 227–8
Kinnock, Neil: 55, 82, 129, 227–8; 1992 election 51, 138–9, 154, 157, 188–9, 227; Sheffield rally 71, 75–6
kitchens – see photo-ops
Kitson, Alec 207
Knott, Herbie 170

L

Labour party: 2015 election 2–9, 48, 153, 159; advertising 18, 22; election strategy 166–8, 187–8, 208; votes at 16 253
Lamont, Norman 51, 243
Landale, James 114–6
Lawrence, Jane 41
Lawrence, Mathew 254
Laws, David 73
Letts, Quentin 117
Leveson, Lord Justice 133–4, 137
Lewington, Charles 19
Liberal Democrats: 119–128; 2015 election 2–9, 13, 35, 40, 48, 66, 123-8, 153, 159, 192, 217–21; election strategy 106, 120–1,

123–8, 168, 186–7; votes at 16 253–4
Lib-Lab pact 185
Lineker, Gary 74
lost deposits – see deposits
Lucas, Caroline 218, 255
Lyons, Damian 161–2

M

MacDonald, Margo 194
Macintyre, Donald 127
MacKenzie, Kelvin 137–8, 160–1
McCluskey, Len 131, 203
MacGregor, Sir Ian 239
MacMaster, Gordon 198
Macmillan, Harold 112
McNeil, Isolda 225
Mail on Sunday 17, 179, 182, 234, 243
Major, John: 120, 124, 141, 149, 238, 242–6; 1992 election 3, 8, 48, 50–2, 76, 82–3, 154, 157–8, 161, 181, 188–9, 228; 1997 election 18, 53, 228; battle bus 28; 'bastardgate' 241; media relations 26–28, 261–2
Major, Norma 228
Mandelson, Peter 19, 139, 190, 212, 229
Market Research Society 160
Marr, Andrew 56
Martin, Iain 135
Mathias, Tania 192
Matthew, Brian 195
Maudling, Reginald 36-7, 73
May, Theresa 179
Mawhinney, Dr Brian 19
Messina, Jim 13,
Miliband, David 131, 136
Miliband, Ed: 2014 Scottish referendum 142, 146, 203; 2015 election 3–7, 71, 76, 78, 85, 114–5, 117–8, 148–50, 153–4, 161,

175, 199; advertising 21-2, 148; and Russell Brand 255; 'Edstone' 72, 74–6; gaffes 72, 74–8, 135–6, 169; media access 114–5, 117–8, 169, 234; media attacks on 129–39, 148–50, 179, 182; Milifandom 172–3; resignation 177; selfies 172–3; televised debates 61, 63, 65, 67, 77–9, 148, 150; votes at 16 172, 253

Miliband, Justine 114–7, 172, 234–5

Miliband, Ralph 135

Mitchell, Clarence 228

Monster Raving Loony party 42–3

Morning Star 225

Morris, James 162

Morrison, Herbert 190

Mullin, Chris 188

Murdoch, Rupert 5–6, 129–39, 244

Murphy, Jim 89

Murray, Al 41–2

N

National Coal Board 53, 145, 239

National Union of Mineworkers 145, 186

National Union of Public Employees 205

National Union of Students 238

nationalists – see SNP

Neave, Airey 24–5

Neil, Andrew 126

Nellist, Dave 44

News of the World 130–3

No Turning Back Group 212–3

O

Obama, Barack 6, 13, 231, 254

Obama, Michelle 231

The Observer 72, 220, 238, 241

O'Donnell, Lord Gus 51–2, 179, 181

Ofcom 12, 60–1

O'Flynn, Patrick 214

Oliver, Jamie 115

online media 12

opinion polls: 153–64, 234; 1992 election 51, 75, 154, 157, 161, 188; 1997 election 158, 161; 2010 election 155, 159, 191; 2015 election 2–8, 153–5, 158, 191; exit polls 3–4, 158–60, 188, 191; Gallup 156; GfK NOP 159; GQR 162; ICM 79; Ipsos MORI 159, 161, 256; Marplan 156; MORI 156, 158–9; ORC 156; NOP 156; Survation 161–2; YouGov 80, 126, 146, 148, 155–6, 159–60, 164, 234, 256

opinion pollsters 7, 48, 59, 149, 151, 153–5, 158–60, 185

Osborne, George 55, 73, 75, 90, 168

Osen, Doris 43

Oxford Mail 25, 214, 224

Owen, David 21, 28–9

P

Page, Ben 161

Patten, Chris 28, 261, 262

Paxman, Jeremy 70–1, 91–2, 254, 265

People 64

photo-opportunities: 83–4, 87, 151, 165–74; animals 167, 170–1; kitchens 72, 109–118; selfies 89–90, 172–3; set-up shots 109–11; walking shots 110

Piero, Gloria de 31

Plaid Cymru 61, 65, 221

Platell, Amanda 107

Portillo, Michael Denzil Xavier: 107; 1997 election defeat 192, 237–8; and David Hart 239–48; leadership ambitions 238–48

posters see advertising Powell, Enoch 209–11, 214–6

Prentice, Reg 259–60, 262

Prescott, John 86, 107, 123
Press Complaints Commission 133
public relations 11

Q

Queen Elizabeth 51, 171, 175–82, 190

R

Rantzen, Esther 261, 262
Reckless, Mark 65, 213
Redwood, John
Reece, Gordon 93,
Rees-Mogg, William 196
Referendums: 2011 alternative vote 219; 2014 Scottish independence 21, 141–6, 164, 179–80, 249–53; 2016-17 European Union 8, 66, 253, 256; votes at 16 249–53, 256
Rentoul, John 163
results night 126, 159
Rifkind, Malcolm 245
Roberts, Bob 172
Robinson, Nick 57, 144–5
Rowling, J K 145–6

S

Saatchi, Charles 18
Saatchi, Maurice 18–9
Saatchi, M&C 18–22
Saatchi and Saatchi 17–22, 261
Salmond, Alex: 65; 2014 Scottish referendum 143–6, 203; 2015 election 65, 142; advertising 21-2, 148; media attacks on 137, 142–5; selfies 173; votes at 16 252
Sambrook, Richard 163–4
Scargill, Arthur 44, 145, 239, 242
Scottish Labour 119, 147, 192, 199, 201–2, 208

Scottish National party: 193–5; 2014 independence referendum 21, 141–6, 249–53; 2015 election 2–9, 21–2, 35, 59, 65, 119, 146–52, 159, 199, 201, 208, 217– 21, 224; heckling 88–9; media attacks on 141–6; online abuse 145–6; Scottish Parliament 60, 142, 253, 256; social media 100–2, 145–6; votes at 16 249–50, 252, 256
SDP-Liberal Alliance 21, 28, 40, 120, 219
selfies – see photo-ops
Selwyn, Jeremy 136
set-up shots – see photo-ops
Shakespeare, Stephan 160
Short, Clare 18
Sky News 87, 96, 158, 167, 191, 256
Smith, Sir Cyril 94–5
Smith, Iain Duncan 247
Smith, Matthew 1
Snow, Jon 106
social media 11–4, 20–2, 81, 83, 99–100, 103–4, 230, 234–5
Socialist Labour party 44
Socialist Workers' party 44, 83
Somerville, Julia 225
Spiegelhalter, Sir David 162
Steel, David: 21, 120–1; 1979 election 24–29, 94; 2015 election; battle bus 24–9, 31
Stewart, Donald 194
Storer, Sharon 85
Sturgeon, Nicola: 2014 Scottish referendum 62, 202–3; 2015 election 5, 65, 142–52, 177, 201–4, 218; advertising 22, 148; media access 117, 173–4; media attacks on 137, 142, 179, 182; 'most dangerous woman' 5, 63, 142; selfies 89, 173; televised debates 61–4, 80, 148, 150
Sutch, David (Lord Screaming) 42–3

Sun 5, 31, 42, 77, 115, 117, 130–1, 134, 136–8, 149, 151, 155–6, 160, 180, 189
Sunday Telegraph 135, 246
Sunday Times 146, 156, 164, 178, 216, 248

T

Taylor, Dr Richard 44
Tebbit, Norman 111
televised leaders' debates: 2010 15, 29–30, 60–2, 84–5, 121–2, 155, 233; 2015 60–7, 77–8, 91–2, 148, 150; independent commission 67
Thatcher, Margaret: 25, 116, 120, 141, 145, 205–7, 238, 241–2, 260; 1979 election 2, 17, 27, 49–50, 53, 89, 93, 167, 206; media access 16, 93, 112, 167, 170
Thorpe, Jeremy 26–7, 186–7
The Times 77, 117, 135, 151, 170, 173, 178, 196–7, 227, 232, 242, 247
Toynbee, Polly 78
Trade Unionist and Socialist Coalition 44
Transport and General Workers' Union 185–6, 206–7, 259
TUC: 202, 204; 1978 Congress 49; 1982 Congress 205; 1995 Congress 204
Twigg, Stephen 238
Twitter 12, 23, 31, 74, 89, 146, 182, 230, 255

U

Unite 131, 203
Unison 203, 205
United Kingdom Independence party: 253; 1999 European Parliament elections 212; 2014 European Parliament elections 60, 124,143; 2015 general election 2–3, 8–9, 21, 41–2, 48, 59, 217–21; by-elections 65, 211; media attacks on 143
Urwin, Harry 207

V

Villiers, Theresa 36
Vine, Sarah 115
voting system – see electoral reform

W

Walker, Carole 232
Watson, Jenny 45
Webb, Colin 198
Wilkinson, Simon 77
Williams, Baroness Shirley 219, 226
Wilson, Harold 2, 111–2, 186, 196–8, 226, 258–9
Wilson, Mary 112, 227
wives of politicians 223–35
Wood, Leanne 61–4, 80
Woodward, Camilla 264–5
Woodward, Shaun 260–5
Worcester, Robert 156, 158–9

X

Xavier – see Michael Portillo

Y

Young Conservatives 71, 93, 251
Young, Janet 225
young voters: 249–56; 1997 election 250–51; 2014 Scottish referendum 249–50, 252–3; votes at 16 249–56
YouTube 12–3, 21, 23, 255

Z

Zelig, Leonard 257–65

about the author

Nicholas Jones is an author and political commentator. He was a BBC industrial and political correspondent for thirty years and has written extensively on the relationship between politicians and the news media. Nicholas is a regular commentator to debates on issues concerning politics and the media and he takes a close interest in issues affecting the standards and practice of journalism.

Nicholas began his career as a journalist in 1960, and after working on local evening newspapers in Portsmouth and Oxford, he became a parliamentary and political reporter for *The Times* in 1968 and joined the BBC in 1972, as a news producer at Radio Leicester and was later a national radio reporter, before being promoted to correspondent.

In 1986 Nicholas was named Industrial Reporter of the Year by the Industrial Society for his reporting of the 1984-

85 miners' strike for BBC Radio News. He was awarded an honorary doctorate by the University of Wolverhampton in 2005 and appointed an honorary visiting professor at the Cardiff School of Journalism in 2011.

His books include Strikes and the Media (1986), Soundbites and Spin Doctors (1995), Sultans of Spin (1999), Trading Information: Leaks, Lies and Tip-offs (2006) and The Lost Tribe: Whatever Happened to Fleet Street's Industrial Correspondents (2011). His four books on general elections: Election 92, Campaign 1997, Campaign 2001 and Campaign 2010: The Making of the Prime Minister.

He has contributed chapters to a range of recent books including Pulling Newspapers Apart (2008), Broadcast Journalism (2009), The Phone Hacking Scandal (2012), What Do We Mean By Local (2013), Is The BBC In Crisis (2014), Freedom of Information 10 Years On (2015), and chapters for books on the miners' strike, Shafted (2009) and Settling Scores (2014).

Urbane Publications is dedicated to developing new author voices, and publishing fiction and non-fiction that challenges, thrills and fascinates. From page-turning novels to innovative reference books, our goal is to publish what YOU want to read. Find out more at

urbanepublications.com